THE NATURE OF THE SELF

Starwalker Press

THE NATURE OF THE SELF

This book is a facsimile reprint of the original edition published by Allan Wingate in London, 1959. It represents one of the crowning achievements of the author, Francis J. Mott, a prolific writer whose work was far ahead of its time, but is now poised to receive the recognition it deserves. His profoundly significant work, long unavailable, is today finding an eager and receptive readership.

Francis J. Mott was born in England in 1901; in spite of ill-health as a child and little formal schooling, he showed a precocious intelligence which eventually led him to study the work of many controversial and innovative thinkers, some of whom he met in person. The list includes Otto Rank and Nandor Fodor, former protégés of Sigmund Freud, and among the first people to write about prenatal experience in a psychological and spiritual context. Francis J. Mott spent time in the USA and Canada, where he found the principal audience for his developing ideas concerning a universal pattern of creation in the natural world, which included human experience. He lectured, conducted group psychology and individual dream analysis, wrote and published several books. As a platform for this work, he founded a group which came to be known as 'The Society of Life'. He served in the Canadian Air Force in World War II, until his discharge in 1945 when returned to England. In 1933, he married Gwendolen Mayhew, his support in every way until his death in 1980; they had two children. Francis J. Mott was intellectually vigorous, pursuing with passion his research and publishing his writings until the last year of his life.

In *The Nature of the Self* Francis J. Mott draws on extensive case material, particularly dreams, to unravel the mysteries of the world of pre- and perinatal experience, and demonstrates how the residue of this realm plays itself out in our post-natal life, reflected in symptoms of various kinds – physical, emotional and mental. He also demonstrates how these intrauterine dynamics inform familiar symbolic and mythological themes. Anyone interested in the development of human consciousness is sure to find Mott's work to be truly revelatory. Artists, poets, psychoanalysts, mythology enthusiasts, anthropologists and students of symbolism will discover here a rich and completely new understanding of the inner dimensions of human experience.

BY THE SAME AUTHOR:

BOOKS:

The Crisis of Opinion
The Meaning of the Zodiac
Biosynthesis
The Universal Design of Birth
The Universal Design of the Oedipus Complex
The Universal Design of Creation
Play Therapy and Infantile Paralysis
The Myth of a Chosen People
Doorknobia
Black Hand Over Europe
    (translation from French, original written by Henry Pozzi)
Mythology of the Prenatal Life
    (privately published monograph, re-published by
    Starwalker Press, 2013)

PLAYS:

The Haunted Woman
The Little Robe
    (a version of Oedipus Rex written in the light of this book)
The Greater Power
    (radio play)

PUBLISHED PAPERS:

Oedipus and Beyond
Drama and the Evocation of Unconscious Images
A Pulmonary Conception Fantasy
The Concept of a Prenutritional Libido
Prehuman Stages of the Libido
The Libido as a Cloak of Intrauterine Affect
Mother Goose and the Gastrointestinal Tract
    The Psychoanalytic Review
    The Journal of Clinical Psychopathology
    The Psychiatric Quarterly

THE NATURE OF
THE SELF

The Human Mind Rediscovered
as a Specific Instance of
a Universal Configuration
Governing all Integration

by

FRANCIS J. MOTT

LONDON
ALLAN WINGATE

1st edition 1959: hardback published by Allan Wingate, London
2nd edition 2012: paperback facsimile edition published by
Starwalker Press, London

ISBN: 978-0-9558231-6-9

STARWALKER PRESS

BCM Starwalker
London WC1N3XX
Email: enquiries@starwalkerpress.com
www.starwalkerpress.com

Printed by Lightning Source (UK, USA and Australia)
Design and cover: Tamara Stamenkovic
Engraving: Robert Fludd *Utrius Cosmi (1617)*
Image: Linda Hall Library of Science, Engineering & Technology

Note: The material in this book is for education,
research and reference only. No part of it is intended to
substitute for appropriate professional treatment of medical,
psychological or other conditions.

STARWALKER PRESS

Books for the healing journey

To
HENRY MONTAGU DOBSON

AUTHOR'S PERSONAL NOTE

THE DEDICATION of this book to Henry Montagu Dobson is the only gesture of gratitude that it is within my power to make. He has shared in every aspect of the book from its inception, and without his constant encouragement, help and advice it could hardly have been made. The same is true of my wife, though her aid has been naturally of a very different order. Her steadfast faith in my work, manifested in unending care for me, is something which I can never repay. If these two people had been the only ones to whom I owe a debt of gratitude my task here would be easy, but there are others who in their different ways have helped me so profoundly that I could easily have dedicated the book to them also. First I want to thank Florence M. Caldwell, who patiently assisted me in my early efforts at mental analysis, and upon whose blameless head I projected the irritations and frustrations at work in my own feelings. Then I have to thank also Florence W. Ireys, Mabel Kelly Nunn and Alma T. Wiley, all of whom have encouraged and supported me with great enthusiasm and generosity. I owe special debts of gratitude to Gertrude E. Huffman, Mae McD. Hummer, Anne Patrick and Josephine F. Peckham. Also to Stig Kempe and his wife Ann. I wish also to thank Michael Mott for giving up hours of his vacation to proof reading. I am conscious that there are many others, too numerous to mention here, to whom I also owe much. I have simply been privileged to be at the center of a web of circumstance and endeavor without which I should never in the first place have begun the researches which have culminated so far in the material of this book.

My earlier books have been published in the United States of America, and some of them were written there. This explains why I, though English, have largely adopted the American forms of spelling. I trust that this minor circumstance will not trouble English readers, nor my occasional lapses from strict American usage appear odd to the reader in America.

vii

The Nature of the Self

I wish to acknowledge with gratitude the considerable help given to me by Mr. George Dixon, who made the drawings for this book. Unless Mr. Dixon had been willing to enter into the spirit of the book, many of the drawings would have been very difficult for me to achieve. It is not easy to convey to an artist the lineaments of a fantasy, and would be quite impossible if the artist were not highly sympathetic.

FOREWORD

IN OUR TIMES it is hard to find a name for mental phenomena that will evoke no war of words. If instead of using the word 'self' in the title of this book I had used 'mind', or 'ego', or 'psyche' or 'soul' I should inevitably have aroused preconceptions. I have therefore chosen a relatively neutral word which indicates without defining the subject of this book. We all know that we constitute a 'self', even if we cannot define it. My purpose here is to describe certain newly-discovered facts which throw light upon the nature and origins of the self.

In order to give the reader an idea of the direction in which this book will carry him, let me offer a brief synopsis of the contents. He will be asked to consider the idea that all external phenomena show signs of having been created in accordance with a common plan. It will be suggested to him that the atom, the solar system, the living cell and, indeed, all forms of external 'nature', bear an imprint in common as certainly as all British pennies bear the imprint of the monarch's head, and all American ones bear the imprint of Abraham Lincoln's. This analogy is, of course, a very naive one, for if the imprint in nature of a universal design were as clear as the print on a penny, this book would be superfluous. It seems wise, furthermore, to warn the reader that this brief synopsis does not follow the same logical order as the book itself.

Having been offered indications in support of this concept of a universal pattern of creation, the reader will then be asked to consider evidence that this same pattern is imprinted in the human feelings, where it appears as the veritable anatomy of the self. The assertion is that the pattern which is common to all external forms is common also to the internal forms of the mind. This assertion is much more than a vague idealist assertion that mind and matter have a common source. It is a claim that a single configuration is demonstrable in both the objective and the subjective worlds of human experience. This claim, indeed, is backed by a specific demonstration that the bodily organs of man subserve the making of this universal imprint in the human feelings. This book shows how it comes about that certain bodily organs assume a role for which they were by no means created, but in the course of which they evoke the sense of self.

These insights have been won by the application of the principles of empirical science to the observation and analysis of the deep feelings. The formulation of hypotheses has been guided by knowledge gained through a new organon of dream analysis. Moreover, each hypothesis as soon as formulated has been subjected to a rigorous discipline of proof by persistent application of the same organon. This may surprise, and perhaps even affront, those who have assumed that a dream is a purely personal phenomenon in the narrow sense of the term. I cannot deal with this objection here, since, although this book offers some hints as to the nature of dreams and of my methods of analysis, a proper exposition of these matters requires a volume to itself. Here I seek only to give the outline of the results obtained over a long period of research. This means that I am compelled to present my facts in a rather dogmatic manner, a circumstance which I find regrettable but inevitable. I have at my back a great mass of impersonal evidence in the form of the myths and *märchen*, and in the first draft of this book this evidence was profusely adduced. But reaction from several sources convinced me that the symbolism of the myths might well obscure rather than illumine this text. I have accordingly dropped almost all the mythological material from this book, though I hope that one day I shall be able to publish it in a separate volume. By itself, this unification of the great myths is a work of enormous potential human importance.

Inevitably I have been compelled to create a conceptual structure into which my new facts can be fitted. But I have kept a tight rein upon any tendency to philosophize or to extrapolate, and have sought to restrict my conceptual picture to that bare minimum necessary to string the new facts together into a meaningful context. Yet I cannot entirely exclude all basic philosophy from this work, since the facts themselves could not have been unearthed had I not had some prior suspicion of their nature and existence. This philosophic framework was originally little more than the conviction that a universal pattern may be traced in outer nature and ought logically, therefore, to be discoverable also in the mind.

In addition to an outline of basic philosophy, I have been compelled to offer a few hypotheses as to the nature of the bodily mechanisms involved in the evolution of the mind. For instance, the reader will find in Chapters One and Two efforts to account for the mechanics of the fetal skin feeling and of the imprint which the umbilical flow somehow leaves in the organism. I cannot make it too plain that my discoveries do not stand or fall upon the correctness of such hypotheses. It is conceivable that the mechanism of the fetal skin feeling is not the lanugo hairs, and that the umbilical cord is not a species of electrolytic conductor. I offer these as hypotheses *faute de mieux*, in the effort to explain the phenomena which I have unearthed in the feelings. But the phenomena themselves are indisputable and they can be demonstrated to anyone by (1) the analysis of his own dreams or of a subject selected by him, or (2) by the symbolic testimony of the myths and *märchen*. My hypotheses are by no means final, and they are not intended to represent the substance of my findings. They are, on the contrary, efforts to explain my findings, and are a challenge to others to find better ones under the discipline of the methods which I have evolved, without the application of which discipline all is mere unsupported opinion.

One unexpected outcome of my researches has been new light upon the relation of mind to body, which is to say the relation between the brain and the mind. When I began my researches I expected to find only mental patterns. I did not at all anticipate that I should find these mental patterns in terms of physical organs and functions. In the end I found that mind is evoked in the bodily organs as a result of their configurational interrelationships. What I mean by this will become clear as the reader goes on. What I have learned makes it quite clear that the self is not the unique product of the nervous system. The self is not primarily evoked by the brain. Other organs than the nervous system play a primary role in the making of mind. Mind and brain ultimately are revealed as standing in a relationship which can best be described as one of 'configurational resonance'. This may sound obscure, but the reader will find the concept adequately explained in the text. At least, I have explained it as simply as I can within the framework of my existing knowledge. It will be evident that any contribution to the solution of the problem of the relation of mind to brain must shed light upon the philosophical problem of the relation of spirit to matter.

I am in no doubt at all that the facts stated in this book will appear strange and often downright ludicrous. It is the fate of a discoverer of new facts to appear to be talking nonsense. This was true even of such discoveries as the round earth and 'curved space', both of which concepts are now taken for granted. I am compelled to the much more dangerous task of making statements about your own feelings which you will at once 'know' to be quite absurd. I hope you will keep in mind that I also, when acting consciously as a private person, find them no less peculiar. I have to go back again and again to my studies to convince myself that what I see in my analyses is real, and is given emphasis and collective status by the great myths.[1] The fact is that neither you nor I can trust our conscious minds to tell us the anatomy of our feelings, because that anatomy was largely formed and done before conscious thinking began. In principle we cannot know by direct introspection anything about the strange things which lie in the depths of our feelings.

I cannot make it too abundantly and emphatically clear that I am essentially an empirical worker in respect to dreams and, I believe, the only one engaged upon pure (as distinct from clinical) dream analysis. It must not be forgotten that we live in an age when even the most scientific minds, once they leave the guiding rails of their own fields of endeavor, have no compunction in expressing utterly unsupported opinions in the most emphatic manner. Everything to do with the mental worlds seems to have become the plaything of human egotism which, excluded from the physical sciences by the discipline of the experimental method, vents its rage in the ever-narrowing fields left to it. I listen with amazed astonishment at the large-scale opinions and windy theories which the most inexperienced people have no com-

[1] See Appendix P for some notes concerning the nature of myths.

punction in uttering on the subject of dreams, their nature and their analysis. Truly the rubber truncheon of tyranny is a fearful thing, but sometimes one wonders just how much less fearful is the mind-rotting and truth-ousting chatter of undisciplined opinion. Our hope lies in the extension of the scientific spirit and method to the field of the mind, whereby the discipline of fact will hush the wild chatter of opinion and achieve the ordered quiet which all truth must have if it is to emerge. I fully believe that by the creation of a new organon of scientific dream analysis, I have taken the first step towards that consummation.

After many years of research in this field I have naturally become so familiar with my facts that they seem to me very simple. And, indeed, they are intrinsically simple. It is only when I come to try and describe them to others that I find that there is no language in which they can be simply described. The very background is missing against which they can be made to fit. I have uncovered a whole new realm of experience, and it is so new that there are no words for its simple and economic exposition. I am in the position of a man who is asked to write a book on chemistry in a language which possesses no name for chemistry, and none for the simple chemical elements. What does the poor fellow do when he wants to refer to oxygen or to hydrogen? Must he call oxygen 'the stuff that makes iron go red' every time he wishes to refer to it? One of the basic experiences with which I am concerned in this book is the manner in which the infant feels or fantasies that his head moves down into his gastro-intestinal tract. In any established science there would be a word for it, because it is so fundamental. But every time I want to refer to it I have to *describe* it. And I dare not invent a word. Neologism is a most presumptuous behavior, and is so often the mark of a crank that it must at all costs be shunned by one whose whole story is so unusual as to be suspect from the very start. For this reason the reader may find the writing in this book labored, repetitive and clumsy. I think that as he perseveres with it he will find that the fault is very largely ascribable to the circumstance described above, rather than to any intrinsic fault in the method of expression. The material is new to every context save the symbolic ones of mythology, so that even the necessary background is missing for its presentation. To the analytical mind of the modern human being all this material is forgotten, not only individually (for we have all been through these experiences) but also collectively, since there is no shared-expression of these experiences available to the modern mind apart from the contents of this present work.

TABLE OF CONTENTS

APPENDICES

The Galileo and the Lavoisier of psychology will be famous men when indeed they come, as come they some day surely will, or past successes are no index to the future. When they do come, however, the necessities of the case will make them 'metaphysical'.

WILLIAM JAMES

Most of us believe—perhaps in large degree intuitively—that there is an underlying, integrating, unifying principle that in some way characterizes the cosmos of which we are a part and makes it truly a universe. Presumably this principle manifests itself in various ways in physics, chemistry, biology, psychology, sociology, history, philosophy, art and ethics. The manifestations are diverse and manifold, but the active principle responsible for them is presumably one.

KIRTLEY F. MATHER
(*Professor Emeritus of Geology, Harvard University*)

Metaphysics could well become man's chief preoccupation of the next century and may even yield a worldwide working consensus on the nature of life and the universe. This metaphysical quest must of course be compatible with the latest proven truths of science, and it is one in which scientists can be useful—but it is not confined to them.

LIFE *magazine, January* 28, 1957

The problem of life will not be solved, I think, by the discovery of specific substances, like the nucleic acids or the hormones. It is not in these that we must seek the secret of life, but rather in the patterns and configurations of matter. . . .

EDMUND W. SINNOTT
(*Dean, Graduate School, Yale University*)

PART ONE

AN OUTLINE OF THE UTERINE ORIGINS OF MIND

Chapter One

THE FETAL SKIN FEELING AS THE PRIMARY PHYSICAL AND PSYCHOLOGICAL FEELING

IN THE COURSE of my analytical work I have unearthed what I believe to be a fundamental principle, namely that every *psychological* feeling derives from an older *physical* feeling. That is to say, I have established a link between emotion and physical feeling. This discovery may not at first seem very impressive, but if the reader will follow me, I think he will ultimately see that it has enormous significance.

In the English language we have a single word 'feeling' to cover two entirely distinct forms of experience. We all know the difference between a physical feeling and that type of emotional experience which I have referred to above as a 'psychological feeling'. Though perhaps we could not all hit upon an immediate and perfect definition, we all know the difference between feeling hot and feeling sad. Possibly we assume that the use of a single word to cover both forms of experience is just a lazy approximation, as when we say that it is our birthday instead of our anniversary, or say that we see ourselves in a mirror instead of our reflection. Superficially the use of the word 'feeling' to cover both forms of experience may be unfortunate, but ultimately there is a very definite justification for it. I shall attempt to describe what I mean by this assertion.

As one sets about the analysis of feelings, one slowly becomes aware that they show an articulation not to be even remotely suspected by the ordinary processes of thought. We speak very loosely and personally of our feelings without having the least idea

3

of their nature or their source. My work has led me to a deep analysis of feelings, and in the course of this analysis I have been impressed by the fact that all emotions (psychological feelings) derive ultimately from physical feelings. This is not immediately obvious even in the course of deep analysis, but I am convinced that it is demonstrable.

Suppose, for instance, to take an actual case known to me, one analyzes a man or woman who has a strong revulsion against receiving help or advice. The tendency is in such cases to suppose either that this characteristic is inexplicable, or that it can be traced back to some older *emotional* feeling such as a revulsion against a dominating father. But I have found that if the feeling be traced back still further it will in the end derive from something much more physical, such as for instance an infancy rejection of the thrust of the mother's nipple into the newborn mouth. This is only one instance taken at random from many, and it is given only as an illustration. But it serves to illustrate what I mean when I say that current psychological feelings can always be traced back to older physical feelings.

I would not want to give the impression that just *any* physical feeling can give rise to an emotional feeling. The matter is not quite so simple as that. There seems to be a dividing line in our young lives behind which physical feelings can turn into psychological feelings, but in front of which this transformation is no longer possible. I do not know where that line is set in our lives. Perhaps it varies from person to person, but I suspect that the variation is not great. I should say, and it is no more than an enlightened guess, that the line is drawn in our lives somewhere between five and seven. I should say that up to that time certain physical experiences can become translated into psychological feelings, but that after that time it is not possible or, at any rate, ever decreasingly so.[1]

I can illustrate what I mean roughly by an analogy drawn from the relation of a piece of coal to the tree from which it was made. We know that coal is the relic of ancient trees which flourished

---

[1] See Appendix J for notes on an essential difference between adult and infancy feeling.

millions of years ago, which fell and through chemical changes were metamorphosed. Every piece of coal, therefore, we know was once part of a living tree. But the converse is not true: not every tree has been turned into coal. In the course of the geological eras a line was drawn behind which it might very roughly be said that any tree could become coal, but in front of which that transmutation was increasingly unlikely. The analogy is not too bad, for it is true that the physical experiences which we undergo from about seven onwards do not seem to make emotional feelings, though they certainly reanimate existing ones. Moreover, the converse is true, namely that the earlier the physical experience, the more likely it is to create emotions.

There is another element involved here which needs to be made clear. That is the fact that these old physical feelings, when they are converted into a psychological feeling, are not transitory. They remain in the organism as a part of its nature. The physical feeling passes away, but the converted impress of it remains in the individual, and acts like an organ of emotion, instead of being just a passing reflection. Let me try to illustrate what I mean by this. Suppose a child of ten falls out of a tree and hurts itself. It certainly may make the child afraid of climbing, perhaps for a very long time, but it will not create an actual emotional organ in the sense indicated above. The child will remember the fall, or he will be in a position to remember it. But when we consider that 'fall' which we have all made long ago, namely the 'fall' from our mother's womb, we find that the physical feelings then experienced have become part of our emotional make-up. Any subsequent physical fall may reanimate this birth shock, which remains in the depths of the feelings as a permanent part of their structure.

I would like to labor this point a little, for indeed it is of vital importance. The difference between the two kinds of 'fall' discussed in the previous paragraph is vital. At the time of birth the infant gets his first sense of weight and of the related pull of gravity. Up to the time of birth the child had felt completely weightless. He had floated in a weightless world without sense of direction. As the amniotic water runs away so the infant for the first time gains the sense of weight, and so also he gains the sense of

5

falling. Slight as the physical 'fall' may be from the mother's body, it becomes the root of our feeling of weight and height. This first impression of weight and height is quite different in character from all that will be ultimately learned by the conscious mind about the pull of the earth and the relation of that pull to height. But every sense of height and of weight, throughout life, will always stem back to the feeling-core formed during the experience of birth. We can never fall or experience the sense of gravity or of height without reanimating this original core of the feelings. Everything we experience in later life flows back to this core as by an irresistible attraction. Every other fall, especially after the age of about five or so, tends to be a transient experience. But this first 'birth fall' remains as a part of ourselves, and forms that organ of the feelings which enables us to react emotionally to weight, height and falling.

The reader will now see clearly what I mean when I say that what we experience currently as psychological feeling is invariably derived from old physical feelings experienced in infancy, which have become transmuted and buried in the depths of the organism. He will understand me when I say that each such transformed physical feeling does not just reappear once-for-all as a psychological feeling, but it acts again and again, just as if it were an organ of the body. To revert to our coal analogy, the piece of coal, once it is burned, dissipates the energy gathered from the sun millions of years ago by the living tree. But the transformed physical feeling of infancy does not dissipate its content merely by giving rise to a current psychological feeling. On the contrary, it has the power to manifest over and over again. In short, it has become not merely a buried feeling, but it has become a literal *organ* of feeling, able to evoke current psychological feeling. It has become a fixed part of our psychological anatomy.

Let us try to explore backwards into the life-story of any human being. It is obvious that if, in imagination, we turn back the clock of a human life, we shall find this individual life involved in fewer and fewer physical experiences as we turn back the clock. If we take the life of a man of, say, thirty years of age, and go back in this way, we shall find that with every eliminated year there is also eliminated a number of physical experiences, emotional experiences and thoughts. Eventually we shall reach a point where rational thoughts become few and scattered, but where feelings, both physical and psychological, are intensified. And if we turn back the clock until we arrive at our man's first birthday anniversary, we shall have him in a state in which the vast majority of his feelings have been stripped from him. Here I must be careful to point out, however, that what has been taken away from him is not really his feeling, but the various *divisions* into which his feeling has been drawn by experience. Let us translate this into the analogy of the reversed motion picture of a plant's growth. The picture begins with the plant at full growth, and as it unwinds it shows the plant shrinking back and ever back to the seedling. As this reverse process continues, we see how the many tendrils and branches into which the plant's energies have been drawn, become increasingly reduced in number, until at last we see only a single little stem. That is the kind of thing I have in mind when I try to depict the way in which the turning back of the clock of a man's life reduces the number of external experiences into which his capacity to feel has been drawn. It is not the feeling itself that has been reduced, but the divisions into which it has been drawn. Not only logically, but also by other indications, I am persuaded that there is an original capacity to feel which is not *increased* by experience, but *divided* by experience. In these terms I suggest that the baby of one year may be regarded as a little ball of feeling waiting to be drawn out into branches and tendrils by experience of life in space.

Now let us turn the clock back the one remaining year, and by this means come to the time of birth. What have we now? We find now a little organism which, after living an aquatic life in the water of the amnion, where it was supplied with its needs through the navel, through which it also 'breathed' and 'excreted', has just recently been extruded from the mother's body to face an entirely different kind of existence. What of its feelings now?

They are all focused upon a relatively few experiences. They are focused upon the eyes which, having so far lived in relative darkness, are now stimulated by electromagnetic radiation. To a smaller extent they are also focused upon the ears which, up to the time of birth, had lived in relative silence, but which now are assailed by air waves. To a still smaller extent they are focused upon the nose and mouth, which before birth had snuffled and gulped an occasional drop of warm amniotic fluid, but which now are stimulated by the passage of a strange, cold gas, and the related molecular irritations which produce the sensations of smell and taste. They are focused also upon the frightful new experience of the opening lungs which, heretofore solid, are suddenly blown out and hollowed by the inrush of air. They are concerned with the contrast of feeling caused by being exposed to the cold air after the warmth of the maternal body. They are concerned with the new sense of weight, insecurity and deprivation caused by the loss of that warm, compressed and weightless existence of the fetus floating in the amniotic water.

All these experiences we might, of course, surmise. But indeed when we analyze any human being we find that all these feeling-experiences are deeply impressed into the very core of our organism. Just what the mechanism of this impress is I am not competent to say, but the fact is that the analysis of dreams makes it very plain that at the core of all our feelings towards the external world there lies this tightly compacted group of feelings caused by the experience of birth. All our reactions to the world are affected by this compact group of primary feelings, and it is a fact of my experience that here we have the source of a great number of human character traits. Indeed, at the very beginning of my analytical work I saw little more, if anything, in the depths of the feelings save these violent impressions caused by the experience of birth.[1] This subject in itself is big enough to fill a large book and to be the basis of a whole psychotherapy. But the object of this book takes us deeper, and so I will leave the subject of birth aside as secondary to our present discussion, and will turn back the clock a little further, whereupon our man now disappears

---

[1] My experience is that birth memories dominate our dreams until they are expunged by analysis. Only then are the deeper and subtler memories able to achieve dream expression. One reason for this domination will appear in Appendix E, but no doubt the major cause is the severity of the traumata and the revolutionary nature of the changes suffered.

from view, and lies curled up in the warm water of the womb.

What of his feelings now? Are they merely *in potentia*? Apart from some possible slight sense in the eyes of a dull red glow through the abdominal tissues of the mother, and some occasional sound through the same covering, has the unborn child no feeling at all of its environment? It was in seeking the answer to this question that I came at last upon powerful evidence which showed me plainly that in the unborn child all feeling for his environment is focused upon the skin.

The skin of the unborn baby is a kind of primary sense organ—an overall organ of touch which touches its limited watery environment equally in all directions. It is this primary feeling, this primary physical feeling, which creates that focal sense, that unified nuclear sense, which eventually will become the psychological feeling of the "I".

I do not want to discuss what other writers on psychology mean by the term 'ego', but insofar as that word signifies the focal sense of self hood in the stream of feeling and awareness, here is the source of it. The *primary* psychological feeling at the core of *all* psychological feeling is the feeling of being an "I" or of possessing an 'ego', and this derives direct from the primary *physical* feeling which was created by the touch of the fetal skin upon the amnion and its water. So we come to the assertion which my analyses reveal, namely that all psychological feeling is derived from once-physical feelings which have become encapsulated and transmuted; and that at the *root* of all psychological feeling is that primary physical feeling generated or stimulated by the touch of the fetal body upon its uterine surround.

The reader may wonder how I know that this primary physical feeling of the fetal skin is indeed the source of the ultimate post-natal sense of the 'ego'. Though I do not wish to run ahead of my story, I will say here that whenever the sense of the 'ego' is analyzed, it is found that it contains deeply buried memories of the fetal self lying in the mother's body. Even that statement is not forceful enough: *the ego itself is composed of this feeling*. Indeed, in the course of this book it will be shown that the brain itself eventually assumes this feeling in a very specific way, the thalamus at the core of the brain assuming the old feelings of the fetal body,

9

so that *psychologically* we all feel that the thalamus *is* our own fetal body lying in the womb, the skull being felt as the womb. This feeling is deeply hidden from consciousness and none of us has any access to it, so that this assertion will inevitably sound incredible. Yet the fact has been demonstrated over and over again in the course of my analyses; myths and primitive notions reflect it; and in some psychotic conditions it bursts through in distorted form into consciousness.

But I am running ahead of my story in order to show the reader the way it is heading. Let me return to my sheep. As I investigated the primary sensations felt by the child at birth, so I became aware that although *physically* they were brand new in the experience of the child, *psychologically* they were felt to be *divisions* of the primary feeling generated by the fetal skin. The eyes *as optical instruments* experienced the stimulation of radiation as an entirely new physical feeling.[1] But *psychologically* the newborn child feels that the sense of light in the eyes is a division of that primary feeling which was generated on the fetal skin before birth. The same is true of hearing. The auditory mechanism experiences the impingement of air waves upon the ear-drums as an entirely new feeling. But *psychologically* the child feels that the excitation thus caused in the brain is a *division* of that primary feeling which was generated all over the fetal skin before birth. The same is true of smell and taste.

Psychologically, therefore, birth involves the disintegration of the primary *physical* feeling caused by the touch of the fetal skin upon its surround. The unified prenatal physical feeling seems to be split by the birth experience into the special senses of sight, hearing, smell, taste and certain other physical feelings. But at the same time (and this is of profound importance) the overall fetal feeling becomes transformed into that psychological feeling which we afterwards experience as the 'ego'. This sense of 'ego' will not appear in consciousness until some time has elapsed after birth. It has to undergo many strange experiences before it can become established in the brain. But this is the first instance of the

---

[1] The reader will understand that I mean that the brain experiences the excitation of the rods and cones of the eyes as a new event. I am not being too precise on the mechanism, as it is my present task to give the overall picture.

changeover from a physical feeling into a psychological feeling, namely the changeover from the overall physical feeling of the fetal skin to the compacted psychological sense of focus we call 'I'.

The division of the primary fetal skin feeling among the special senses is supported by a strange fact which my analyses have revealed, namely that underneath the primary feelings of seeing, hearing, tasting and smelling there can always be discovered traces of the fetal skin feeling. Dreams not infrequently present the symbolic figure of a man who has eyes all over his skin, or of an animal skin covered with eyes. Although, as explained in the Foreword, I am omitting from this volume my mythological evidence, yet I feel compelled to point out here that this symbol of the eye-covered skin is to be met with in mythology.[1] I have always found in the analysis of dreams that such symbols fit neatly into a context dealing with the feeling at birth that what once was felt all over the skin is now felt in the eyes. It was indeed a dream of this order, presented to me by an untutored maid-servant, which first alerted me to the existence of the fetal skin feeling underlying the special senses, and set my mind upon the track which has bit by bit uncovered the whole content of this book.

What is true of the sense of sight at birth is true also, though in a lesser degree, of the sense of hearing. Under the sense of hearing there can be unearthed the memory of the fact that at birth the fetal skin feeling seemed to be assumed in part by the sense of hearing. Quite frequently in dreams and allied associations a drum is used as the symbol of the skin that becomes associated with noise—a very apt and clever piece of symbolism! And in mythology we find what might be called 'musical skins', as witness that of Marsyas, whose skin was torn from him because of his failure in a *musical* contest, and which after death would quiver to the strains of certain *music* dear to its late owner.

The same thing is true also of smell and taste in rapidly descending order of importance. Dreams represent the fact that under the sense of smell there lurks the primary feeling of the fetal skin. I have seen this symbolized in dreams by means of such things as an

[1] See Appendices A and D.

improperly-cured lion's skin which became offensive to its owners, and hence made a splendid symbol for the conjunction of skin and smell. Dreams also reveal that the memory of the fetal skin underlies our sense of taste, a condition which I have seen symbolized by a 'tasty' skin, as in a dream which told of eating the 'crackling' of pork.

The symbolism frequently takes a still more concrete form. Dream symbolism sometimes suggests the feeling that the fetus itself, or its skin, has actually migrated into the eyes, the ears, the nose or the mouth. This peculiar illusion we can understand quite easily if we stop for a second to realize what has taken place, and imagine the results which might easily accrue as a result of a cataclysmic revolution in the sensory apparatus of the newborn child. First of all we must rid ourselves of any assumption that the newborn child has the least means of orientation. He simply does not know where he is, and if we would try to understand his bewildered feelings, we must imagine ourselves slightly stupefied, drugged, blindfolded, then taken up in an airplane and hurled about the sky in an aerobatic performance. With no visual or auditory perceptions to check the testimony of his feelings, the newborn child is susceptible to the weirdest confusions. So that when the skin ceases to act as the unique sense organ, and its role is suddenly assumed by the previously quiescent organs of the head, there is no logical reason why the child should not feel that his fetal skin has suddenly appeared in those organs, so that the fetal self now resides in the orifices of the head.

By this time the reader will have had his credulity stretched to its utmost, but I can assure him that I have not imagined the testimony which has stared at me again and again from the symbolic forms of dreams and associations. Moreover, I can assure him that this same experience is testified to in myths and folktales, the best instance known to me being found in the story of *Little Snow-white*. In this story the child is shown as fleeing in wild despair and fear from the knife of the huntsman. She rushes through dark and confusing woods, only to come at length to the home of the seven little men. The flight of *Little Snow-white* from the huntsman's knife symbolizes the terrified feelings of the newborn child as the knife cuts away the umbilical cord. The house of the seven little men symbolizes the seven orifices of the head (two eyes, two ears, two nostrils and the mouth) wherein the feelings of the fetal skin seem to lodge. The seven little men are simply seven little divisions of the fetus, signifying the fact that the fetal feeling has been divided among the seven orifices of the head.[1]

While on the subject of the special senses in relation to the fetal skin feeling, I should mention the fact that inevitably the sense of sight claims a predominant share of the fetal skin feeling. I say this is inevitable because, of all the senses, that of sight is vastly the most powerful. And it is a fact that at birth the lost fetal skin feeling becomes very closely identified with the sense of sight. I presume, though of this I have no absolute certainty, that this is the reason why the fetal skin feeling is in dreams and myths persistently symbolized by light or by a brightly-colored garment or by a majestic shining figure. That is to say, I assume that what happens is that the awakening of the feeling of light in the eyes, plus the 'migration' thereto of the fetal skin feeling, results in a sort of composite feeling of fetal skin and light, so that in effect our most direct and poignant feeling-link between the prenatal state and the postnatal state is this sense of light. Because the eyes and their association with light receive so large a 'share' of the fetal skin feeling, we tend in our feelings to look back at the fetal skin feeling as a cloak of light.[2]

If one contemplates the Heroes and the Saviors of the past, one is immediately struck by the fact that a very large proportion of them not only have associations with light or with fire, but also possess the most marked fetal undertones. I will mention here only the Semitic Hero Samson, whose name derives from a Hebrew word meaning 'sunshine'. He is betrayed by Delilah, whose name is related not only to night but also to the sense of a spiral twist and to the sense of something dangling at the end of a line. In other words, she has definite etymological associations

---

[1] This does not imply that every newborn child essentially feels that its lost skin feeling is divided up into seven parts—it merely feels a division.
[2] See Appendix D.

with the placenta and the spirally twisting navel-string; which is supported by the fact that Samson met her in the valley of Sorek, a name which is related to the vine, to red wine and to eye-piercing red light.[1] These few words may serve to show the reader what I mean when I say that mythology is full of men of Light or Fire, all having marked fetal undertones.

I revert again to the fetal skin feeling in its original (prenatal) condition. How is it generated? This question has not unnaturally exercised my mind a very great deal since the day in 1946 when I first became certain of its reality. I have always supposed that it might be related to the fine hairs (*lanugo*) which cover the skin of the fetus from the fifth month onwards. Since each of these hairs has at its root a nerve-ending, there is every reason to suppose that the movements of the fetus, and of the mother, might cause these hairs to become gently titillated, so that they would evoke neural currents that would impinge upon the thalamus. Though such currents might be small, we must set against that the fact that the unborn thalamus may be specially sensitive. This I say because it is known that the thalamus, when not inhibited by the cerebral cortices, magnifies every incoming signal, so that (to quote a writer on neurology) every unpleasant feeling becomes agonizing, and every pleasant feeling voluptuous. That the fetal thalamus feels the fetal skin impulses with intensity seems to follow from the fact that the cerebral cortices of the fetus are not fully active. In the first place they are not as fully oxy-genated as they will be from birth onwards. In the second place they are designed to deal with the varied demands of postnatal space, and have thus presumably little work to do *in utero*. Such considerations incline me to the belief that although the actual irritation of the fetal skin may be relatively slight, the feeling engendered in the thalamus will be disproportionately powerful for the reasons shown.

The feeling registered in the fetal thalamus is a very simple one. It evokes the sense of a nucleus lying within an undifferentiated

[1] For the reason explained in the Foreword I have deferred publication of my mythological material, though in it the myth of Samson is fully analyzed. See Appendix D for a brief discussion of the figure of The Shining One as fetal symbol.

14

periphery. It does not matter whether we think of this nucleus as the whole fetal body lying in the uterus, or whether we think of it as the thalamus lying at the focus of a rain of neural impulses. The result in the feelings is the same: the fetus gains as his basic feeling-experience the sense of a nucleus within a periphery. This sense is burned into his feelings by an intensity of neural concentration which few human beings ever postnatally attain. For what must seem an eternity the fetal thalamus receives a monotonously persistent drizzle of neural impulses arising on the fetal skin. This is a neural condition which contrasts sharply with that of the postnatal organism, which becomes the focus of almost endlessly variant stimuli. This prenatal experience may be thought of as 'burning a basic feeling' into the very core of the organism. It is my belief that this primary, intensive feeling of the fetal thalamus, unable to be given any orderly discharge through the cerebral cortex, turns, as it were, inward and establishes a veritable tie-post in the feelings. It is this focal spot 'burned into the feelings' which is the primary physical feeling of man, and which after birth becomes transmuted into the primary *psychological* feeling, which is precisely the sense of being a focus, a point in the midst of life, which is to say an "I", a self. It is this primary 'clot' in the feelings which serves to arrest the subsequent (postnatal) flow of feelings and to gather them about itself to form the "I". By this instrumentality the otherwise endless flow of feeling-events is converted into a persistent entity which defies the flow of time. By rough analogy the fetal skin feeling is like a tree which, felled into a torrent, gradually collects the flotsam of the stream and converts it from a sequence into a persistent integration. The fetal skin feeling creates in the feelings that nuclear focus to which may gather the events which otherwise would merely pass in the torrent of experience.

The reader may be relieved to know that I am fully aware that the nervous system was created for no such purpose as here outlined. It was evolved as a rudimentary organic telegraph to enable the organism to act as a whole. There was no foreshowing in it of the human "I". The nervous system, evolved for one purpose, has become enlisted in another. In this there is nothing new, for the history of evolution is lavishly sprinkled with similar adaptations. Who could have predicted that the lungfish would lead to Caruso, or that the fins, forerunners of the hands, would ultimately make possible a Heifetz! The fact is that whenever we say "I", the feeling at the back of it is the feeling of our own fetal body lying in the womb. For several reasons this feeling is inaccessible to consciousness. For one thing, our postnatal consciousness did not begin until this basic feeling of the fetal skin was done for. Moreover, since this basic feeling is the very instrument of consciousness, consciousness cannot penetrate it. One cannot think oneself into the feeling of the "I" any more than one can look into one's own eye.[1] My analytical methods permit the examination of the "I", and although it is impossible to demonstrate it here, it is a fact that such examination always reveals the "I" to be the impacted memory of the fetal self *in utero*. The great myths support this contention to the hilt. All the great gods and heroes of mythology show strong signs of being not only the representatives of the human "I", but of being also the representatives of the fetal skin feeling. This I have demonstrated conclusively in my work of mythological analysis.[2]

The reader will undoubtedly be feeling that my description of the human 'I' denigrates it to the level of a mere physical feeling. How could the oganization of feeling upon the fetal skin or in the fetal thalamus ultimate in the genius of a Beethoven or the personality of a Winston Churchill? The answer offered by this book is that the fetal skin feeling is only the *instrument* of the self. It acts as a kind of 'configurational resonator' by means of which the pattern of creation is evoked in the depths of the feelings. The focal feeling created by the fetal body lying in the womb, and carried on after birth by the relation of that focal feeling to postnatal experience, creates in the depths of the self a configuration strikingly like that which dominates the whole field of external phenomena. If we look at the external world we shall see that it is

[1] We may certainly see our own eye by using a mirror. So also can we see into our own "I" if we use the mirror provided by my analytical methods. This whole book is, in fact, fundamentally a report of what is to be seen.

[2] In this book I have restricted the use of this material to a few brief lines in Appendix D.

everywhere dominated by the simple pattern best represented by the sun lying amid its ring of planets. This basic pattern is common to all creation, and is not peculiar to the solar system. It is the pattern also of the atom, of the galaxies, of the living cell, of society and even of the total cosmos. All this I shall amplify in Chapter Four. This same pattern is provided in the human feelings by the fetal skin irritations and their impress upon the fetal thalamus. The resultant sense of "I" thus created also in turn achieves the same pattern, since it eventually gathers about itself a periphery of postnatal feelings to which it acts as the nuclear core. Thus the nervous system provides the configurational analogue of the basic pattern of the cosmos itself. My conclusion, which I shall develop further, is that creation is done by a brooding spirit which creates by imposing a single design upon all its creations. It is this pattern which the configuration of the fetal skin feeling registers.

However, the matter is not quite so simple as this chapter might seem to imply. I myself at first thought that the fetal skin feeling creates in the nervous system a bias which was sufficient to permit a condition of resonance between the nervous system and the cosmos. But later I discovered that this was an over-simplification. The fetal skin feeling merely sets the stage for the much more complicated experiences which will be outlined in Chapter Two.

Chapter Two

THE DYNAMIC EFFECT UPON THE FETAL SKIN FEELING OF THE CIRCULATION OF BLOOD IN THE UMBILICAL CORD

I BEGIN THIS chapter by reasserting that the picture of the 'ego' presented in Chapter One is only a partial picture. It represents, in fact, roughly the kind of picture which I had been able to construct after the first four years of my researches. Although I did not realize it at that time, it is essentially a *static* picture, but to this day it makes an excellent way of approaching the total picture now to be developed.

The picture of the uterine feelings was converted to a dynamic one by the discovery that the fetal organism is only a *part* of the original 'mind-making apparatus'. The *whole* apparatus is to be found in the total uterine organism, consisting of the fetus, the placenta and the umbilical cord. I shall presently show that the circulation of blood between the fetus and the placenta through the umbilical cord is the full instrument of the evocation of the 'ego'.

The discovery was revolutionary in more ways than one. Not only did it transform my whole picture of the origins of the 'ego', but it also emphasized the fact that mind is not the special product or phenomenon of the nervous system. For the umbilical cord has no nerves: no nerves connect the fetus with the maternal body or with the placenta. Yet I uncovered consistent and persistent evidence to show that it is the beat of blood in the umbilical cord which evokes in the fetus those primary elements of feeling which form the basis of mind. These elements, imposed later upon the nervous system, form the mind. *Mind is a configurational imposition upon the brain. It is not the product of the brain itself, and on the whole the nerves are not primarily concerned in its evocation.*

I ought perhaps to say at once that I am in no doubt as to the origins of the uterine organism. I am aware that the fetus, the placenta and the umbilical cord were orginally evolved for much more mundane purposes than the evocation of mind. Something over fifty million years ago the egg-laying mammals found themselves hard pressed to preserve their eggs from the predatory reptiles and lizards. In response to this challenge, they appear to have evolved a sort of internal nest, the womb, in which their eggs could be deposited and fertilized, and where the resultant embryo might be reared. To enable the embryos to live in this maternal enclosure, means had to be evolved to supply them with the necessary chemicals, and to carry away their waste products. This was done by evolving the placenta, a flat, cakelike organ in which the blood of the mother could pass *close to* the embryo's blood, enabling chemical exchanges to take place between them. At the same time, a system of flexible tubes was evolved to enable the blood of the embryo to reach the placenta and return again. This uterine complex of organs was thus originally a survival mechanism pure and simple. It had nothing directly to do with mind at all, nor did it possess any obvious attributes which would fit it to become the instrument of mind. Yet the back-and-forth flow of blood, as I shall presently show, has become the means of the evocation in us of the primary elements of mind. Therefore I can but assume that the umbilical circulation, like the nervous system itself, has had imposed upon it a configurational function which is entirely different from the physical function for which it was evolved, yet this superimposition has not involved any observable change in the anatomical structures.

The discovery of the new facts in no way diminished the importance of those outlined in Chapter One. Rather, they increased their importance but changed their emphasis. Whereas previously I had seen the fetal skin feeling as the unique instrument of the ego's making, I saw now that it played a vital role in a larger mechanism. For unless the fetus had first been made to feel

The Nature of the Self

nuclear by the fetal skin feeling, and thus had been polarized in its feelings *vis-à-vis* the uterus, the umbilical circulation could not have created the alternating sense of polarity which is the essence of the 'ego'. The point is so vital that I feel I must make it absolutely clear:—

The circulation of the blood in the umbilical cord would be just a physical fact and no more unless some starting point had been established in the feelings which would endow it with configurational meaning. The crucial starting point was, I am inclined to think, the nuclear sense evoked by the fetal skin feeling. Because the fetal body felt to be nuclear to the womb, it became possible for the umbilical circulation to modulate that nuclear feeling by constantly interrelating it with the peripheral feeling offered by the functions of the placenta. As I shall presently show, the umbilical flow of blood causes an alternating emphasis and reduction in the nuclear feeling of the fetus *vis-à-vis* the placenta. The reader may be puzzled to understand why such a rhythm between the nuclear fetus and the peripheral placenta should be of importance to the evocation of mental elements. I shall show as we go on that mind is a reflection in man of the basic structure and rhythm of the cosmos, and that these are of the same *order of relations* as the basic structure and rhythm of the uterine organism, these being in both cases the structure of a nucleus within a periphery, related by the rhythm of a two-way flow of energy.

All that I have said in Chapter One applies here, save that all is now converted into dynamic terms of flow and response. Thus, for instance, the fetal skin feeling, which is nuclear in a static sense, as indicated in Chapter One, is converted by the umbilical flow into a dynamic sense of thrust and penetrant power. The umbilical arterial flow[1] increases the fetal sense of nuclear status, and endows it with a dynamic sense of being able to thrust something (i.e. blood) into the 'hollow' placenta and to occupy that hollowness. Thus in the umbilical arterial flow the fetus magnifies and expands its static nuclear sense into a dynamic and

---

[1] The umbilical arterial flow is the outgoing flow of blood from the fetus to the placenta. It is carried by two small tubes twisted helically around the umbilical vein. See Appendix L.

penetrative sense, and in this way reaffirms its own nuclear status and at the same time also affirms the peripheral status of the placenta. It is in these terms that dreams have shown me how the umbilical arterial outflow converts the static skin feeling of the fetus into a dynamic sense of being nuclear, hence penetrant and occupying.

I soon discovered that there is a complication. The fetal blood, having reached the placenta, and having rid itself of waste and taken aboard fresh material, then moves back to the fetal body through the umbilical vein. Physically, this pulse of returning blood into the navel is the source of life to the fetus. *Configurationally, it is the source of dismay, for in this vascular inflow the placenta is felt to become the solid and nuclear agent, while in like degree the fetal body is felt to be made hollow.* The tables are turned. Whereas in the umbilical arterial flow the fetus felt to be aggressively nuclear and penetrant, in the umbilical venous flow he feels to be the victim of placental aggression, and to be hollowed out and occupied.

The circulation of blood in the umbilical cord thus sets up an alternating reversal of primary feeling in the relation of the fetus to the placenta. The alternation is between solid and hollow, which is to say, in other terms, between nuclear and peripheral, or penetrant and penetrable. Here I must pause for a moment to admit that I have used the word 'feeling' in this paragraph in an unorthodox way. For since the umbilical cord has no nerves, and since by the word 'feeling' we generally refer to something related to neural activity, some adjustment must be made. This will be made clear later when I make what explanation I can of the link between blood and nerves.

Another complicating factor must now be mentioned. Up to this point I have presented the dynamic picture of the fetal feelings in terms of penetration and counter-penetration. That is to say, I have presented the picture of the fetus as a kind of perpetual jouster, who constantly strikes out at his periphery with a succession of blood-pulses, and just as constantly is the recipient of similar pulses back from the periphery. That picture is certainly not wrong, and it certainly is one aspect of the fetal feelings, but it is not the only one. In addition, the fetus feels that he himself travels down the umbilical arteries and enters the placenta, where his nuclear virtue is somehow dissipated, but from which he recovers and returns to the fetal body via the umbilical vein. This constant sense of 'journeying' is very real, and it seems able to go hand in hand in the feelings with the simpler sense of the 'jouster' as outlined above.

This raises a vital question: How can the fetal skin feeling, which is in itself evidently of neural origin, become so identified with the blood that it feels to journey down into the placenta and back? I can account for this only on the supposition that the fetal skin feeling is not the simple neural feeling previously described, but that it has *two* distinct component parts. The first of these is precisely that neural feeling described in Chapter One. The second is created by electrical activity in the blood. For this hypothesis I claim no more than the status of an enlightened guess. It is one of those necessary but deliberately tentative hypotheses which every researcher must create in order to avoid working and thinking in a total vacuum.

There can be hardly any doubt that the fetal skin *is* the seat of electrical polarities. One possible source of such charges is the heart itself, which generates action-currents that are conducted to the skin by the electrolytic activity of the blood.[1] Another possible source is the generation of 'diaphragm currents' and 'pore membrane currents' which are formed when an electrolyte (in this case probably also sodium chloride) is forced through capillaries by the heart's action. In addition to this, we may remember that in the postnatal body friction between the skin and its clothes may generate static charges up to as much as two hundred volts. It is hardly conceivable that the fetal skin can be without some frictional charge, and whereas ordinarily such a charge would be dissipated in the salty water of the amnion, it is a fact that the fetal skin is covered from about the fifth month onward by a 'cheesy varnish' called *vernix caseosa*. This varnish is a specific electrical insulator.

[1] That is, by the electrolytic activity mainly of sodium chloride (common salt) dissolved in the blood.

Umbilical Cord as Solenoid

It is my suggestion that this fetal skin potential, whether generated by one or by several means, is prevented by the *vernix caseosa* from dissipating into the amniotic fluid, and finds its discharge by passing down the umbilical arteries, where it discharges at the placental barrier. I suggest that this makes a fair working hypothesis to explain the undoubted fact that the fetus feels that some virtue resident in his skin is drawn away down the umbilical cord and destroyed.[1]

Another fact seems to align itself naturally with the electrical hypothesis. The structure of the umbilical cord is virtually that of an electrical solenoid. A solenoid is formed when an electrical conductor is wound back upon itself in a helical fashion, or when helically wound around a soft iron core. The umbilical vein is a relatively straight vessel, and around it the twin arteries are twisted in a helical fashion. Many reasons have been given for this peculiar fact, but none has so far been proved conclusive.[2] A solenoid is one of the most important devices in all electrical practice. I am compelled to wonder if the umbilical cord may not in degree act as a solenoid.

The reader may suppose this to be *sheer* guesswork. It is rather *enlightened* guesswork, for there are several facts which give it backbone. One of these is the fact that this umbilical pattern not only is clearly imprinted somewhere deep in the feelings of us all, but that wherever it appears it evokes most powerful feelings. In every one of us the triple structure of the umbilical cord is registered. We all show a deep awareness of the fact that the umbilical cord is composed of one large and two small vessels. We all remember clearly that the two small vessels were helically wound around the relatively straight vein. Why? Why should this umbilical pattern have made so deep an impress in us all? I suggest that it is because this pattern has played a vital role in the making of the 'ego'. What we call "I" bears a deep imprint of its origins in this 'fleshly solenoid' we call the navel-string or umbilical cord.

---

[1] The weakness of this hypothesis is that it offers an explanation for the sucking away and the destruction of the fetal skin feeling, but so far none for its restoration through the umbilical venous return-flow.

[2] See Appendix L.

The Nature of the Self

The universality of this umbilical imprint is confirmed by the fact that mythology is full of the mysterious serpent on the tree of life, or of the twin snakes upon the staff. The basic myth of our Western civilization is that of Adam and Eve as the first parents of mankind. Here we have the immemorial couple, symbolizing the fetus and the placenta, occupying the garden of the womb with the magic tree and the serpent.[1]

In the days before electricity was understood there could be no possible objective referent for this coiled serpent who haunts the depths of our feelings. But now I think we are probably in a position to begin to understand his significance. He probably represents not merely the umbilical cord, but the subjective impression created by the electrical or electromagnetic phenomena engendered in it. It is perfectly conceivable that the *ions* in the blood may interact as they pass in the two-way flow of the cord. Let us imagine a positively charged *ion* of *sodium chloride* moving in one of the umbilical arteries, and being whirled around in the helical stream of blood. Let us imagine also a negatively charged *ion* of the same substance moving in the opposite direction in the umbilical vein. Is it not possible that the two *ions* might interact electromagnetically through the tissues of the umbilical cord, each influencing the other? I am not suggesting that this interaction could in itself convey or evoke anything akin to human mind. But it could be part of the mechanism of the configurational dispostion of electrical charges which would provide the shimmering pattern of relations that could be influenced by the space-time structure. I am sure that this picture is unsatisfactory, but I am also sure that a sympathetic expert in electronics might with a few deft touches put it into reasonable shape. Certainly there is no medium better fitted than electricity to register the delicate play of nuclear and peripheral relations, for electricity itself is nothing but that very thing. Electricity appears only when an atomic nucleus loses part of its periphery.

I should perhaps add here that I have frequently seen in dreams elusive symbols which might well be susceptible of interpretation

[1] These few words are but a tantalizing excerpt torn from the context of my mythological interpretations; see Appendix I.

24

on the above lines. Again and again one comes upon the symbol of *three* things in which *two* are opposed to *one*, and in which the two affect the one and *vice versa*. For instance, in order to be specific, let me make up a composite dream fragment from typical material known to me. A man dreams that he is walking along a straight road. Suddenly he sees two drunken men coming towards him, lurching and weaving about the road. They seem to threaten him, and he hurries past them, but they leave on his mind a sinister impression. Experience shows that such a dream, when analyzed, is highly likely to yield strong umbilical symbolism. The straight road will turn out to be the umbilical vein, and the two men will turn out to be the umbilical arteries, or the blood in these arteries, their weaving being but a way of representing the umbilical arterial twist. This is the kind of material I have in mind when I say that there are not wanting indications that the blood flowing in the umbilical arteries does in some way affect the venous blood as the two pass in their separate vessels.

It now remains for me to give some indication of a possible mechanism of linkage between the fetal skin feeling described in Chapter One, and the electrical skin charges suggested in this chapter. How could they interact? I suggest that the fetal skin may well be a transformer from electrical to neural energy. Such a concept would certainly fit the facts revealed by deep analysis of dreams. That the skin is equipped to play some such role there is hardly any doubt. The true skin (the corium) is rich in nerve-endings and in blood-vessels. The skin has been described as an important medium for transmitting physico-chemical substances and electro-magnetic fields to the blood and the nervous system.[1] My own suspicion, for what it may be worth, is that the blood in the small capillaries of the skin exerts an electrical influence upon the nerve-endings.

In this way, it seems to me, the two separate components of the fetal skin feeling may come into conjunction, and may achieve an identity so that the experience in the blood, which involves the constant dissipation of electrical energy from the fetal skin in the placenta, may become identified so closely with the (neural) fetal

[1] Tromp. *Psychical Physics*. p. 173.

skin feeling that it appears as if the fetal skin itself (and with it the fetus as nuclear agent) is sucked down into the placenta and destroyed there.

These are truly suppositions, and are no more than an effort to weld together certain facts into a tentative whole, to stimulate and to permit of experiment, and also to make possible a meaningful presentation of the facts. These suppositions may not turn out to be wholly right. But it should be clearly understood that any uncertainty I may feel about these hypotheses does not affect my complete certainty as to the facts. These facts are that deep in our feelings may be found indications that the umbilical arterial flow seems at one and the same time to increase the fetal nuclear status by demonstrating its power to penetrate the hollow placenta, while at the same time it seems to threaten the fetal energy with dissipation. Similarly, the umbilical venous flow seems to reverse this process, and to cause the fetus itself to feel penetrated and hollow; yet at the same time it seems to restore the fetal nuclear energy again.

There is a double ambivalence here which will bear repetition:

1. The umbilical arterial flow increases the fetal nuclear sense by adding to it the dynamic sense of penetrant power.
2. Yet at the same time it seems to draw the fetus away from its high place and to destroy its nuclear virtue.
3. The umbilical venous flow restores the fetal virtue to itself—the fetus feeling like a traveler who has gone away and returned again.
4. Yet this same venous flow makes the fetus feel as if the placenta is now nuclear and penetrant, while he is hollow and punctured.

In essence, to sum up, we have been considering certain basic representations in the feelings concerning the relation of the nucleus to the periphery. The nucleus feels solid and impenetrable, and thus at his right place at the focus. The periphery at once heightens and protects that nuclear sense but, at the same time, threatens it. The number of feelings generated in the umbilical circulation is very small. But they constitute the feeling-nucleus by which ever more complex patterns of feeling can build up. I propose now to outline the primary feelings which are evoked in the fetus by the umbilical circulation, and to show that they have in them the seeds of mind.[1]

The primary sense generated by the umbilical flow is the relation between giving and taking in the simplest sense. This is, of course, closely bound up with the feelings of being solid and hollow, since the recipient must accommodate what is given to him and must in some degree provide a condition of recipient hollowness. It is closely related also to the twin senses of feeding and excreting. The umbilical cord is the instrument of the first 'feeding' in the very widest sense of the term, as it is also the instrument of the widest possible sense of excretion. The umbilical vein is the first 'sucking mouth' and the umbilical arteries are the forerunners of the rectal and urethral tubes.

The back and forth of the umbilical flow is felt by the fetus to increase and to diminish his nuclear status, and even to reverse it, making him feel hollow and peripheral. The blood which leaves the fetal body is felt as a thrust of nuclear energy which enhances the focal feeling of the fetus. It enhances this feeling because it inclines the fetus to feel that he has the power to go forth and to pierce and occupy the placenta. At the same time the fetus feels the opposite sense of this outflow, namely that it causes a diminution of his nuclear status, and a fundamental loss of self. Thus the outward flow of blood down the umbilical arteries acts both to increase and to diminish the fetal sense of nuclearity. And this ambivalent feeling will later be explored in some detail to show that it is the basis of a complex which combines three elements, namely (1) the sense of excretion,[2] (2) the sense of aggression, and (3) the sense of loss of self.

The blood which returns to the fetal body by the umbilical vein diminishes the nuclear, solid feeling of the fetus. The ingoing blood causes the fetus to feel not only less nuclear, but at the same time hollow. It seems, indeed, that the feelings of solidity and

---

[1] To understand what I mean by 'the seeds of mind', one must remember that mind is synonymous with configuration. In principle, it is my conviction that whatever serves to establish the universal design in the feelings will tend to evoke the echo of the cosmic pattern and so create mind.

[2] The umbilical arterial flow is the primary excretion.

hollowness are completely in balance, inasmuch as everything which diminishes solidity creates the feeling of hollowness, the converse being also true. The fact that the fetus feels the returning venous blood as an invading nuclear element (able to pierce him and occupy him) creates the sense of fear and loss. Since at the same time the inflow of blood feeds and oxygenates the fetal body, another complex is set up in which the following elements are found: (1) the fetus feels a sense of aggression against himself; (2) a consequent diminution of his nuclear status; and (3) a sense of ingestion and restoration.

All the foregoing represents the fetus as an entity who is doing things via the umbilical cord to another entity, the placenta, and who at the same time is having things done to him. Yet, as I have said before, at the same time the fetal nuclear feeling actually seems to travel down the umbilical arteries into the placenta, to be engulfed and destroyed there. Along with these feelings go counter-feelings of restoration of the nuclear self through the umbilical vein. In this sense it is not the fetus as an entity who is 'doing things' to the placenta. Instead, the fetal nuclear feeling appears to travel through the cord back and forth between the fetal body and the placenta, being constantly destroyed and renewed in the process.

All these strange primal feelings[1] are interwoven in the core of the self. There they become the basis not only of our fundamental sense of pattern, but also the source of potential complexes. In order to recapitulate these primary feelings and to define them more accurately, I propose to restate them in terms of the fetal reactions to the placenta:

1. The placenta is felt to be the recipient of waste and excretion —hence a valueless thing.
2. The placenta is felt conversely to be a feeder and life-giver —hence a thing of paramount value.
3. The placenta is able to be pierced and to be occupied by the thrust of umbilical arterial blood—hence it is a perpetual victim, hollow and occupied.

---

[1] As already explained, I call them feelings for convenience only.

4. The placenta is able to pierce and occupy the fetal body with the thrust of venous umbilical blood—hence the placenta is a ruthless and persistent aggressor.
5. The placenta is felt as a blood-sucking monster able to engulf and destroy, and hence a place of death, a tomb.
6. The placenta is felt as a restoring benefactor by whom the nuclear sense is renewed.

Try as one may, it is impossible to avoid importing postnatal overtones into the above descriptions or, indeed, into any discussion of the prenatal life, since we can know of these fetal reactions only by peering back at them by means of symbolism drawn from the individual in his postnatal state.

From the conjunction of the above elements arise a number of primary complexes of feeling which I shall now try to tabulate in a comprehensive though brief manner.

1. *A basic confusion between eating and excreting.*

It is perfectly obvious as a physiological fact that the placenta is both the 'eating pot' and the 'excreting pot' to the fetus. It is taken for granted that this unpleasing and undignified identity has no place in our postnatal feelings. Nothing could be further from the truth. I have found that the separation in the feelings of these two functions is perhaps the biggest single element in the struggles of infancy and childhood. Indeed, it persists in many an adult, and many a fad or fancy in regard to eating can be seen by analysis to be a mechanism of defence erected against the intrusion of this horrible primary identity.

The little child suffers considerable anxiety concerning his eating and excreting, and does so very often in connection with the body of his mother. Mother's body inevitably tends, after birth, to assume for the child the functions which the placenta carried out before birth.[1] The child very often tends to require the actual presence of his mother (or her surrogate) not only for his eating but also for his unworried excretion. Mother's body, like the placenta, has become the 'eating pot' and the 'excreting pot' in

---

[1] See Chapter Seven and Figure Sixteen.

one.[1] When the human being fails to separate these umbilical feelings, they can form a malignant mental condition which can dominate and impair the mind. The best instance of this known to me comes from the writings of a psychologist who reports a patient as saying that:

> 'He and his mother formed one being originally. If they had been cut into halves they would both have ceased to exist. Love flowed from mother to him in the shape of milk and from him to mother as urine.'[2]

Here we see the mother's body playing its placental role in the feelings of an adult. It is not only the source of milk, but also the 'chamber pot', and the victim reveals the umbilical origins of his fantasy by his declaration that he and his mother originally formed one being. In actual fact, it was not the mother who formed this pristine unity with the child, but the placenta. The fetus and the placenta actually *do* constitute a primal unity, having as their bond the umbilical circulation of eating and excreting. It was this two-way umbilical flow which Hoffman's patient still preserved in his feelings in terms of a two-way flow of milk and urine between his postnatal body and his mother.

2. *A basic confusion between excretion and aggression.*

Freud long ago pointed out the deep-rooted relation between the act of excretion and the feelings of aggression. The concept of anal aggression is a familiar one in modern depth psychology. Freud explained this complex of feelings on the grounds that the infant uses his rectum as a primary weapon, presumably in default of being able to develop the striking and kicking reactions. It was Freud who first drew our attention to the specific link between these two diverse matters, and it is not his fault that his approximation has become hardened into a dogma. The real

[1] One of my own children used constantly to say when very small, 'Would she make a good mummy?' of every woman he met. This was said with some anxiety. We discovered by careful observation that underlying this worry was a concern both about eating and excreting.
[2] From the writings of E. P. Hoffman, quoted by Géza Róheim in his book *War, Crime and the Covenant.*

link between excretion and aggression is to be found in the umbilical arteries, and the repetition of this link at the postnatal rectum is but one instance among many of the transfer of umbilical feelings to postnatal organs.[1] At this point I feel I must anticipate my narrative by mentioning a very potent link in the chain of relations between anal action and aggression. There is a direct feeling-link between the umbilical arteries and the legs, and this means that there is also a strong link between the sense of the outthrust of the legs in kicking and the outthrust of umbilical arterial blood. This link seems to be almost certainly due to the fact that the umbilical arteries and the femoral arteries of the fetus are directly linked.[2] This linkage between the feelings of the umbilical arteries and the legs is later complicated by the fact that after birth a powerful link develops between the legs and the excretory ducts—the rectum and the urethra.[3] In this way there is established a fantasy not only of excreting at the feet, but also of being able to kick with the excretory ducts. The confusion, not unnaturally, works both ways.

3. *A basic confusion between excretion and death.*

Since the placenta is not only the 'excreting pot' but also the destroying monster and the 'grave' there is a strong link developed between excretion and death. In dreams the feelings of the anal excretions are closely linked with the fear of death. Feces are frequently related with dead bodies. The toilet is the grave. The perpetual uterine feeling of being slain and engulfed by the placenta is transferred postnatally upon the anal feelings.[4] This association appears to be amplified by fears of birth, in the course of which the fetus feels to be wholly destroyed by 'excretion' from the maternal body.[5] The catastrophic feelings of birth assume all the umbilical feelings of death and excretion. It is as if the perpetual cycle of death felt in the umbilical excretions is summed up in one

---

[1] As will be shown in detail in Part Two.
[2] See Chapter Seven and Figure Six.
[3] This will be given detailed consideration in Part Two.
[4] For reasons not yet understood, this does not seem to apply to the feelings associated with urination.
[5] A full statement of this aspect of the feelings must be deferred to Part Two.

31

grand horror at birth and encapsulated into the birth-shock. This is no doubt the reason why we have also the strange phenomenon of anal birth, in which the child and the adult represent themselves as born over and over again with every act of defecation.

4. *A basic confusion between food and the dead.*

Since the placenta is not only the 'eating pot' but also the place of death, there is a strong and horrifying link between the sense of feeding and the sense of 'eating the dead'. There is deep-buried in the feelings of us all a horrifying sense of being compelled to eat not only from the 'excretion pot' but also from the 'grave'. Being perhaps the most revolting and really horrifying of all these basic confusions, this one is usually deeply repressed and brought out from the feelings only with the greatest difficulty. The understandable reluctance to bring so terrifying a confusion anywhere near to conscious admission ensures that it is invariably repressed with all possible efficiency. But there it is, deep in the self, as I have had occasion to see again and again. Yet it is only by 'eating' from the placenta in spite of these horrible links, that the fetus can be perpetually restored not only physically but also in the sense of a perpetual restoration of the nuclear self. For the flow of blood up into the fetal body is felt to bring back again the nuclear fetal self who was lost and destroyed in the placenta. We may see this reflected in one of the most solemn rites of the human being, coming from the most immemorial antiquity and still current even among the most civilized people. It is widely believed, and deeply felt as true, that only by eating the body of the slain god and by drinking his blood can the individual partake in the resurrection of the god. This deep feeling, which long antedated the Christian religion, is by no means a mere superstition, nor is it negligible. It is, in fact, the very core of the umbilical complex. For in the flow of blood down the umbilical arteries the nuclear fetal feeling (the very core of the sense of self!) is engulfed and destroyed, and only by 'drinking back' this flow of blood through the umbilical vein is it resurrected again. The placenta is felt to be the destroyer of the nuclear feeling and, **through the act of 'feeding', to be its restorer.** Hence in the rite of

sacramental eating the very deepest feelings of doubt and confusion are played out and given the seal of salvation.

5. *A basic confusion between eating and being victimized.*

Since the placenta, in the act of 'feeding' the fetus, is felt as
an aggressor who pierces, invades and occupies the fetal body,
making it seem hollow, which is to say less nuclear, there is a
strong sense that feeding is aggression. These feelings come out
very strongly in dreams, and are frequently associated with the
dim memory of the taking of the nipple after birth. There can be
hardly any doubt that the very common reluctance of the newborn
baby to accept the nipple stems back to this primary confusion.
In this particular instance we have supporting evidence from the
mother herself, since I have again and again seen evidence to
show that the nursing mother senses the inthrust of her nipple
into her baby's mouth as an act of aggression. This maternal
confusion links back, in the mother's feelings, to her own fetal
sense of placental aggression, and provides her with a means of
playing out (of course, entirely unwittingly) her own umbilical
fears. Indeed, one may often observe in the behavior of mothers,
not only when breast-feeding but when bottle or spoon-feeding
their children, a strong element of aggressive feeling which cannot
be wholly accounted for by impatience. Indeed, upon analysis, I
have frequently found these feelings to be linked with the fetal
memory of placental aggression.

I have already said several times that mind is evoked in the
uterine organism[1] because it offers a configurational analogue
to the structure of space-time. So far I have not made this assertion
specific, but I now wish to adduce certain facts which I have
uncovered during the course of my analytical work, namely that
the fetus actually *does* gain a distinct primary sense of space and
time both through the skin feeling and the umbilical flow. It is a
fact, of course, that this cosmic sense is mixed and confused with
the highly personalized feelings evoked by the umbilical flow and
enumerated in outline above. This is not unnatural when we
consider the nature of man, and indeed it probably accounts for

---

[1] By which term I mean the fetus, placenta, cord and amnion as a whole.

the strange blend of the earthy and the sublime in the human character.

It was shown in Chapter One that all our special senses (those of seeing, hearing, tasting and smelling) feel to be psychologically derived from, or to be underlaid by, the primary sense of touch evoked by the overall fetal skin feeling. Thus all our postnatal means of orientation may be said to derive psychologically from the first sense of touch. Nor is this neurologically peculiar, since all our special senses, though not subjectively felt as such, are essentially senses of touch, highly refined and highly specialized. Even the sense of sight, which appears to us so etherial, is at root the product in the brain of the 'touch' of the delicate nerve-ends of the retina upon the radiation of certain electromagnetic frequencies.

What is true of these special and refined senses of touch is true also of our gross senses of touch as mainly carried out by the fingers. In the touch of the fingers, and the primary sense of space to which it gives rise, there is also deeply buried the original sense of touch all over the fetal skin. Indeed, I have uncovered persistent evidence to show that our primary sense of touch, namely that associated with the fetal skin feeling, is also the creator of our first sense of orientation, and hence of our first sense of space. Our first sense of ambience derives from the amnion, and we touch it all over—we look upon our small universe all at once, as it were with an all-seeing eye. And to this primary sense of space the umbilical periodic beat adds our first sense of time. It is thus that in the depths of the feelings we acquire the first sense of the space-time structure, which also is the structure of mind. The fetus feels to be the 'time nucleus' which is forever permeating space (the womb[1]) through the beat of time (umbilical beat). This is identical with a primary sense of the geometrical elements—of the point which develops within the sphere of space. This primary sense of space created while *in utero* becomes encapsulated into the feelings, where

---

[1] The fetus actually does not permeate the womb with the umbilical beat, but that specialized part we call the placenta. However, at one time the placenta occupies as much as one half of the internal surface of the uterus, so that the physical basis for the undoubted identity between placenta and womb felt by the fetus is adequate.

it assumes the character of our 'inward space'. We all feel to have a space inside ourselves, and there is not wanting evidence to show that this derives from the impacted memory of the fetal body (as time-point) moving and relating itself to its uterine space. In this way we gain, I believe, a primary schema of the nature of space-time. It was Kant who asserted that the mind possesses two basic categories of perception, namely space and time, and I think it will be found that he was speaking in an intuitive and philosophic manner of the two basic elements of mind which derive from the primary feeling of the fetal body as a 'time nucleus' active and developing within the womb as 'space sphere'. My present assertions are, however, neither intuitive nor philosophic, but are an effort to report what I have seen in the deep human feelings. I have been impressed again and again by indications in dreams which show that the roots of our orientation are fetal. In every perception we make of our environment there is an underlying fragment of the uterine feelings. In order to make this emphatic, let me put it that we all see, hear and touch our post-natal environment through at least a faint uterine haze. It is as if some infinitesimal trituration of the amniotic skin still surrounded us like an invisible sheath. This feeling is very strong in children, and can be discerned at the root of some of their most persistent fantasies. The uterine origins of the sense of orientation come out very clearly in many ancient beliefs and systems. I can think of no better example than the emotional dependence of the ancient Greeks upon such a city as Delphoi. The very name of the city means something like 'place of wombs'. It was founded by Apollo, whose fetal nature is unquestionable on the grounds of internal evidence and also of the context in which he appears in ancient thought.[1] The grave of the fabulous snake at Delphoi was marked by a stone that was known as the *omphalos*, a word which means the navel. And it was this *omphalos* that was regarded as the center of the world, a clear indication of the fetal nature of the sense of

[1] Apollo was from early times, among other things, the divinity of radiance and light, and at last came to be identified with the sun. He is thus one of the Shining Ones, see Appendix D, but in my work on mythology I have shown him to have other striking fetal characteristics which I have no space to adduce here.

orientation in the ancient world. From this Delphic center went out not only the directing and controlling word for action, but also the sacred fire for the lighting of the sacred fires of Greece. Here we have clearly a sense of geographical and even of political and economic orientation expressed in uterine symbolisms of the most patent order. In case the reader may suppose that this Delphic symbolism is unique, I would mention that the tomb of Romulus in the Roman Forum had a precisely similar utero-topographical significance, and was called the *Umbilicus Romae*.

At first I thought that the primary orientation of the human being derives merely from the general sense of the fetal body lying at the core of its uterine surround, but my subsequent discovery of the 'umbilical feelings' greatly amplified my views of the primary spatial orientations of the fetus. For I saw that if the umbilical flow is able to register and to record impressions related to the nuclear position of the fetus, then it must prove a more delicate and sensitive touch-mechanism than the fetal skin. For if the fetal skin may be regarded as a great blunt finger feeling around the circumambient walls of its enclosure, the umbilical flow may be regarded as a sensitive electric tentacle surveying and recording the space in which the fetal body lies.

I have shown already that the umbilical flow imports into the fetal feelings a dynamic sense of the contrast between solid and hollow. I have shown in outline how the alternation between the sense of solid and hollow gives rise to some of the primary human feelings. It is only in recent years that I have seen evidence that the alternation in the feelings between solid and hollow is not simple, but complex—more articulated than I had at first supposed. By this I mean that the changeover caused in the feelings by the umbilical flow is not a simple changeover from solid to hollow, but is rather a graduated changeover. The fetal body does not feel, as a result of the umbilical beat, to pass over from the solid state to the hollow state and back again, but feels to achieve this alternation through a simple gradation. In the course of this graduated sense of change the fetus becomes aware of the primary geometrical elements of point, line, plane and solid. I will try to describe the sequence.

The fetal body feels to be solid, but feels its navel as a point.

36

Umbilical Geometry and Periodicity

From this umbilical point the blood flows out in a thin stream, and from this there develops the primary sense of the line. Upon reaching the placenta, the umbilical blood disperses into a thin sheet which at one time covers as much as one half of the interior surface of the womb, and from this develops the sense of the plane. But the backflow of blood from the placenta once again develops the navel sense of a point, whence again develops the sense of a line in the umbilical vein. Upon reaching the fetal body, the inflow of blood causes the evocation of a hollow feeling, which again evokes the sense of a plane.[1] From this the fetal solid state is again restored. It is surprising how frequently, and how clearly, dreams symbolize this primary acquisition of geometrical awareness. In myths there are many links between the uterine and the geometrical elements, and in the Hebrew language there is a most emphatic etymological link between the uterine organs and the primary geometrical feelings.[2]

Important as this geometrical awareness is, it sinks into relative unimportance by contrast with the sense of cyclic periodicity to which it gives rise. It will be realized that the essence of the umbilical feeling is that of cyclic change. But this picture of the umbilical beat was greatly amplified by the realization of the involvement of the 'geometrical feelings'. For now I saw that there is in the umbilical beat a sense of a *sevenfold* series of changes. The feelings of the fetal body are changed from solid to hollow and back through *seven* stages which are repeated over and over again.[3]

This periodic cycle of feeling in the umbilical cord seems to develop in the following manner:

1. The fetal body feels solid and nuclear to its environment.

2. The blood passing out of the solid-feeling body at the navel generates the sense of a point.

3. The blood flowing in the narrow umbilical arteries evokes the sense of a line.

---

[1] A hollow is essentially a spherical plane.
[2] The demonstration of which must unfortunately await the publication of my mythological analyses.
[3] I have assumed, and still assume, that each feeling-cycle is probably the product of a single pulse of the fetal heart.

37

4. The blood dispersing into the thin, flat placenta generates the sense of a plane.

5. The blood, as it begins its return to the fetal body, passes through the 'placental navel' and again evokes a sense of a point.

6. In the passage of the blood through the umbilical vein the sense of a line is again evoked.

7. Upon reaching the fetal body, the blood is felt to create a sense of hollowness, which also evokes the sense of a plane.[1]

After completing the seventh stage, the blood becomes associated again with a sense of fetal nuclear solidity (see Stage One above), thus beginning a new cycle which presumably goes on and on with every beat of the fetal heart. I have given a rough schematic view of this umbilical geometry in Figure One.

This sevenfold rhythm in the umbilical flow is very positively represented in the myths, where we find the number seven connected over and over again with umbilical symbology. In Chapter Eleven I have suggested that it is the imposition of this umbilical periodicity upon the nervous system which ultimately creates our human sense of color and of music.

The more I see of the feeling associated with the umbilical cord, the more am I convinced that these are the source of a great deal of that 'number-mystification' which has for so long bemused the mystics and infuriated the rationalists. I feel sure that both will ultimately find in these basic uterine feelings a hitherto inconceivable basis for the abandonment of their extreme positions. Both the number three and the number seven have been the special concern of myth, religion and mysticism, and I am convinced that this deep bias in the feelings is umbilically generated. However, as I shall show in Chapter Four, this bias is not merely physiological, for especially the number seven is the product of a definite 'resonance' between the beat of fetal blood and the structure of the cosmos. In the beat of the umbilical blood the fetus undoubtedly senses the nature of space-time in terms of a

---

[1] A hollow, as I have said earlier, being a spherical plane.

rhythmic interaction between itself as developing point and the ambient space-sphere in which it lives—see Figure One.

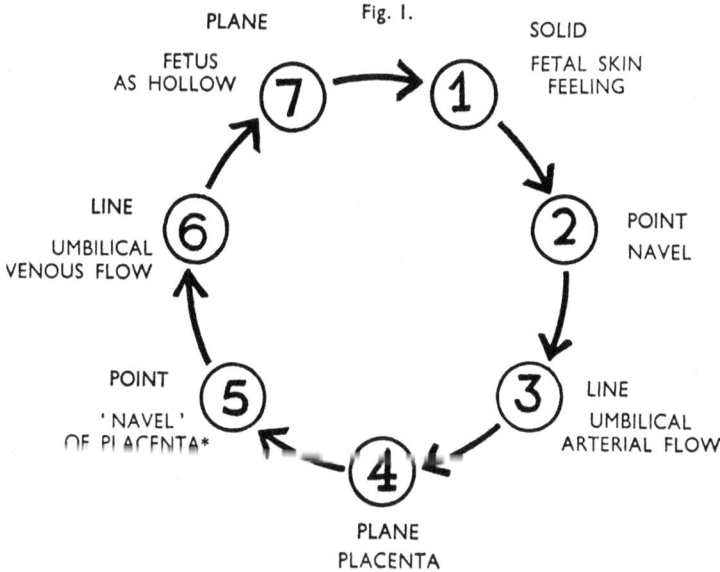

PLANE   Fig. I.   SOLID
FETUS   FETAL SKIN
AS HOLLOW   FEELING

(7) → (1)

LINE   POINT
UMBILICAL   (6)   (2)   NAVEL
VENOUS FLOW

POINT   LINE
'NAVEL'   (5)   (3)   UMBILICAL
OF PLACENTA*   ARTERIAL FLOW

(4)

PLANE
PLACENTA

* By the term 'navel of placenta' I seek to indicate the sense of the blood focusing back to the point of re-entry into the umbilical cord.

Another facet of the umbilical feelings needs to be reviewed in the light of the present chapter; namely, that the fetus feels *itself* to be a traveler. As I have already shown, the fetus does not feel merely to be a nucleus which reaches out into its periphery through the umbilical cord, but that (for reasons already indicated) he gains the sense that *he himself* travels down the umbilical arteries, is destroyed in the placenta and restored again. This means that the fetus not only gains the sense of spatial orientation, but that he feels that *he himself* travels back and forth from the 'time point' of his solid fetal state to the 'space sphere' of the placenta. The fetus feels that *he himself* is a wanderer who constantly goes forth and journeys, and suffers and then is restored again to his place. In the course of this journey he experiences not only all the strange feelings indicated earlier, but also the sense of *space*

39

in contrast to the focal point of *time*. He senses as a constant traveler the geometrical nature of space and his relation to it in terms of the development of a point into a line, a plane and then into a 'restoring' solid. In this way he gains a sense not only of traveling and of geometry and periodicity, but also the sense of life and death, opposition and synthesis. All these become bound up together in the very core of the self, which is the product of the concentration of a nuclear, focal feeling through this same uterine conditioning.

It is a fact which has never previously been rationally explained, that the great heroes of antiquity tended to be endless travelers. Upon analysis the myths clearly reveal an underlying link between this traveling and the umbilical flow. In the course of this traveling the gods and other fetal representatives suffer and are restored. There are even strong indications that in the course of this traveling they become by turns solid and hollow, which is to say male and female.[1] The legend of Teiresias is particularly plain on this point, for in the course of his travels he comes at different times upon copulating serpents, and through this experience is changed from a boy to a girl and then back again. Not only is Teiresias blind (as the fetus may poetically be said to be!) but his experiences take place at intervals of *seven years*, which is a typical instance of the sort of symbolism in which the myths tell the tale of the umbilical experiences of reversal of polarity in association with a sevenfold periodicity.

There is a very good reason why this sense of fetal traveling should be so strong in the postnatal organism. Our basic sense of traveling after birth is gained through the use of the legs. No matter how much we may be carried and variously transported on wheels, our organism registers its basic sense of postnatal traveling through the use of the legs in walking. The infant struggles to its feet and strives to take a few steps, and in this way evokes the very deepest feelings, especially as these concern his legs. Now, as I have shown, the very deepest feelings concerning the legs are those generated by the link between the umbilical and the femoral

---

[1] I shall show in Chapter Thirteen that solid and hollow are identical in our feelings with male and female.

arteries.[1] The legs of the fetus are closely related and even confused with the umbilical arteries, and this confusion persists into the postnatal state, long after the umbilical arteries are gone. The child, in walking, must overcome this primary sense that the legs are umbilical arteries. This struggle leaves its deep imprint in us in feelings which present themselves in a familiar form in dreams. Most people are familiar with that kind of bad dream in which one cannot walk because one's legs are stuck in a strangely soft and yet adhesive substance. This is simply the confusion between the legs and the umbilical arteries, whereby the former are made to feel that they are affixed to the placenta. The legs in walking therefore bring along with them the umbilical sense of travel and, in a strange retroactive sense, the fetal journeying through the cord is thus felt in terms of a primal walking forth into the world and back. In this way the primal feelings of travel evoked in the blood, along with the feelings described in the foregoing chapters, take on a very concrete postnatal sense.

It is very noticeable that in this sense of wandering and spatial exploration strong emotions link space with destruction. Space is the destroyer. The plane (namely the placenta) is the place of destruction and of death. This fact peeps out at us not only in dreams and human feelings, but also in the myths, where we find persistent indications that the 'flat place', the plain (the plane) is not only the place of food, where the crops grow and the cattle graze, but also the place of death and destruction.[2]

*   *   *

The reader will see that there is a fundamental difference between the contents of the pregnant womb regarded in their physical and in their configurational natures. In their physical aspect, which is their original and obvious aspect, the fetus is the all-important entity, and the placenta and the umbilical cord are

---

[1] See especially Chapter Seven and Figure Six.
[2] In the mythological work which I have prepared, I have shown this link between placenta, plane and death to underlie such things as the Rape of Persephone upon the plain, and the mythology of Lot and his 'salt wife' and the destruction of the 'cities of the plain'.

41

but ancillary organs. But in their superimposed configurational aspect all three organs are of equal importance, since all are integral parts of a single unit. This single unit I have called by the name of 'the uterine organism' to distinguish it from the fetal organism. As I am now compelled by the facts to believe, this uterine organism is a little generator of configurational feelings. This it becomes by virtue of the setting up of a polarity between the fetus and the placenta and the constant alternation of that polarity through the two-way flow of the blood in the umbilical cord. I have suggested that the mechanism of this alternation of feeling may be electrical, and I have adduced certain facts which seem to offer a *rationale* for this view, but whether that particular hypothesis be true or not, the facts of the feelings are undoubted.

The polarity of this uterine organism is simple: the fetus is felt as nuclear to the womb and placenta, the placenta being the 'operative' part of the womb. The two-way flow of blood in the cord constantly increases and then decreases the nuclear feelings of the fetus to the point of complete reversal, so that the fetus feels by turns not merely less nuclear but even in degree peripheral.

Why should this umbilical alternation be the instrument of the evocation of mind? Because, I believe, this alternating rhythm between the nuclear feelings of the fetus and his sense of the peripheral placenta is the 'imitation' of the basic pattern of the cosmos and its rhythms. In Chapter One I showed that the fetal sense of being nuclear to a surround is a reflection of the basic pattern of creation. But in this chapter I have shown that the static pattern was only a first appearance: the pattern of the feelings generated in the uterine organism is not simply that of a point within a sphere, but of a point linked in a state of alternating relations with a sphere. This alternating pattern is, I believe, even more closely imitative of the basic pattern of creation as reflected in the forms of the external universe. In Chapter Four, after a digression in Chapter Three, I shall outline the indications of a universal pattern to be seen reflected in external creation—for this is the pattern which I believe imprints itself upon the internal relationships of the uterine organism, and so creates the phenomenon called the human self.

Chapter Three

SOME DEFERRED CONSIDERATIONS

THERE ARE TWO matters which from a strict contextual point of view ought to have been dealt with in Chapters One and Two, but which could not be profitably discussed until the reader had considered the new discoveries outlined therein. For until the reader had grasped the contents of Chapter Two he could not possibly sympathize with my reasons for being willing to believe that human beings perceive not only with their nerves but with their blood. Indeed, until I became convinced that the origins of mind may be found largely in the umbilical cord, I myself could not have been induced to consider the matters discussed in this chapter. I had been brought up to believe that only the nerves can serve as instruments of perception. My discoveries have compelled me to doubt this view, and therefore have made me amenable to the consideration of alternative views. I hasten to add, however, that I have not thereby been made amenable to any and every unorthodox alternative, but I am no longer convinced that mind is essentially related to the brain.

I am convinced indeed that mind is a configurational influence or state which will come into manifestation wherever the appropriate integrative conditions are provided. The reader will by now know what these conditions are, namely that a nucleus and a periphery must be provided and must be linked together by a two-way flow. When this is done, then mind is 'tuned in'. That is the only concept which seems to fit all the facts as I know them. Unless this were true, it could not be possible that the umbilical flow could evoke elements which, when transferred to a similar configuration in the brain,[1] appear in us as mind.

What I have thus discovered and placed in the context of modern knowledge was evidently felt by older peoples. For myth and *märchen*, primitive rite and religion, are full of emphasis upon blood. The blood is presented as having a mysterious ability to evoke spiritual or magical powers. Nowadays the suggestion that this is anything but an old wives' tale is regarded with scepticism and even scorn. We accept with tolerance the statement that as a man thinketh in his heart so is he, because we make an unconscious correction in the terms, and take it as a poetic way of saying that as a man 'really feels', so is he. It hardly occurs to us that the statement may be almost if not quite literally true. When Hitler cried 'We Germans think with our blood', it was regarded as one of his quainter ravings. Hardly anyone suspected that it might have a dangerous foundation in fact, namely that he was appealing to an atavistic state of mind utterly antagonistic to the highly 'neural' conditions of modern life, but one perfectly prepared to employ the scientific achievements of that 'neural' state to reassert the primacy of the old blood-linked tribe.

That the very core of the mind begins in the fetal skin feeling does not contradict the view that in the early stages of life the perceptions of the blood are dominant. For the fetal skin feeling not only has both a neural and a vascular component, but the latter dominates the former because it is able to change it in a periodic manner as indicated in Chapter Two. In the light of this fact I feel that I should restate certain matters indicated in Chapter One, and also that I should mention a matter which may be of the greatest importance to an understanding of man and his evolution.

I. *The Relation of Blood to Nerve in the Development of the Feelings.*

In Chapter One I asserted that physical feelings experienced before a certain period in the life of the child tend to become impacted in the nervous system and to become metamorphosed

---

[1] See Chapter Eleven.

into organs of feeling. These metamorphosed and impacted feelings, I asserted, form the actual substance of the self. I suggested that a line might be drawn across the developing life somewhere between the ages of five to seven, and that prior to the drawing of this line the transmutation of physical feelings was possible, whereas *after* the drawing of that line this transmutation became less and less likely, and indeed largely impossible. This may have given the idea that I was thinking in terms of a sharp barrier

Fig. 2.

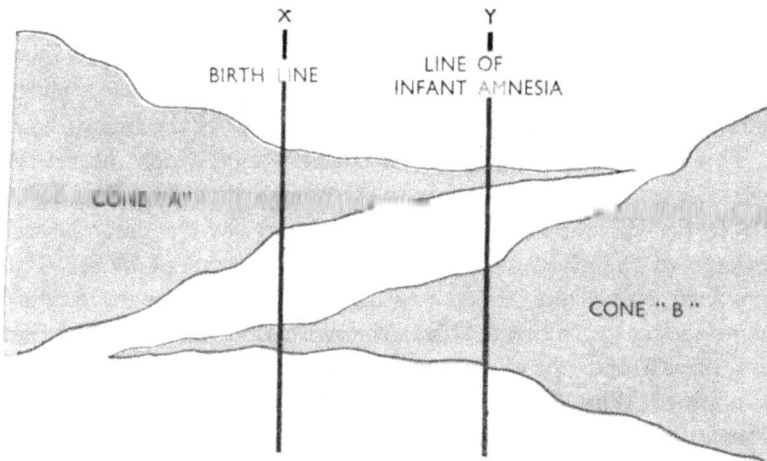

which suddenly shuts off the child's past. Such an idea is, in fact, implied in the Freudian concept of the relatively sudden onset of infant amnesia. It seems to me that what really takes place is that between the ages of five and seven a gradual process suddenly reaches a point of climactic change. This view I have tried to render schematic in Figure Two, where I have shown two straggling 'cones', which represent two forms of feeling, one trailing off into nothing as the other increasingly opens up. Cone 'A' represents the old feelings originating in the blood; cone 'B' represents the new nerve-feelings.

E   45

The Nature of the Self

In the light of what I have written above, it seems pertinent to ask whether the real division in the feelings (represented by the two 'cones' of Figure Two) is not as between blood-feeling and nerve-feeling. Is it possible that only feelings either derived from or dominated by blood, can actually become impacted in the terms described in Chapter One and illustrated by the 'cone' A of Figure Two? I cannot finally say that this is so, but there is much that points to the truth of it. It seems highly likely that the real distinction between the conscious mind and the so-called Unconscious is at root a distinction between neural feelings and blood feelings. In that case, the period of infancy might be regarded as a period of struggle between the two systems of feeling, the climactic point represented by the vertical line 'Y' of Figure Two, being simply the moment at which the sharp, pencilline feelings derived from the nerves submerge the feelings of the blood.

This view is strengthened by a circumstance which the reader will encounter again and again in the course of reading Part Two. There he will observe a constant tendency for the early neural feelings of the child to be represented in terms of blood. The newborn child, and the young infant also, appear to confuse nerve-feelings with blood. Why, otherwise, does the infant feel that not breath but blood is moving back and forth through his windpipe? Why does he feel that he first suckles blood? Why does he feel that the neural activity of legs and arms is bloody? Why does he feel that his excretions (of urine and feces) are blood? How can he feel that his eyes exude blood? How can the neural processes be so laden with blood feelings in the infant? I suggest that the answer is probably given by Figure Two, and that at first the infant is overwhelmed by the experience of blood-perception, and not yet truly reconciled to the relatively newer method of unadulterated feeling by nerve.

The reader may very naturally say that I am creating the question as well as offering the answer—that it is I alone who assert the existence and primacy of the blood feelings. But I would direct his attention to ancient symbolic material which very clearly shows that the pattern of the blood dominates the infant. *Little Snow-white*, for instance, whose story I have already mentioned, is closely related to three mysterious drops of blood which fall from her mother's finger. These drops of blood represent, I believe, the three columns of blood in the umbilical cord. The story is telling us, in effect: 'Watch what happens to the girl who is related to this blood, and you will see what happens to the feelings of the child after birth'. This conclusion the rest of the *Snow-white* story thoroughly supports.[1] Nor does this story stand alone in respect to its emphasis upon umbilical blood. The story of *The Juniper Tree* also contains the same elements of blood dropped on the snow. Though in this case there is no mention of *three* drops, the context of the story plainly shows that a symbolic reference to umbilical blood is intended. The story of *The Goose Girl* very markedly contains the reference to three drops of blood, which in this case the girl's mother lets fall upon a handkerchief, and which she specifically states to have a magical value. The tale of *Cinderella* is full of blood, for the feet of the two wicked sisters fill the golden slipper with blood, and both their eyes are pecked out by birds at the wedding of Cinderella, so that they bleed profusely.

There is no lack of symbolic evidence in myths and *märchen* to support the idea that blood is important in a way that would find no credence in physiology.

II.   *The Maternal and Fetal Bloods as Instruments of Heredity.*

I have found in dreams subtle but persistent indications that the fetus gains more from its mother's blood than oxygen and nutriment. There are persistent indications that the fetus feels the placenta to be conveying to it some form of information. I certainly should not have been willing to follow up the first clues to this had I not already been convinced that the umbilical cord is the instrument of a form of consciousness. Having this conviction, I was not averse to following up clues which suggested that the fetus feels the placenta to be a source of knowledge. In Chapter Two I asserted that the fetus feels the placenta to be a number of diverse things. To this I must now add another: the fetus feels the placenta to be a teacher.

[1]   As I have shown in my as-yet-unpublished book on mythology.

47

The Nature of the Self

The fetus definitely feels that it gains from the placenta, through the umbilical vein, an inflow not only of oxygen and food, but also of knowledge. This knowledge is evidently not that which could be chemically conveyed, as a hormone triggers off reactions in a distant organ, because there is a distinct sense that the placenta conveys to the fetus something akin to ideas. What these 'ideas' may be I have not yet been able to determine, because up to the time of writing I have not done more than to bring dream contexts into synthesis with related external facts known (or ascertainable) by me, thus amplifying both and creating a new picture. If, for instance, I am given a dream containing birth symbolism, I am able to link its subjective elements with the objective facts of birth known to me already. If I see a dream in which I am offered information concerning the brain, I can (after many years of checking and comparing) now recognize the meaning of the symbolism, because it compares with something I can find out about by external means. But if I see in a dream symbolic forms which indicate some sort of learning from the placenta, I cannot possibly interpret that symbolism unless I know what kind of thing the placenta might 'teach' the fetus. This by no means signifies that these possibly deeper dream symbolisms are undecipherable. If they are, as I strongly suspect, a fact, then there is no reason why their meanings should not ultimately be made clear. Indeed, were I a highly competent embryologist or biochemist, it is entirely possible that I might myself be able to get at least a rudimentary idea of what it is that the placenta conveys to the fetus in this sense. It is my hope that one day my methods of dream analysis may be used as instruments of orthodox embryological research. And, let me say this at once, I am strongly of the opinion that what in fact the fetus 'learns' from the placenta is related to inheritance. I am convinced that the placenta is an instrument of inheritance. It transmits (possibly from the mother's blood) a deep organic knowledge stored in the blood or in some way related to the blood.

This being so, the reader will understand why it is specially hard for me to interpret the symbolisms which might offer some clue to the nature of this transmission of inherited factors. Unless one knew roughly what kind of 'teaching' might be involved, one would find it hard to know how to take the first step in unravelling the symbolism. In dream analysis it is specially true that it is the first step that counts.

I do not think that this suggestion is at all without at least a tentative niche in the field of orthodox biology. For who can doubt that there is a definite gap in our knowledge of the mechanisms of inheritance. We know that the inheritance of bodily factors passes via the genes, those minute molecular forms which seem to carry the compressed organic 'memories' of the biological past.[1] We know that this is the sole means of inheritance of the oviparous animals. Once the egg is laid it is cut off from the maternal body. It has rather been assumed that the placental mammals are organically limited to a similar mechanism of inheritance. To the best of my knowledge no biologist has suggested that there might be an *organic* mechanism of inheritance lying in between the genes and the postnatal teaching of the parent. My discovery that the umbilical cord is able to convey some sort of mental impressions offers the possibility that I have uncovered a third mechanism of heredity lying, as it were, between the genes and the act of parental teaching.

This novel view of the placenta is by no means neglected in mythology. One of the most powerful representations is to be found in the person of Cheiron, the Centaur. Cheiron was alleged to have lived in a mysterious cave, where he taught almost all the Heroes of Greece. The Hero in the Cave with the Centaur already offers strong uterine symbolism. I had for a long time noted how many placental characteristics adhere to the figure of the centaur. The symbolism of Sagittarius is perhaps the most obvious, this centaur being plainly placental in the context of the zodiacal symbolism.[2] But on every hand in myths one sees the centaur (or the horse) and expecially the chief centaur Cheiron, in a placental relation with a fetal Hero. And I observed that Cheiron was always regarded as a *teacher*. That is precisely what I had seen in dreams about the placenta. And what did Cheiron teach

[1] Genes are believed to be big spiral molecules.
[2] See Appendix D.

the Hero? The list varies from myth to myth. Most of the subjects are strongly umbilical in the most immediate sense. For instance, Cheiron taught the Hero the arts of the chase, especially the use of the bow and the spear. This certainly fits the umbilical context, since we know that the fetus feels to thrust out and to pierce the placenta, and to be pierced by it in turn. Then the Centaur also taught music: and we know that the fetus gains his first sense of the periodic beat from the umbilical pulse.[1] The Centaur also taught the Hero the arts of healing. This is particularly impressive, because we know that the very father of Greek healing was Asklepios, whose sign was the snake-twined staff—that perfect symbol of the umbilical cord. And we know that at root Asklepios was himself originally a magical snake. We know, too, that the umbilical cord constitutes the primary 'leech', sucking away the impure blood, and that it also supplies the building materials for the body. What doctor could do more than to detoxify and to reinvigorate his patient! The healing art is truly umbilical in its origins in our feelings. But in addition to all this, Cheiron taught the Heroes the old, mysterious wisdom of the race. This seems to me to symbolize very well the situation which my investigations suggest, namely that the placenta is the universal human 'Teacher' who conveys to the fetal Hero the imprinted wisdom of our *human* past—a level of inheritance too inorganic for the action of the genes, and too organic for the conscious mind of the parent to be able to convey to us after birth.

[1] See Chapter Ten.

Chapter Four

EVIDENCE FOR A UNIVERSAL DESIGN OF
CREATION IN EXTERNAL FORMS

I HAVE ALREADY indicated that my approach to the analysis of
the mind was inspired and guided by a strong conviction that all
creation is done by means of, or according to a simple and
unvarying plan. It was the desire to trace this same pattern or
design into the origins of the mind that led me to my long quest
and sustained me in it. It is therefore important that the reader
should know something of this background to my quest, for otherwise he will not be able to understand why I sought what I did
or why I recognized it when I found it.[1] This chapter is an effort
to condense this vast but simple concept into a comprehensible
capsule.

Every man knows out of his own experience that a gathering of
people influences the behavior of all who take part in it. It can
easily be demonstrated that this influence is not just the outcome
of the action and reaction of the individual persons upon one
another. There is a *pattern* at work in the behavior of the
individuals, and although it may not be possible to find that pattern
in the behavior of any one individual, yet the nature of it is
clear enough from the *result* which invariably follows the gathering
together of people. The result referred to is the formation of a

---

[1] Those unacquainted with the spirit of experimental inquiry may hastily
assume that to commence an inquiry with an hypothesis is inevitably to
invite the trap of finding what one is looking for. But no inquiry without a
preliminary hypothesis can possibly be fruitful, however inadequate the
hypothesis. Columbus set sail Westwards to find India and found what was
to be America. Even a wrong hypothesis can lead to truth, and is dangerous
only if it be held unchanged beyond its point of usefulness.

pattern of relations which we loosely sum up under the word 'government'.

Whenever people gather together, especially when they come together into any sort of permanent relationship, the pattern of government at once asserts itself. In its simplest form it is satisfied by the existence of a single individual who acts the focal role. In its most complex form government may assume such a character that the source of ultimate authority almost defies analysis. But the essential principle of government always remains the same: it is a pattern of relations which may be represented schematically by a point or nucleus lying within a circle or sphere. This book is based upon the theory that this pattern of government is not fortuitous or pragmatic, but that it is the response of a human gathering to a universal influence which seeks to do now, in the human present, what it has done already to nature in the evolutionary past. Evolution may be summed up, according to this theory, as the development of this pattern in form after form, upon level after level of behavior.

The immanence of this pattern in human social behavior is demonstrated, as I have said, by its *outcome*. The outcome of human gathering is always the appearance of this pattern in some form. Every effort to deny it ends not in its non-appearance, but in its distortion. This is well seen in the way in which all efforts to reduce men to a flat level through theoretical socialism, communism and anarchism, end in the creation of a social form in which there is too much and not too little nuclear function. The fact is that the appearance among men of this pattern of government is not the product of mere pragmatic necessity, or of the machinations of would-be rulers, but it is the response of human social aggregation to the universal trend which has created all forms.

The same pattern may be observed at work as between any two human individuals, though on this level it is much harder to perceive, and often almost impossible to identify. Let me say bluntly and dogmatically in what I believe it to consist: It consists of a simple struggle to occupy and to become nuclear to the other person in some form. This struggle is the basis of all games, which seek in some way to permit the penetration of one individual by another.[1] Games in their modern sublimated forms tend to conceal this basic intent, but the rougher and more primitive the game, the more clear the intent becomes. The fight, the duel, the joust, all tend to make it clear that what is intended is a demonstration of who can penetrate the guard and even the body of the opponent. Even in the politest of games this intent is clear, as in a game of tennis, but it is masked by the polite atmosphere in which it is played. Yet the intent is to thrust a ball through the opponent's guard. And even where the game involves no physical thrust at all, but is purely mental, as in a card game, the intent is to 'get inside the other man's mind', as it were, and to direct his will or to forestall it. The most powerfully and intimately organized of all such relations is, of course, the sexual relation, in which the male is specifically organized for penetration, and the female for occupancy. Yet the strange mental and emotional accompaniments of sexual activity and feeling, when analyzed, show us plainly that the original functions of reproduction have been taken over by this ever-present configurational need. The reader will, of course, recall the struggle of feelings generated in the umbilical cord, and will link these to the above statements, as indeed is entirely proper for, as I shall show later, the mental feelings of sex derive direct from the umbilical feelings.[2] The relation of sexual organization to non-sexual functions is plain enough in homosexual and perverted practices. It is plain also in the so-called pecking order of the hen run. For where there is no cock bird to provide the organized function of sexual penetration, the hens will themselves set up a quasi-social configuration in which one hen pecks all the others, and each of the other hens (save one wretch whom everyone pecks) pecks at least one other. The thrust of the beak is, I believe, an effort to satisfy the essential drive behind all animal association, namely the need to penetrate.

It is this essential relation which overshadows, if it does not dominate, the relation between any two persons. But it is radically

[1] And of all group games, also, though here I am dealing specifically with individual games.
[2] See Chapter Thirteen.

changed as soon as more than two people become involved. Then at once there are no longer potentially three individuals (or more) interacting *pari passu*, but one individual who seeks to make the others (even if unwittingly) peripheral to himself. That is, he seeks to penetrate them collectively by being the core of their integration. This drive is, I sense, the meaning underlying the old phrase 'two's company, three's none', or its variant, 'two's company, three's a crowd'.[1] Two persons are essentially company in the sense indicated above. That is, each acts direct upon the other. But immediately a third person is added, then there will be found potentially a situation in which one leads the other two, or in which two continue to be 'company' by thrusting the third into the cold. This configuration can be masked, as it frequently is in everyday life, by the demands of kindness, politeness and necessity, but it is always present. And it grows in intensity as each new individual is added to the group, until at last it can be hidden no longer, and in the end it leaps into full and accepted manifestation as the configuration of government, in which a minority stands at the focus of the majority, having 'penetrated' to the focus of the group. This same relation between penetration and government may be seen in primitive human groups and animal groups. There is discernible a distinct tendency for the focal government of a prehuman or a primitive group to center in the person of the Big Male—the one who can penetrate. There are not wanting some signs that primal human organization may have taken the form of a Big Male surrounded by females.

While I wish to avoid the least suggestion of mysticism, I cannot very well ignore the fact that human groupings tend to take on a distinct personality of their own. The common existence of national figures such as John Bull and Uncle Sam, and the emotional identity between the individual and the national group, not to mention the flags and songs which act as the symbols of this identity, serve to indicate, though not to prove, the tendency for a group to acquire an integrative personality of its own. That vast

---

[1] This saying is most commonly used in respect to the desire of the boy and girl to be alone together. But it will be seen from the above paragraph that this meaning is all of a piece with the wider connotation here suggested.

human groups do thus form an organized entity is suggested by the fact that civilizations tend to go through quite distinct life-cycles of their own, as both Spengler and Toynbee showed.[1] Regiments and ships'-companies generate or evoke an *esprit de corps*. Indeed, that very phrase may be taken as possible only because of the principle here adumbrated. I suggest that in the pattern of human government, namely that of a focal center in the midst of the mass, we have an instance of how an aggregation of similar parts always eventuates in an integration brought about by the distillation of a focal center standing in contrast to the peripheral mass, both of which are thus differentiated out of a prior state of undifferentiated aggregation. It is this pattern alone which makes for wholeness, and which permits the evocation of that sense of unity which we call *esprit de corps*, and which also can operate upon us quite unconsciously to impel us to play our role in the life-cycle of a social organism.[2]

There is another factor in human social integration which deserves a word here, and that is the manifest longing of ordinary people for a social focus. There is a deep need in the hearts of men and women for some public figure in whom they can focus their most powerful feelings. That such a need often results in the most disastrous accommodations is beside the point. That kings and queens have not satisfied the desire; that gods and saviors have failed; that idols of stage and screen have feet of clay—this does not alter the desperate need. Dictators have risen upon the need. False prophets have misused it. But it is there, and it represents, however falsely accommodated, the need of man to see beyond the endless proliferation of ordinary men to some product—to some human *point* in the endless aggregation of men.

All that I have written above may be summed up in terms of a fundamental need to satisfy the requirements of the pattern of the point within the sphere. It is the primary impress in our feelings, placed there by the universal pattern of integration sensed in the

---

[1] Though Spengler represented them as plants in which the individual was as helpless as a cell, and Toynbee tried to get the best of both worlds by speaking at one and the same time of cycles of history while yet denying the organic nature of society.

[2] I have dealt with this in some detail in my book, *Biosynthesis*.

fetal skin and the blood while *in utero*.[1] It endows us each with the need, varying enormously from individual to individual, and influenced immensely by our sexual structure, to be either penetrator or penetrated or, at any rate, to take part in a drama of interpenetration. And when we gather together into groups (or are born or impelled into them by forces beyond us) then these feelings are the ready-made inner links which respond to the same configurational force at work in human social forms.

*   *   *

You may incline to the idea that what is written above of men in society is plausible but not demonstrated. You may even consider it *highly* plausible, but you may believe that it is a situation peculiar to human beings. May I invite you, then, to look into an older level of social form, and to see how the same pattern has worked there long ago in essentially similar terms. I refer to those non-human animal societies, the beehive, the anthill and the termitary. In all these societies there is to be observed an organizational pattern which bears a strong configurational resemblance to the fundamental pattern of human society.

The familiar beehive is typical of these societies, and there we may see the lineaments of the universal pattern of integration expressed not only in terms of social relations, but in terms also of bodily function. Each of these societies is divided primarily into two major types of insect, namely a minority of active males which perform no day-to-day work, but which have the power to reproduce, while on the other hand there is a majority of sterile females which do all the day-to-day work of the hive. The reader may feel that I have improperly omitted any mention of the so-called 'queen', but I think it can be shown that this creature is not really either male or female, but is essentially both, so that her function is rather that of a synthesis between the male minority and the female (sterile) majority.[2]

[1] See Chapters One and Two.
[2] In the case of the 'queen bee', for instance, we have a creature who not only lays the eggs like a female, but who like a male releases the sperm from a sac wherein they have been stored since the nuptial flight.

Fundamental Division in Animal Society

It is intriguing to observe that whereas in the case of human society the division between the governmental minority and the governed majority is purely mental in nature, in the case of these social insects the division has involved the modification of the bodily structure. The female population of the insect society has been deprived of the power to reproduce, and their functions have become collectivized in the body of the so-called 'queen'. The male population alone has been allowed to retain their power to reproduce, but they can reproduce only in an indirect fashion upon the body of the 'queen'. Two things are significant here, quite apart from the configurational aspects presented by these insect societies. The first is that the integrative focus is identical with the reproductive focus. The second is that the females (that is, those who normally produce the peripheral ovum) are the instruments of the social periphery; while the males (that is, those who produce the nuclear sperm) are identical with the reproductive nuclear social minority.

This coincidence of social and sexual configurations is most interesting, because it provides a highly suggestive link between two different levels of expression of the same basic pattern. It helps to support what I have noted in respect to human beings and their social forms, namely that the configurational roles played by the male and female are linked with the configuration of society itself. That is to say, I have shown that between individuals the drama of penetration and reception which interlinks with the drama of social configuration is most naturally provided for in the structure and function of the sexual organs.

Unlike human societies, which we can experience today at work around us, the insect societies are completed. The evolutionary impulse which took place in their creation is saturated and no longer is at work. Human society operates within the light of consciousness, however dim, and its destiny is susceptible to some measure of control, however small.[1] But the insect societies are mechanisms left functioning without any conscious link with their formative principle. As an analogy, we may think of human

[1] The Author believes that the universal design can be harnessed in society for the evolution of human destiny—see *The Myth of a Chosen People*.

57

society as a coral reef in which the insects are still at work, whereas the insect societies are the residual coral structures from which the living and formative 'insects' have departed.

What makes the insect societies of special interest in this context is that, at least in the case of the bees, the history of the process is in part demonstrable. Biologists have been able to trace the existence of bees in several states of social existence, running from the purely free-ranging state to that of the completely collectivist state that has not stopped at the mere 'brain-washing' of such intellect as they possess, but which has involved the structural change of their very bodies. The picture which biology presents of this development of the hive is that of a free-ranging insect which gradually was drawn into closer and more persistent family aggregation, until suddenly the creatures were 'seized upon' by the configurational trend of integration, and the pattern of creation stamped not only into their social relations but into the very bodies of the individuals. Similar histories are not traceable, I believe, in the evolution of the anthill and the termitary. These stand isolated from any evolutionary stages. Their 'missing links' are irrevocably missing. But I do not think that there is any zoologist who would care to assert that the formation of the anthill and the termitary took place in any way fundamentally different from that of the beehive.

*   *   *

With these simple facts in mind, let us look deeper still into the evolution of the animal forms of this planet. There is plenty of evidence to suggest that what happened to the insects in the course of their socialization is not only the direct analogue of our own human social configuration, but also is the equally direct analogue of the evolution of all animal bodies above the level of the ameba. The facts are not in dispute, and I will content myself with indicating them, leaving it to the reader to check and amplify them as he will.

At one time on the surface of this earth, in the waters of the cooling planet, the highest form of life was the unicell. Still today these ancient cousins of ours live by the trillion in the damp places of the globe. The evidence shows that at some time in this unicellular world some of these lowly creatures were impelled together by an aggregative impulse. Cells came together and formed colonies, and a new and lowly form of existence was brought into being. Cell colonies still flourish in the waters of the earth. But, in perfect conformity with the theory here adumbrated, one or more of these aggregations of cells were suddenly 'seized upon' by the integrative pattern, which expressed itself in their economy in a manner surprisingly like that which eons later was to give rise to the insect societies. This transformation of the cell-societies from mere colonies (aggregations) to organisms took place by dividing them into two specific types, namely into a majority of somatic cells and a minority of reproductive cells.

The somatic cells are essentially the body cells, which have the role of maintaining the organism in its present spatial aspect. They are the majority, the 'workers' of the organism. The reproductive cells have no part in the work of the present time in the narrow sense, but are charged simply with the task of carrying forward the life of the organism in the stream of time, not by *continuance* of form, but by *renewal* of form. The analogy between the socialization of the cells and the socialization of the insects is not only close, but it is admitted on all hands by biologists. The insect societies exist as integrated entities *because* they possess a sterile majority which presents the living form of the hive (anthill or termitary) in the present and in space, and a germinal minority which is parasitical in the present but which alone has the power to reproduce the *whole*. The living animals which exist above the cellular level owe their integrated existence to a precisely similar configuration expressed in a precisely similar division of labor: namely in the existence of a majority of 'worker-cells' which maintain the organism in the present, and a germinal minority of gametes which are parasitical upon the body, but which alone have the power to *reproduce the whole*.

We have every reason, therefore, to trace the evolution of all living forms in terms of the recurrent manifestation of a simple configuration. It is a configuration which governs the integration of living parts into new living wholes. How may we sum up this simple common element which all these levels of integration share? It may be expressed quite simply, I think, in terms of a response to space and time. Thus we can see that in each case the instruments of majority-action are spatial in their primary function. The somatic cells, the sterile insect workers, and the mass of the human governed, all have as their primary role the maintenance of form in space. They form the instrumentality of space-occupancy and of persistence in space. Against them we may in each case contrast the instruments of minority function in terms of a struggle for permanence in the stream of time. The majority, it appears, is always peripheral in its attention, always concerned with the problems of the present moment and of spatial activity, always tending to expansion in space. Contrasted with the majority, the minority is always nuclear in attention, always concerned with the unfolding future, however slightly, always tending to withdrawal from the mass.

This basic division of labor represents, in my view, the response of living forms to the pattern of space-time. The very fact that the 'time-people' are always the minority seems to link them with a shrinking away from space. The fact that the 'space-people' are always a majority seems to identify them with an expansive tendency which leads them away from time and unfoldment, and identifies them with massive accretion in space and to fixation of form. All life and all struggle eventually may be seen in terms of this basic struggle between the time-few and the space-many, the former seeking to restrain expansion and to dissolve form in order to unfold new meaning, while the latter seek to repress change and new meaning, and to demand the perpetuation of the 'already-achieved'. This can be seen at work in individuals with especial clarity in the relations of the sexes, where on the whole it may be said that man seeks to change by destroying and recreating, while woman seeks to preserve and maintain. There is nothing so ferociously conservative as the woman. This was expressed collectively more clearly in older times than now, when the walled city (universally associated with the woman) was constantly threatened with assault by the warring males. Nothing links the two things more clearly than do such legends as the rape of the Sabine women, where warlike penetration was 'sublimated' into the penetration of the women. The same motif is to be seen at least dimly in the story of Troy and the abducted Helen. Toynbee, in his *A Study of History*, has suggested that the evolution of the historical cycle emerges through minorities, and goes through expansion to fixation and the emergence of new minority creative impulses. The process is seen clearly at work in the life-cycle of the higher plants which, like the higher animals, are the outcome of the same essential process.[1] It was Goethe who first seems to have formulated at least an approximation to the rhythmic expansions and contractions of the plant, all of which may be seen in terms of a centrifugal thrust of time into space and a centripetal withdrawal. Whether or not the formula of Goethe is correct, it is evident that there is an overall rhythm of the plant from seed to seed, the interval being occupied by an expansion into space. The life-cycle of the higher plants seems to represent in a very simple manner the basic rhythmic relation between the time-point and the space-sphere. We may see, indeed, in the growth of the plant a periodic rhythm rather different from that noted by Goethe. The plant in the course of its cycle seems to respond to the geometrical elements of point, line, plane and solid; the seed being the analogue of the point, the stem of the line, the leaf of the plane, and the fruit of the solid. The plant, as it unfolds from the seed, thus may be seen as expressing in geometrical terms the centrifugal thrust from time into space. Meantime, as the expansive cycle comes to its close, a counter-rhythm may be found developing in the interior of the fruit, namely the preparation of new seed, which in itself has an analogous fourfold series. Thus the zygote is the primary point, from which develops the radicle as the line, followed by the cotyledon as the plane, resulting in the formation of the solid testa around the miniature plant, which testa, in turn, becomes the seed-point to a new generation.

[1] All that I have written above of the metazoic animals could be said of the metaphytic plants, namely that they are cell-communities which have achieved organic integration through a basic germ-soma division of labor among the cells.

The Nature of the Self

This geometrical cycle of the plant's life can, I think, without any 'pythagorean juggling' be represented as fulfilling two four-fold cycles which combine into a composite sevenfold cycle. This is more easily represented by the diagram, which appears here as Figure Three.

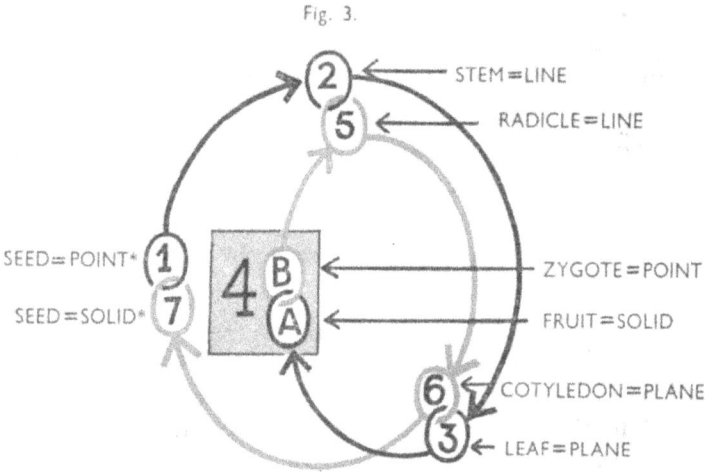

Fig. 3.

* A seed represents the solid culmination of the process of seed-making but represents the germinal point to the development of the plant.

It is, I think, highly significant that the plant not only seems to respond to the geometrical structure of the space-time universe, but that this response is similar to what we find in dreams concerning the primary human umbilical response to the same elements.[1] It is also, I think, of importance to note that the plant's life-cycle is specifically related to, and governed by, the relation

[1] See Chapter Two, Figure One.

of the earth (as part of the sun's periphery) to its solar focus. For, as I shall presently suggest, the solar system itself is at root a response to the same configurational necessity as has produced the plant. The plant, which in itself is a living representation of the relation between nuclear seed and peripheral expansion into leaf and fruit, may be thus seen as a synthesis between the radiant energy of the solar nucleus and the 'coldness' of the peripheral earth.

*   *   *

Up to this point I can fairly claim to have on my side the experience of observable facts. It is an observable fact that human beings in society are dominated by configurational necessities which issue at length in what I have called the governmental pattern of directing minorities and directed majorities. It is an observable fact that insect societies show signs of having come into being through an ancient response of free-ranging insects to a similar necessity. The biological facts strongly support the idea that all animal (metazoic) and plant (metaphytic) organisms have come into being in a not dissimilar fashion. My interpretation of these facts does no violence to any positive aspects of science. Indeed, it illumines them and welds them into an integral whole without recourse to any kind of mysticism or magic. We have a grip upon a basic principle of organization covering the integration not only of cells into bodies, but of insects and of men into society. It is a principle which gives all moral and biological evolution a direct link with the space-time pattern.

I now make bold to extrapolate this principle into a realm of creation inaccessible to ordinary observation. I suggest that every living cell has come into being in the same way, namely by the integration of molecules into a rhythmic interrelationship between nuclear and peripheral elements. It is quite true, of course, that there are entities such as bacteria which are indubitably 'alive', but which are not cellular and have no nucleus. But, then, so are there bees which are not hive-bees, and so also are there cells which are not parts of higher organisms. It is possible that such forms as

63

the bacteria, and such things as the viruses, are the early stages of molecular integration which never have achieved the cellular state. They are collections of molecules in some kind of aggregation which never has received the ultimate impress of the universal pattern.

It is my suggestion that the living cell was the *ultimate* in the rhythmic integration of molecules—ultimate because it received the 'impress' of the universal pattern, which acted upon the constituent molecules to divide them into nuclear particles and peripheral (cytoplasmic) particles. The living cell with its central nucleus and its cytoplasmic surround is plainly a chemical representation of the universal design. Moreover, signs are not wanting that the nucleus is the instrument of time within the minute cellular economy, the cytoplasmic surround being the instrument of space. For the cytoplasm by itself is powerless to reproduce itself in the living stream of time. A cell from which the nucleus is removed dies. Yet a nucleus left with a minute fragment of cytoplasm will regenerate itself. Furthermore, all cellular reproduction commences in the nucleus, where lie the mechanisms of heredity—time-past bound into an arrangement of molecules: a physical memory!

Unseen in the economy of the cell (as in that of all living organisms), but invisibly present, is a factor too often neglected in the formulation of any comprehensive view of creation, namely the relevance of the solar system to the cell's very existence. But for the existence of warmish water the cell could neither exist nor have been evolved in the first place. And this warmish water depends for its existence entirely upon the prior existence of the solar system, itself a larger manifestation of the universal design. We tend to take warmth for granted, especially if we live in a temperate clime, for even on this earth it is by no means universal. As for the wide universe, the existence of warmth is a rarity of the highest order, and indeed we have no absolute certainty that it exists anywhere but on the surface of this earth. For the most part, the universe knows only incandescence or near-zero temperature. Warmth, and especially rhythmic warmth as known on this planet, is a cosmic miracle.

Origins of the Solar System

The solar system represents a majestic instance of the universal pattern of creation. The central sun, boiling with hydrogen transformations, radiates its energy to a periphery of far-flung planets and planetoid bodies. Its creation has always been a puzzle, and in degree still remains so. One of the first theories to account for its creation was offered by Kant and Laplace, who asserted that it came into being as a small 'nebula' of gases which condensed a fiery ball at the center (which became the sun), leaving the cooler peripheral gases to condense into the planets. This theory lost favor owing to technical difficulties, and for a time was replaced by the 'collision theory', which represented the solar creation as an accident caused by the near approach of two stars which tore lumps from one another and left them revolving as planets. Now, once more, the Kant-Laplace theory in a modified form seems to have gained favor. With respect to all these theories, I make bold to say that everything suggests that the creation of the solar system took place by essentially the same universal impulsion as has governed the creation of the cells, the cell-societies and the animal societies. This seems to imply that there was first of all an aggregation of atoms followed by their integration into the familiar pattern of (solar) nucleus and (planetary) periphery. Vastly different are the actual physical forces which were instrumental in the making of the beehive and the solar system, the living cell and the human society. But I submit that these physical forces were in each case the instruments of a more primary force, namely the universal principle which compels integrations to assume the structural form of point and periphery.

It would appear, therefore, that the modified 'nebular hypothesis' of solar origins comes close to what in the light of this general theory we might expect, namely that there was first an aggregation of atoms; a drawing together of atoms from the dispersed wisps of gas which still fill all interstellar space, followed eventually by their division into the two kinds of bodies which form the solar system, namely the radiant sun (as nucleus) and the non-radiant planets of the solar periphery. Reflecting on this process, one sees how each level of the manifestation of the Universal Design automatically and inevitably prepares the raw materials for a yet new manifestation of the same fundamental pattern.

With even greater temerity I extend my general principle to cover the creation of the atom, that veritable brick of which all physical forms are made. It would be quite presumptuous of me to comment upon the several theories which attempt to explain the actual detail of the formation of this fundamental form, but the fact remains that the *outcome* bears the same essential configurational imprint as has been seen in all other forms. Whatever may have been the actual history of the evolution of the atoms, it is undeniable that the pattern of their integration is precisely that which we have already observed in the structure of human and insect society, in the cellular societies which we call plants and animals, in their constituent cells, and in the solar system. In assessing this statement the reader should make allowance for the vast differences of appearance which hide the central simplicity and unity of pattern. The phenomena mentioned above are outwardly so diverse that one is inclined to be struck rather by their differences than by the less obvious unity of pattern.

Fig. 4.

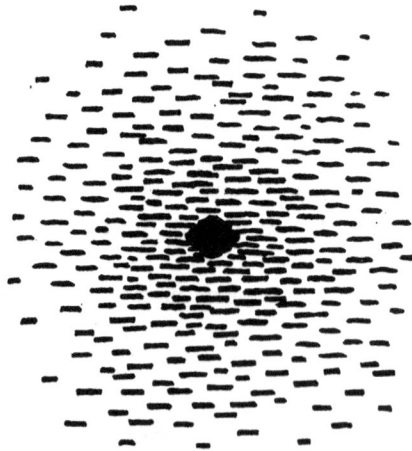

Figure Four represents a rough wave-mechanical picture of the hydrogen atom, and is based upon an illustration in Professor George Gamow's book 'The Birth and Death of the Sun'.

The Universal Design in the Atom

There was a time, only a few decades ago as I write, when the atom was represented in terms of a miniature solar system, the nucleus being represented as analogue of the sun, the electrons being shown as so many planets revolving about it in their miniscule orbits. Indeed, so close was the analogy drawn that comparisons were possible between the orbit of the planet Mercury and the orbit of the single electron of the atom of hydrogen. But now this delightful analogue is swept away by new discoveries concerning the complex nature of the nucleus and the indeterminate nature of the electrons and their orbits. Figure Four represents a fair effort to give a pictorial idea of the atom.

It is evident that the modern concept of the atom represents less the analogue of the solar system than of the beehive. Indeed, whereas the older picture was satisfied with the existence of two simple particles, the electron and the proton, which might be equated roughly with the planets and the sun, the new picture of the atom requires a much larger number of infinitesimal particles, including such now-familiar entities as neutrons, positrons, neutrinos and a whole family of mesons. Moreover, some of these particles have but a fleeting existence, and some are the products of a constant rhythm of change. There is evidently an orderly confusion and buzz of particles in this subatomic world. But whatever that confusion and buzz may eventually turn out to be, and no matter how many or how few the constituent particles, it is indubitable that they are under the control of a universal configurational force whose imprint does not differ in essence from that to be seen on all other levels of creation.

Whether the subatomic particles predated the formation of the atoms, as the free-ranging bees predated the formation of the hive, being drawn into the atomic structures and modified by their new status in the whole, or whether they appeared as integral parts of the nascent atoms, is naturally beyond my knowledge. One modern theory tends, with variations, to the idea that all the atoms were created suddenly, at the moment when an infinitely dense mass of primal nuclear energy suddenly burst forth into spatial expansion—its effects being still perceptible in the retreat of the galaxies to some distant periphery.

67

The Nature of the Self

As to the origins of the material universe, we may note here the two opposing cosmogonies hinted at above. The first, which appears to exist in several variant forms, is cataclysmic. It predicates a primal state in which all matter was condensed into an infinitely compact nucleus. From this nucleus exploded the universe, and it is still going on exploding.

The opposite theory is that although the universe is truly expanding, the old matter, as it reaches the far periphery, simply goes out of existence. But this does not mean the end of the universe, since new matter, in the form of hydrogen, is being created all the time, and is being aggregated and integrated into galaxies, condensed into stars, in the hot depths of which the hydrogen is then built into the heavier elements.

While I am in no position to enter the lists where the mathematical giants wrestle with such concepts (and one another!), I can without presumption point out that *both* these theories and their variants potentially satisfy the universal concept which I have propounded. The first-mentioned theory would represent the cosmos as a fiery chick that had come bursting out some two thousand million years ago from its infinite compression in the nuclear egg, and is still growing. You will note that this picture satisfies the general configurational concepts here laid down, namely that all creation is done through the establishment of a nucleus within a periphery, and by the centripetal and centrifugal reactions between them. Such an explosion must either have created space, or that space must have been in extension at a prior date. In either event, it must surely be true that the structure of space-time is essentially the relation between the primal nuclear point and the ultimate peripheral expansion which it can achieve. It seems to me, therefore, that an interesting comparison may be seen to exist between the alleged primal explosion of the universe from its nucleus, and the contemporary expansion of a plant from its seed. The plant's structure may be seen to evince signs of a response to the fourfold elements of point, line, plane and solid. But these very elements themselves, surely, may be none other than the products of the invisible architectonics created by the original cosmic explosion.

The Universal Design in the Unicell

It is worth noting here that a similar fourfold and sevenfold rhythm appears to have been involved in the emergence of the individual atoms, for these rhythms are manifest in the periodic structure of the atoms. There are not wanting signs to suggest that the plant is still annually obedient to a time-pattern which at earlier epochs guided the emergence of the universe and each constituent atom. Such facts argue strongly for a fundamental common source from which all forms derive their nature and their emergence. Such a concept has been immensely strengthened by the discovery that the beat of blood in the umbilical cord 'detects' in some way a fourfold and sevenfold periodicity.[1]

I turn now to the second theory of cosmic origins, namely that the universe is constantly 'fraying off at the edges', but is as constantly being recreated from within by the emergence of new hydrogen atoms 'out of nowhere'. This view also satisfies the configurational concepts here outlined, but substitutes the continuous creation of hydrogen atoms for the once-for-all explosion. The hydrogen atom is peculiarly suited to play this emergent rôle, and I have in fact elsewhere described the whole of the atomic forms as 'a great tree' that has burgeoned from the 'hydrogen seed'.[2]

*   *   *

For fear that the reader may be a little lost in the relative complexity of the foregoing, I will recapitulate my story in a slightly different way. I have presented the 'brick' of all material forms (namely the atom) in terms of a universal configuration, and likewise the 'brick' of all major organic forms—the living cell. Both these 'bricks', the living and the non-living, contain the same fundamental design of the nucleus within the periphery.

The 'living brick' (the unicell) is, of course, like all material forms, built up of 'non-living bricks' (atoms). And it seems highly significant to me that the coincidence of these two 'bricks'

[1] See Chapter Two, especially Figure One.
[2] *Biosynthesis.* Part One. (A book now out of date as regards my psychological concepts, but still useful in its comments on the universal pattern.)

depends upon a manifestation of the same configuration which characterizes them both, namely the solar system. The solar system, like both the atom and the living cell, is a representation of the universal pattern of the nucleus and the periphery. It is this solar representation alone which permits the existence of those conditions in which the 'non-living bricks' (atoms) can develop into the 'living brick' (the cell). The solar system, through its configuration, creates conditions of balance between nucleus and periphery, giving rise to the condition of warmth.

It may seem extravagant to describe warmth as the symptom of a balance between nucleus and periphery. And yet this is what it manifestly is. Extreme cold is a characteristic of space. Extreme heat is a characteristic of those nuclear centers which everywhere dot the cosmic prairies with points of fire. The solar system permits of a balance between one of these nuclear points of fire (the sun) and the ambient cold of space. This temperature balance, which we on this planet think of in terms of warmth, represents one instance of a synthesis between nuclear and peripheral elements. It permits the emergence of water, which can exist only within a narrow temperature range, and it is water which permits that molecular state from which came the colloids and their susceptibility to chemical rhythm which is the basis of all living matter.

*   *   *

My concepts manifestly have something in common with the *holism* of the late Field-Marshal Smuts. I believe that all creation is done by making new wholes out of available parts. But whereas Smuts gave no more than the concept of integration, I have shown that integration always takes place in accordance with an unvarying configuration. Every transformation of an aggregation of parts into a new whole is done by creating a fundamental division of labor between the parts, whereby a few become agents of the nuclear function, the majority becoming agents of the peripheral function. Every mass thus becomes an integrated whole by the polarization of a nuclear few whose natures and qualities suit them to play the focal role. On each level the qualities differ, so that it is difficult, save on a configurational basis, to see what can possibly be shared by an atomic nucleus, the sun, the cell-nucleus, the drones in a hive, and a governing minority in human society. The fact is that it is probably impossible to discern any concrete physical element which these diverse phenomena share, such as would give them a single category. All that they possess in common may be purely their configurational status—all being nuclear agents on their appropriate levels. But is configurational status concrete? Has it any claim to reality?

It is my view that configuration *is* the primal element of all form, even though its tangibility is negative. In the ultimate analysis there is nothing *but* configuration. Modern man is able to dissect and analyze matter to its ultimate constituent. And when at length he arrives at the final analysis, what does he find but a feverish play of subatomic particles guided by 'pilot waves' particles which often behave as if they too were waves!

Creation is pattern woven into pattern and woven yet again into pattern. The particles are integrated into the pattern of the atoms; the atoms are woven into the pattern of the stellar systems, the crystals and the cells; the cells are woven into the patterns of the plant and animal bodies; the animal bodies are woven into the pattern of society. Pattern is woven into pattern and into pattern again. *But the miracle is that there are not many patterns; not even several patterns, but one pattern repeated over and over again.*

This impels me to offer the generalization that the Creator is a brooding Spirit which makes only one demand upon Creation, namely that it bear the imprint of the universal design, and faithfully carry out an unvarying rhythm of interrelation between its fundamental parts. *This is the supreme demand laid upon the cosmos, and it has no physical basis, for it creates the physical forms 'out of nothing' by the weaving of its primary substance—configuration.*

One of the biggest stumbling blocks to any acceptance of this view is the fact that people either know too much about the universe or they know too little. The vast majority of mankind knows too little about the cosmos, so that even so simple a statement as this chapter will appear unbearably complex and learned.

The Nature of the Self

The rest tend to know too much, so that this chapter inevitably will appear too simple and naive. This is the tragedy of modern man, and it is a tragedy which this concept of integration alone can solve, so that all men, learned and simple, may unite in a common human understanding of the creative method that has worked in the past to create 'nature', and now works in these same men themselves to create mind and society.

Thinking people lament the gap which exists between laymen and the men of science. Efforts are made to educate the laity in popular science and to provide 'humanities' courses for scientists. Such efforts have a value of their own, but they merely tinker with the larger problem. The natural answer lies in the organization of man's collective realization of the universal pattern of creation.

So simple it would be to teach every child that God has established one pattern and one rhythm in the universe, and that all things bear this imprint. In that simple knowledge all mankind could find a factual religion that would offer the basic explanation of the nature of all things, inorganic, organic, moral and spiritual and would provide the basis for a new unified philosophy, a new epistemology and a new unity of feeling among men.

Because the specialist knows so much about the 'trees', the layman assumes in his ignorant simplicity that if he (the specialist) cannot see the 'wood', then who else can? This helps to vitiate all such efforts as mine which, made by a non-accredited thinker, are inevitably (and properly) suspect from the start. One physicist to whom I put my concepts replied: 'As to the supposed likenesses between the beehive and the atom, the solar system and the cell, this does not *interest* me—I am *interested* not in their similarities, but their differences.' The reader will note the emphasis upon the factor of *interest*. It is not that the scientific man dismisses what I say. He does not deny my interpretation of the facts. He merely is *not interested*. This is the voice of the analyst speaking. It is not the authentic voice of science as understood by Bacon and Galileo. It is the voice of the specialist who has mistaken laboratory method for the empirical method, and pragmatism for truth. It is the cry of the man who cannot see the wood of *meaning* for the trees of *fact*.

72

The Kingpin of Integrated Education

Yet I have been encouraged to find that in New York there has been set up a Foundation for Integrated Education, which has upon its board of directors a number of men bearing good names in science. Of the purpose of this foundation its distinguished president has written:

'Most of us believe—perhaps in large degree intuitively—that there is an underlying, integrating, unifying principle that in some way characterizes the cosmos of which we are a part and makes it truly a universe. Presumably this principle manifests itself in various ways in physics, chemistry, biology, psychology, sociology, history, philosophy, art and ethics. The manifestations are diverse and manifold, but the active principle responsible for them is presumably one. Just what it may be, no one is sure. But we are committed to the search for it. Recent progress in widely separated fields gives hope that the search may not be in vain. There is much encouragement from those who work on the far frontiers of knowledge that the basic marching orders for the organization of the universe are not only very potent and profound, but also very meaningful and simple. To lay our hands on them, and to transmit them in terms comprehensible to all thoughtful persons would be a contribution of superlative merit to the welfare of mankind.'[1]

It seems to me that I have come upon the underlying, integrating, unifying principle which characterizes the cosmos and makes it truly a universe. Moreover, so far from my concepts being a mere derivation from popular science, I have actually created my own specialist field and my own organon for its penetration, and what I have found there sets the seal upon what I have written above. With all due respect to organizations of scientists aiming at synthesis, their efforts cannot lead to ultimate success unless they be co-ordinated by the kingpin of a cosmic science of the mind that creates the specialisms.[2]

[1] Mather, Kirtley F., Professor Emeritus of Geology, Harvard University. President of the Foundation for Integrated Education.
[2] See Appendix O.

73

The Nature of the Self

I spent nearly twenty years of my life in pursuit of evidence for a universal design of creation in external nature. By the year 1940 I had reached the conclusions which I have adumbrated in this chapter. My picture of universal integration was as complete as I had power to make it save for one important detail: *I did not know how to demonstrate that the human mind itself is the product of the impress of the universal design.* I could not believe that the external world could be created in one fashion and the internal world of mind in another. Accordingly, from about the year 1940 onwards, I set myself to try to find evidence of the universal design of point and sphere in the structure of the mind. There were tantalizing superficial indications, for who could deny that the sense of the mind is that of an 'ego point' within the stream of consciousness? But this was not enough. I wanted to find, if possible, specific indications that mind is due to the impress of the same pattern that already had left its impress upon external forms.

Obviously my first need was to find a reliable method of analyzing the mind. I looked far and wide, but could see nothing which offered any possible lead save perhaps the work of Jung, who predicated a system of archetypal mental patterns which he apparently discerned chiefly through the analysis of dreams. I wondered if I, by means of similar efforts, might discover a unitary pattern or archetype of mind, but I was reluctant to follow this lead because all that I had read of dreams and their analysis seemed to me to be contradictory, opinionative and trivial. At length, however, by routes too involved for discussion here, I was driven to try dream analysis, at which eventually I won some expertise, and for the achievement of which I perfected certain techniques. It was by this method that I came at length upon definite indications which strongly suggested that the fetus feels itself to be nuclear to the womb, and that this feeling is the origin of the sense of self.[1] I found that the fetus gains in some mysterious fashion the awareness that this pattern of uterine relations is the analogue of the basic nature of the cosmos itself. That is to say, the fetus senses the universal design, and is somehow aware of what he experiences.

[1] See Chapter One.

74

The Universal Configuration

Because the fetus feels himself to be configurationally nuclear, it follows that if my theory is correct, he is thus *configurationally identical* with the atomic nucleus, the sun, the cell nucleus, and hence the male sperm[1] and the governing focus of society. I fully appreciate that it sounds extreme, but the fact is that dreams reveal an intuitive knowledge of these configurational identities. Not that the fetus knows anything about these external objects, but the fact is that every child and every adult produces evidence to show that he possesses an intuitive sense of this configurational sympathy. This comes out in the persistent tendency of us all to represent the fetus in dreams in terms of (1) *the sun,* (2) *the male, especially one's own father,* and (3) *a king or other male ruler.* It will be observed that in each of these symbolic representations the fetus is identified with a nuclear function. The sun is nuclear to the solar system; the male is the carrier of the sperm, which is essentially a cell-nucleus; the father is not only the bearer of the cell-nucleus (sperm) but is also center of the home; while the king or other male ruler is nuclear to a social grouping. It is quite impossible for me to say upon what basis we make these identities. I assume that at least some of them must be retroactive, being the product of postnatal association. But the identity between the fetus and its father may not be postnatal. I have no warrant for declaring one way or the other. Nevertheless the fact remains that we all reveal these identities existing deep in the feelings. That they are not peculiar to a few strange people, or to our generation, is demonstrated by the fact that myths and *märchen* all employ them in almost unvarying form. The sun in myths always yields a contextual significance when interpreted as the symbol of the fetal skin feeling. The Hero (the supreme male) or Kouros likewise. So does the Father, whether he be a magnificent figure like Abraham or a humble father in a fairytale. The figure of a king invariably fits the fetal interpretation, and is not infrequently equated with the sun. It can hardly be a mere accidental coincidence that all these symbolic figures or entities are distinguished primarily by their focal or nuclear characteristics and possess no other discernible common element.

[1] See Chapter Thirteen for evidence that the fetus always feels male.

75

The Nature of the Self

How could this deep impress be made in our feelings while *in utero* except on a configurational basis? How could it be possible that I could look for and find the same pattern in the feelings that I had found already in external phenomena, unless all these impressions had a common source? My psychology, it must be noted, is the outcome of the application of the empirical method of science to the field of mind, where so far no other effort has been made to apply it. I started my researches with a specific hypothesis, namely that if a common configuration may be traced, however sketchily, in all external forms, then it is fair to assume that it must be possible to trace that same configuration also into the mind. I created or perfected the methods necessary to the quest for this pattern in the feelings. I found that pattern through step by step of hypothesis and proof. At every step each new hypothesis, arising from prior steps, was submitted to the discipline of dream observations.[1]

When I began my researches I had only the barest hope that I might find some sort of mental patterns which by implication could be said to derive from a universal source akin to that which I believed to have created the physical world. I had not the least suspicion that I should find a whole new 'anatomy' in the sense that I should find the evocation of mind in terms of the configurational use of purely physical organs. I had no idea that the fetal skin would prove to be the organ of nuclear feeling, or that the placenta would prove to be the organ of peripheral feeling. I had no idea at all that the umbilical cord would prove to be the organ of synthesis between these two poles, or that it would be found able to 'tune in' the cosmic rhythms and the sense of space-time structure.

All that I found in the feelings, as due to the configurational use of the physical organs, served to convince me that I was on the right lines when I postulated that the basic essence of creation is configurational. For what other answer fits all the facts? I am convinced that anyone who without prejudice takes all the facts under survey, will ultimately reach the same conclusion. In a word, the fetus, through the configurational nature of his uterine

[1] See Appendices H and P.

76

relations, and through the sensitivity of his position, is able directly to register the operation upon him of the same configurational influence that has created the atoms, the solar system, the galaxies, the cell, the plant and animal bodies, the insect and human societies. The universe is one in this creative imprint and method, and its substance is configurational.

When at length I found that the human 'ego' is indubitably the original uterine impress transferred to the nervous system and the brain, then I knew that I had discovered the essence of the relation of mind to brain. Mind is configuration. It does not originate in the nervous system. It originates mainly in the blood, which somehow senses that the pattern of its umbilical flow is in resonance with the cosmic configuration. All arguments about 'spirit' and 'matter' at once became as outdated as pre-evolutionary concepts of 'nature', or as pre-Copernican discussions of astronomy. The real dichotomy is not as between spirit and matter, but as between Point and Periphery. These are the two great primal categories, for which reason we respond deep in our hearts to the idea that God is Father and Mother, which is to say, Point (sperm) and Sphere (egg). All creation is built of these two basic elements of Point and Sphere, interwoven again and again into unbearable complexity, but ever retaining their basic simplicity. Mind and matter, spirit and form are but different levels of the same creative pattern.

That this verges upon the religious I do not doubt. But how can it be otherwise? For in the ultimate analysis what can we know that is not from this primal Source which we may without violence call 'the anatomy of God', the pattern of all being. Certainly this is not religious in any superstitious, dogmatic or magical sense, for it stands square upon a picture of the external world that does no violence to science, but offers a new, universal and unitary philosophy that can save science from its own specialism. It offers also a new epistemology, simple and natural, namely that we can comprehend 'nature' because our minds are the product of the same configurational forces that had earlier created the external forms which are to be comprehended.[1]

[1] The reader's attention is drawn to Appendix B.

The Nature of the Self

When the reader eventually has digested Part Two of this book, and thereby has gained an idea of the tortuous processes by means of which the original uterine pattern is carried through the postnatal body to the brain, he may perhaps turn back to this chapter and recall with astonishment the lengths to which the human organism goes to retain in its scattered feelings the primary (uterine) impress of the cosmic pattern. He may perhaps reflect upon the miracle that every human being *knows* the contents of this book in his feelings, no matter how little his conscious mind may know or care about a unifying philosophy. He may feel disposed to notice a parallel between the present state of the cosmos and that of every man alive. For he may reflect that just as the wide cosmos takes its source in the simplicity of the Universal Design, the presence of which is hidden in the complexity of forms, so also the human self has a like origin, though the memory of it lies hidden in the complexity of feelings generated by the processes described in Part Two.

Chapter Five

A BIRD'S-EYE VIEW OF THE FOREGOING
MATERIAL

FIFTY MILLION years or so ago a radical development in the methods of animal reproduction took place. Up to this time, the best method had been the laying of a hard-shelled egg which could be hatched by the warmth of the mother's body and led from the newly-evolved mammary glands. But so great was the pressure of the predatory reptiles, that a method was evolved whereby a mother could retain her eggs inside her body, and 'hatch' them there and 'rear' the young inside her. A bag of flesh was evolved to meet the need. In this bag the egg could be 'hatched' and the young retained. But the evolution of this bag demanded the ancillary evolution of a placenta, an organ which could permit the blood of the young to 'feed' off the mother's blood, and to 'excrete' into its cleansing flow. This in turn required the provision of a free link between the placenta and the occupant of the womb, a requirement which was met by the evolution of a set of tubes called by us the umbilical cord.

This reproductive mechanism, after serving its physiological function for millions of years, became involved in matters which quite transcended its original purposes. Presumably because it proved to have a configurational similarity with the creative pattern of the universe, this reproductive mechanism found a 'resonance' with the primary architectonics of the cosmos. Because the fetal body in its 'bag' imitated the focal nature of the creative nuclear element of the cosmos, this became 'imprinted' in the fetal organism. And because the relation of the fetal body to the womb and placenta through the umbilical cord, imitated the universal pattern of relations between nucleus and periphery, the whole uterine experience became invested with deep and unexpected intimations of the nature of the cosmos.

The primary sense thus evoked seems to be that of a constant cyclical reversal between the sense of being nuclear and the sense of being peripheral. The fetus, having acquired the sense of being solid and nuclear, felt that the umbilical arterial flow of blood away from his body was a means of demonstrating his nuclear power to thrust out and to pierce and occupy the placenta. Yet at the same time he felt that this arterial 'outthrust' carried away his nuclear virtue and achieved its dissipation in the placenta. The return flow of blood from the placenta seemed, on the contrary, to restore the energy of the fetus, and yet at the same time to 'hollow out' the fetus and to make it feel non-nuclear, which is to say, peripheral. Thus there was set up an oscillation of feeling which swung from a sense of being nuclear to a sense of being peripheral and back again. This experience seems in some way to match the basic process of the cosmos itself, which shows signs on every hand of a tension between nuclear and peripheral forces (contractive and expansive oppositions), the evidence of which is to be found on every level of creation.

The relation between the nuclear and peripheral forces is always shown in dreams and myths in terms of two streams of energy moving helically around a single stream. It is not possible yet to say whether this is imposed upon the cosmic impress by the umbilical instrument, or whether it is inherent in the cosmic flow itself. This subject is expanded in Appendix L.

In addition to this configurational element, superadded to the ordinary physiological functions, the fetus also seemed to gain a new mechanism of heredity, namely from something in his mother's blood which came to him through the placenta. This communication does not appear to be merely chemical, as would be the case with a hormone transmission, since it carries with it distinct mental elements.[1]

[1] See Chapter Three.

Recapitulation

The primal feelings generated in the fetus by the umbilical arterial flow may be summed up as follows:

1. This is sensed as the primary act of excretion, and so becomes the root for all later experiences of excretion.
2. It is felt also as a dual aggressive thrust from and by a nucleus into a hollow.
3. But at the same time the fetal virtue itself feels to be drawn away into the placenta and there dissipated.
4. From which arises the strange sense that it is the fetus itself which travels forth, enters the placenta and is there destroyed.
5. From this 'journey' the fetus gains the primary sense of orientation, and of the structure of space-time.
6. The umbilical arterial flow is always associated in the feelings with the sense of two thrusts and their helical twist.

The primal feelings generated in the fetus by the umbilical venous flow may be summed up as follows:

1. This is sensed as the primary act of ingestion, and so becomes the root of all later experiences of eating and drinking.
2. This is sensed as an aggressive thrust from the placenta, as if it were constantly piercing the fetal body. Allied to this is the sense that the placenta, having been hollow and receptive, has suddenly become nuclear and aggressive.
3. The fetal virtue feels nevertheless to be restored through the life-giving activity of the placenta in the act of this venous thrust.
4. The fetus, having felt to go forth into the placenta and to be destroyed therein, now feels to be renewed and restored from the same source.
5. In this return journey, as it were, the fetus supplements its sense of the pattern of space-time and, in the total cycle of back-and-forth, gains a resonance with the cosmic process.
6. The umbilical venous flow is always associated with a single straight thrust.

As a result of this activity, the placenta is sensed by the fetus to be playing the following highly ambivalent roles:

1. It is a receptacle for excretion.
2. It is the instrument of food.
3. It is a hollow and helpless creature which can be pierced and occupied.
4. It is a solid and aggressive creature which can pierce the fetal body and occupy it.
5. It is a blood-sucker and a destroyer of nuclear virtue.
6. It is a life-giver and a restorer.
7. It is the 'wide world' into which the fetus may 'travel' and from which it may 'return again'.
8. It is a mysterious 'teacher', which transmits to the fetus organic or quasi-organic hereditary factors.

From these ambivalent feelings eventually arise a number of primary complexes, in the course of which the most conflicting and rationally impossible and even disgusting associations potentially derive. All these associations are made entirely without the intervention of the logical mind. They are associations made in much the same way that a pun is made. In fact, the Unconscious is a great maker of puns. This process goes on in the depths of the most illustrious minds, though it is strictly the mental process of infants and savages. Typical such complexes are:

1. The sense that one feeds from the place of excretion.
2. The feeling that one feeds from the place of death.
3. The sense that excretion and death are the same.
4. A feeling that one's own self is excretion.
5. The feeling that to feed is to 'eat oneself', since the umbilical vein is not only the feeding tube, but also the tube through which the fetal 'wanderer' returns to himself.

While it is generating these all-too-human elements of primary feeling, the cyclic flow of blood in the umbilical cord is also acquainting the fetal organism with the structure of space-time, so that it may be said that the flow of blood through the navel and along the umbilical cord, recapitulates the essential configuration of the cosmos. By this is not meant that the fetus senses the movements of the contemporary physical universe (though this also may be true), but rather that the fetus senses the original pattern from which the physical universe was derived.[1]

The fetus feels to be a nuclear point which throws out a line, achieves a plane, and then experiences the reversal of this geometrical development in the back flow of the blood from the placenta. In this 'vascular geometry' the fetus gains much more than a static sense of the structure of space-time. The fetus senses that he has lived through the experience of the unfoldment of the cosmos from the time-point to the space-sphere, through the line and the plane. The fetus gains a concrete sense of the manner in which creation is always done, namely by the setting of a point into a sphere. He senses this, moreover, not in terms of something once-done, but in terms of a persistent interrelation between point and sphere, in the course of which a rhythm is set up, a rhythm that runs from point to line, from line to plane, from plane to solid and to the point again. This the fetus feels in terms of a sevenfold complex, for reasons which I have explained.[2] The fetus in this way gains a specific insight into the creative pattern and method. Thus the umbilical cord is the instrument which evokes not only extremely personal and earthy feelings, but also the most elevated and cosmic ones. This coincidence of the 'earthy' and the sublime is a marked feature of the human self.

Subjectively, all this fetal impress takes on a highly personal and poetic color. The fetal skin feeling is represented in dreams as a majestic cloak or garment of light, color and nuclear pride, a representation which the myths also make, most naturally since they are but a collectivized version of the individual feelings. The fetus or, at any rate, the nuclear feeling reposed in him by the cosmos, is felt as the Shining One, King of the universe, who occupies the focal position in all things. Yet this majesty has a seed

[1] See Appendix B.
[2] See Chapter Two.

of tragedy: this Great One has an Achilles Heel. For his virtue is being constantly drained from him and destroyed. Moreover, the instrument of this destruction is also an aggressive enemy who constantly pierces the Great One and hollows him out. The instrument of this inquietude is a mysterious Twin, whose nature is tantalizingly ambivalent. There is another complication in the life of this Lordly One, who symbolizes the subjective sense of our own fetal existence. He feels himself to be a monarch sitting upon a throne and dominating his periphery, but he is also a wanderer doomed forever to go forth and to return again. He is humbled and brought low; he is destroyed; but he is restored again to new life and to his central place.

The reader will recognize in this sketch of the subjective sense of the fetal life the lineaments of the mysterious saviors and gods who have in the past received the adulation and hope of the world's millions. This is no mere sacrosanct fiction. It is an answer to the longing of the human heart, which is to find somewhere on earth, or in heaven, the glorious one they once knew before birth, and whom they mysteriously somehow lost. This feeling is ever with us, no matter how battened down it may have become by the rational mind. For this strange medley of primary feelings, as enumerated in these chapters, though it is cut off by birth, is not lost. It is separated by birth from the familiar organs and processes which first evoked it and then maintained it, but it is not destroyed. The uterine pattern lives on in the body after the disruption of the organism that evoked it. This it does by selecting certain postnatal organs, which it induces to feel as though they were the lost pre-natal structures. I do not pretend to be in possession of all the details of this great changeover, but I know a great deal of the way in which the prenatal pattern bridges the chasm of birth and attaches itself to other organs and processes.

It will be the task of Part Two of this book to outline, to the best of my knowledge, the story of what happens to this complex of feelings at birth, and to show how it eventually arrives in the brain, where it gives rise to the sense of the self.

PART TWO

AN OUTLINE OF THE NATAL AND POSTNATAL
DEVELOPMENTS IN THE BODILY
CONFIGURATIONS

Prologue to Part Two

THE PATTERN of feeling evoked in the umbilical cord survives the experience of birth. Were it not so, this book could not have been written, since it is by unearthing the relics of these feelings in the the human adult that I have been able to reconstruct the experiences of the fetal life.[1] What I have learned about the fetal feelings is obviously not learned direct from the uterine state, but from the products of that state carried over into the postnatal body.

This carry over is achieved in a most surprisingly simple manner, or so it appears to me. Indeed, the methods are so naive that they will inevitably be suspect on that account alone. I myself, as each new discovery of these methods began to dawn upon me through my analyses, was often tempted to feel that nothing could be quite so naive as the hypothesis I found myself impelled to formulate.

The method of carry-over of the prenatal feelings into the postnatal state amounts to this: the feelings select three organs or parts of the body which can play the roles of fetus, placenta and umbilical cord. They then invest these ordinary bodily organs with their own peculiar configurational elements. For instance, at birth, as I shall show in detail, the newborn head swiftly becomes enlisted to play the role of fetus; the lungs are impressed into the task of representing the placenta, while the windpipe and its two-way flow of air assume the representation of the umbilical cord and its two-way flow of blood.[2]

Let me make it very clear that to the newborn child this

---

[1] Of course, I could go much further and say that but for the survival of this umbilical pattern there would be no human mind at all, but this would be begging the question.

[2] See Appendix R.

superimposition of new values upon orthodox anatomy assumes the most concrete form. The newborn infant has no truck with analogies or anything of an abstract character. To him it is not true that his head *feels* to be the fetus. What is true is that his head *is* the fetal self. The lungs are not *felt* 'as if they were' the placenta. The identification is complete: the lungs *are* the placenta. The same is true of the postnatal identity between windpipe and cord, air and blood. The breath is not merely felt 'as if it were' the umbilical blood. To the neonate the breath *is* the umbilical blood. This simple fact must be kept in mind, or the reader will not be in a position to appreciate what follows.

As to the basis upon which these organs are selected to play their configurational role, I can say no more than that it appears to be one of pure feeling-association. Taking the above instance as my example, I suppose that the newborn head feels to be the fetus because whereas before birth the whole skin was the source of 'touch', this sense now becomes concentrated at the special organs of the head. In the same way I suppose that the neonate feels his lungs to be the placenta because the effect of oxygenation derived from both these organs is similar. Given this situation, how inevitable that the flow of air between head-as-fetus and lungs-as-placenta should be felt as the two-way flow of umbilical blood! It is a relatively simple process of feeling-association, and it bears no more relation to the formal anatomy and physiology of the body than a brilliant pun bears to the body of formal logic.

Yet this irrational nature of the method of 'feeling migration' must not mislead us into supposing that it is without a logic of its own. Indeed, that logic is the structure of our very minds, and without it there could be no mind. Moreover, it is a *strict* logic, and it demands satisfaction in the body in the shape of strictly formal accommodations. It demands this satisfaction in a specific and orderly manner—in a logical sequence that is fulfilled by the migration of these feelings to new and yet newer sets of organs until at last they reach the brain.

Not just *any* three organs or bodily parts selected at random can fulfil the demands of this configurational process. At birth, for instance, certain organs or bodily parts *always* play the same roles.

Prologue to Part Two

The configurational anatomy of the body is just as rigid as its gross physical anatomy. *The same organs always play the same roles in each one of us.* Unless this were so, there could be no such things as the myths, for the myths confirm what dreams suggest, namely that the configurational anatomy of the human being is consistent. Moreover, the very age of the myths shows us that this consistency is not of recent date, but that it stems back into the far past. And where myth abandons us, primitive rites and beliefs carry us still further backward into the mists of human origins, suggesting that indeed this configurational consistency of bodily parts and functions is the nature of man as mind.

The organs which take up the uterine pattern at birth do not normally retain it, or more than a lingering hint of it, but they pass it on to another set. This set, in turn, passes the 'torch' on to yet another set of organs until at length the brain takes up the major role and weaves the entity we call "I". There is, so to say, a migration of these polar feelings through the body from birth until about seven years of age. It is the story of this migration which forms the subject matter of the following chapters.

Wherever this configurational polarity awakens in the body, there inevitably appears the original pattern of the womb.[1] There is always found to be an organ that is playing the fetal role, another the placental role, and yet another organ or process that is playing the role of the umbilical link between them. Moreover, what I said earlier of the head, the lungs and the windpipe remains true, namely that the organs invested with this configurational pattern actually *feel to be* the fetus, the placenta and the cord. The identity is *never* abstract, *always* concrete and absolute.[2]

Part Two will give an outline of the way in which birth effects the transfer of feeling from the prenatal to the postnatal state, and will in addition give an outline of how the uterine feeling moves or migrates through the body until at last it reaches the brain. The reader may suppose that this persistence of the old uterine feelings is merely a nuisance, to be brought to an end at

[1] See Appendix R.
[2] It is, in fact, the transformation of this identity which forms, as I see it, the major task of psychological engineering.

89

the earliest possible moment. On the contrary, it seems impossible to avoid the conclusion that the loss of these uterine feelings means almost literally the loss of the soul. Yet at the same time it is true that if we retain the old feelings unchanged in form, we become emotionally deranged, as in the case of the mother-tied adult. The proper course seems to be to retain these feelings and to strengthen them, but at the same time to transform them. The extreme of losing them seems to be almost as bad as the extreme of retaining them unchanged in form. Both extremes are danger-ous. What we need to do is to retain but to transform the uterine sense of cosmic pattern. We have to keep the pattern but to lose the influence of the organs of the womb. This need to retain the uterine feelings is probably the influence lurking behind the superstitious awe with which many primitive people (and some of our own peasant ancestors) regarded the placenta and the umbilical cord. These were (and still are) preserved or disposed of with great respect, since they were believed to exert a powerful influence over the child's future. I presume that this care of the actual physical relics of birth was the outcome of a failure to distinguish between the discarded organs and the configurational elements of which they had formerly been the instruments.

The reader undoubtedly needs some slight indication of what he will be offered in the following chapters. Lacking any such indications, he would hardly grasp the import of what he is reading, so fantastic to the conscious mind must these chapters appear. I offer, therefore, the briefest outline of the material picture which the following chapters will draw. They will assert that the newborn head becomes in feeling as if it were the child's own recently-lost fetal self. They will assert that this head-fetus (or 'head-as-fetus') feels as if it is sucked down into the stomach and then 'born' out at the bottom. They will assert that this head is then 'reborn' again up through the shoulders, and so appears as the newborn self which has been on a long and hazardous journey down into the depths and back. They will assert that when it feels to be in the stomach, the head-as-fetus becomes identified with the heart, and that when it eventually is reborn at the top end, then it feels to be a piece of hollowed-out excrement.

Fig. 5.

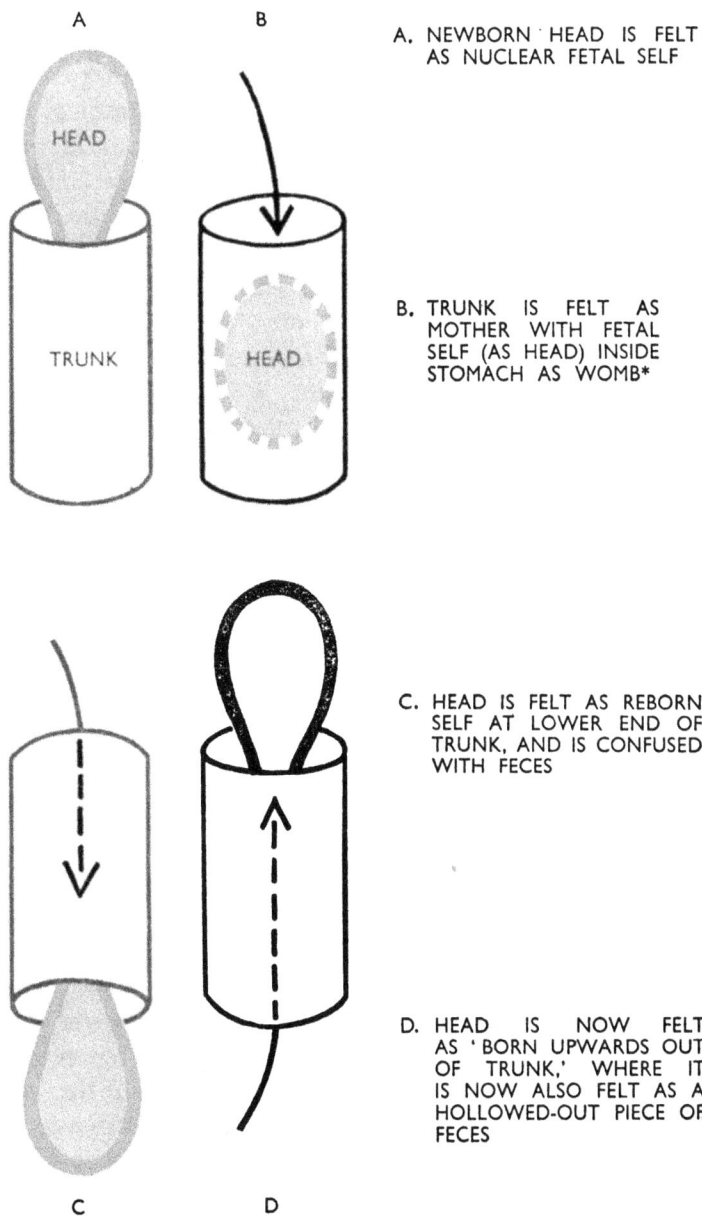

A. NEWBORN HEAD IS FELT AS NUCLEAR FETAL SELF

B. TRUNK IS FELT AS MOTHER WITH FETAL SELF (AS HEAD) INSIDE STOMACH AS WOMB*

C. HEAD IS FELT AS REBORN SELF AT LOWER END OF TRUNK, AND IS CONFUSED WITH FECES

D. HEAD IS NOW FELT AS 'BORN UPWARDS OUT OF TRUNK,' WHERE IT IS NOW ALSO FELT AS A HOLLOWED-OUT PIECE OF FECES

The Nature of the Self

For the sake of relative clarity, the outline of this strange feeling-evolution is given in schematic form in Figure Five. Four stages of this peculiar 'pilgrim's progress' are shown, and all ancillary complications omitted. This framework map will be enough to permit the reader to understand with a minimum of trouble the import and tendence of what he is reading. No doubt these drawings may appear at first to be as fantastic as some of the more fanciful forevisions of space-travel. It is therefore of the greatest support and comfort to me to find that the schema offered opposite might also be regarded as a schematic outline of some of the most revered myths and of the most familiar and beloved fairy tales.

I will mention here in outline one of these representations, taken from the Grimm collection. It is the famous tale of the Princess and the Frog, which I will briefly outline. A princess is wont to play with a golden ball by a well. One day she drops the ball in the well, and as she is lamenting bitterly, an ugly frog peers over the well-top and offers to restore it to her if she will promise to let him eat from her golden plate, drink out of her goblet and sleep in her bed. The princess promises this, and the frog retrieves her ball. The princess forgets her promise, but the frog turns up at the palace and demands to eat from her plate, drink from her goblet, and to sleep in her bed. The princess shudderingly permits the first and the second, but when the loathsome creature appears in her bedroom and demands to be *lifted up*, she throws him hard against the wall, but when he falls down from the wall, he is a handsome prince. He had been bewitched. The couple are married, and as they drive away, they hear three strange noises, one after the other. It is the three iron bands bursting from around the heart of the prince's servant—iron bands which he put there when his master was bewitched.

This fairy tale may be understood perfectly in terms of the four little sketches in Figure Five. The first sketch represents the princess playing by the well with the golden ball: the well is the trunk (or gut) and the golden ball is the head-as-fetus—that bewitched royal fetal 'prince' we all once were! The second and third sketches represent the ball lost in the well. The frog is the loathsome 'head-at-the-bottom' represented in Figure Five-C. The frog 'lifted up' and 'flattened against the wall' and transformed into his original self, is represented in Figure Five-D, which shows the sense of the fetal nuclear self 'lifted up' and 'flattened' (hollowed) and restored. The bursting of the three iron bands from around the servant's heart is a symbolic representation of the fact that the fetus-as-head, when it is felt in the stomach, becomes identified with the heart,[1] an identification which must be broken if the evolution depicted in Figure Five is to proceed.

*   *   *

The following chapters will amplify and fill in the outline offered above. I am quite certain that the facts which I shall state are correct. I am satisfied that on the whole I have the sequence of feeling-development rightly stated. The only thing I am not always sure about is the exact *age* at which these feelings occur and the *length of their duration*. In some cases, of course, the chronology is fairly well dictated by obvious considerations. For instance, we may be sure that the date of the occurrence of birth phenomena in the feelings was set by the hour of our birth. Similarly, we may be sure that the experience of the first gastrointestinal feelings dates from the time we began to suckle. But when, for instance, do we undergo the experience of feeling that we have the head at the bottom?[2] I have never yet been able to determine exactly when this takes place. Possibly it varies widely from individual to individual.

As to the duration of these feeling-experiences, this also is in some cases fairly well indicated by external events. The length of time which elapses between the newborn feelings of the head and the sense of the sucking down of that head into the gut, seems to be fairly well indicated by the time which elapsed between birth and suckling. But as to how long the head-as-fetus

---

[1] The reader will not understand the involvement of the heart in this situation until he has read Chapter Seven and understood the significance of Figure Seventeen.
[2] See Figure Five-C.

feels to be at the backside is anyone's guess so far as my present information goes. It may be seconds or weeks, minutes or months. It may vary widely from child to child. It may linger partially in some, and receive a clean cut-off in others. I just do not know.

All I can say for certain is that the events which are described in the following pages *do* occur in the bodies of every man and woman. That there are variations goes without saying. Some things are done that ought not to be done, and some things are improperly, imperfectly or insufficiently done. My experience suggests that these improperly, imperfectly and insufficiently done things are the cause of a great deal of human sickness; physical, emotional and mental.

Chapter Six

THE EXPERIENCE OF BIRTH AND THE SENSE THAT THE HEAD IS THE FETAL SELF

I STATED IN Chapter One that the newborn child feels that his fetal self has suddenly become divided and switched into the orifices of his head. The reason for this strange evolution of feeling seems plain. It is the subjective aspect of the fact that the head-senses suddenly assume at birth the role prenatally played by the whole fetal skin.

We all know tricks which can cause even the most alert and educated adult to suffer a distortion of his feelings. Two crossed fingers placed upon the tip of the nose give rise to the sensation that there are two noses. The juxtaposition of certain lines can make squares appear oblong and oblongs appear square. The newly-awakened senses of the head play even more drastic tricks upon the brain. Up to the moment of birth the brain has known only one source of external stimulation, namely the fetal skin surfaces. Suddenly it is asked to accommodate powerful new impulses arising from the eyes, the ears, the nose and palate. At first it cannot sort out the skin stimulations from those arising from the special organs of the head. In consequence it links the organs of the head with the fetal skin. It places the fetal skin, and hence the fetus itself, in the orifices of the head. Two crossed fingers placed on the nose create the sense of *two* noses, but the sudden switch of feeling at birth creates the sense of *several* fetuses; one lurking in the eye, another in the ear, yet another in the nose, and so on.

I have no idea as to the duration of this strange illusion. It may be moments only. At any rate, it seems to be quickly followed by the sense that all these dispersed little fetal selves are united. As a result of this development, the whole head is felt as the fetal self. What causes this change in the feelings I do not know. I have no idea what causes the head-orifices to seem to lose these little fetal inmates and to become instead part of the head-as-fetus. It is as if a number of little part-selves suddenly ran together like pools of water coalescing into a single pool.

As I have said before, it seems to be a condition of the uterine feelings that they must retain their integral nature. There must always be the sense of the total uterine organism—fetus, placenta and cord. Hence, wherever the fetal feeling migrates, there also follow it the feelings originally associated with the placenta and the umbilical cord. The truth of this is apparent in the fetalization of the feelings of the head. As soon as the head feels to be fetal, there appear at once also the feelings of the placenta and the umbilical cord. The accommodation is total. I have hinted already at the nature of this accommodation. As soon as the head assumes the status of the fetus, the lungs are felt to play a placental role in respect to it; the head and lungs being related through the meta-umbilical movements of the breath in the windpipe. This condition of feeling is already partly prepared through the fact that with the first breath the lungs are felt as though they were the placenta that had suddenly been sucked inside the trunk and divided into two.

It must be remembered that the newborn infant does not necessarily have any awareness that the feeling associated with his breathing is caused by a gaseous substance which enters and leaves his body. All he feels is the nervous excitation of the mouth and throat by the cold air, and the movement and feelings of the lungs. There is no sensation that he is taking in air and passing it back to an external atmosphere. To the newborn child the sense of the movement is entirely internal, from the head to the lungs and back.

All the feelings originally evoked in the uterine state are now remobilized in the feelings of the head and the lungs and the relation of the two through the rhythm of the breath. The very breath itself is first felt to be blood. There is, I must repeat, no mere abstract feeling in these evolutions. Whatever is *felt*, immediately *is*. The head is not just *felt* as fetus, but it *is* the fetus. The lungs are not merely *felt* as placenta, but they *are* the placenta. The windpipe is not just *felt* as the umbilical cord, but it *is* the cord. The breath is not merely *felt* as blood, but it *is* blood.[1] The feelings recognize no analogy, but only identity.

The breath now evokes all those feelings which once were specific to the umbilical flow. The breath takes on all the alimentary, excretory and aggressive elements which before birth were evoked by the flow of blood in the umbilical cord. The most important element of these respiratory-umbilical feelings is that the head is sucked down into the lungs with each ingoing breath and restored again by each expiration. We all feel to conceive a child in the lungs through this ingoing breath, and to bring him to birth with each expiration. Before birth the fetus felt that his nuclear virtue was drawn down through the umbilical arteries and destroyed in the placenta, being restored again by every venous pulse. This same feeling is evoked by the breath. Put very concretely, the newborn child comes swiftly to feel that he breathes his head down into his lungs and then breathes it back again.

In addition to this feeling, the head-as-fetus is felt to thrust aggressively into the lungs-as-placenta and to hollow it out, and the lungs, with every expiration, are felt to carry out the same aggressive thrust against the head. The head feels to excrete into the placenta and to receive back a revivifying flow. There is no need to complicate this narrative by repeating all that I have written earlier about the primary umbilical feelings, for whatever I have written about those feelings applies in very large measure to the first feelings awakened by the breathing rhythm. There is only one reservation: from all I can gather the newborn child already has acquired a rather puzzling sense of change; he seems to sense a strange disturbance in the fact that the placenta has suddenly become divided into two, and the fact that the taking of air into the lungs, though felt as excretory in umbilical terms, is not excretory in effect, but the reverse.

[1] See Chapter Three.

The Nature of the Self

It is the imposition of these umbilical feelings upon the breath which gives the newborn infant those qualities of character already apparent to the keen observer in the early crying. The reader may well be sceptical of such an assertion, since he must wonder how I could determine any such thing. But I have seen the early cries of the child represented so often by his later adult self, and have been able to analyze the content of those cries so easily, that I am quite sure of my facts. Many times people have come to me with a dream in which some peculiar noise appears in association with certain events. Many times it has happened that the nature of the events, when analyzed, turns out to be natal, while the patient, upon being asked to imitate the peculiar sound, gives a realistic imitation of a baby's crying which, in some cases, he himself recognizes for what it is. One might say that in the analysis of all that can be demonstrated to represent the early crying, one is dealing with the original umbilical pattern in its first postnatal manifestation. Dr Arnold Gesell has written that the breathing pattern of every child is completely personal.

I do not know how long this experience persists. But I do know that it is offset by an entirely new experience as soon as the child begins to suckle. At once the child seems to feel that he is sucking blood into his mouth from the placenta. This placenta is represented to him best by the maternal breast, but the representation is easily displaced upon whatever form of suckling he is offered.[1] The mouth is now felt as the navel. But what really seems astonishing is that the return flow from the head (the head-as-fetus) is felt to be made *through the eyes*. Therefore the eyes of the child are felt as umbilical arteries, while the mouth is felt as the umbilical vein. The milk is definitely sensed as blood. The reader will remember that I said in Chapter Three that all the early postnatal neural feelings were identified or confused with blood. I have already indicated the relevance of this to the breath, and now I am suggesting that the same thing applies both to the eyes, and to the mouth as the alimentary orifice. All the early neural feelings of the infant are identified with blood or

[1] I cannot say definitely, but I have a suspicion that all surrogates for the maternal breast are configurationally undesirable.

98

in some way confused with it either totally or partially—this is a fact which I cannot too strongly emphasize.

The problem now before us is not therefore as to why the sucking mouth should feel to suck blood, or the eyes to be associated with blood, for this, in terms of Chapter Three, is an inevitable association. The problem is as to why the eyes should feel to be specifically umbilical arteries to the venous feelings of the mouth. Why should this particular pattern of sanguinary feelings arise? Why is it not the *ears* and the mouth, or the *nostrils* and the mouth that become involved together?

I offer such tentative help as I can on this point. I think most people know that the act of swallowing tends to produce a reaction in the eyes. I do not mean the eyes as optical instruments, but in the wider sense in which we know them. It is as if the act of swallowing excites the eyes in some way—again, I do not mean optically. My suggestion is that this is due to the fact that the trigeminal nerve on each side of the face links together the jaws and the eyes. I will state the situation as simply as I can in its application to the new sensations aroused in the newborn child by the act of suckling. Each trigeminal nerve is divided into three parts.[1] There is the ophthalmic nerve which, as its name implies, serves the eyes. There is the mandibular nerve, which serves the lower jaw, and the maxillary nerve, which serves the upper jaw. It is my supposition, which I offer with all trepidity, that the act of suckling, which inevitably excites the nerves of the jaws and gums, also causes an excitation of the ophthalmic nerves. In this way there is set up an interrelation of feeling between eyes and mouth which provides an accommodation for the ever-present sense of the umbilical pattern of flow.

In order to understand *why* the trigeminal nerve should serve in this configurational sense, we must bear in mind the background of feeling against which the accommodation takes place. The primary pattern of intercommunication set by the umbilical cord is that of two arterial streams or pulses of blood running in the opposite direction to a single stream or pulse of blood. This seems to set up in the feelings a demand for the satisfaction

[1] As its name implies!

wherever possible of this simple numerical relationship.[1] This satisfaction is offered whenever a flow in one direction can be related to two flows in the opposite direction. It is offered equally well in cases where these conditions are only partly satisfied, or where they can find a sufficient basis for the creation of a fantasy. I think this last is true of the feeling that the suckling mouth is taking in one stream of blood and that the eyes are passing out two streams in the opposite direction. Bizarre as it seems, this is what I have seen frequently in dream symbolism, and what the myths confirm to be a universal human experience.

All the feelings which were once evoked in the umbilical flow now tend to invest the feelings of the sucking mouth and the sense of the bleeding eyes. Just as I believe that the newborn cry expresses in sound the result of the umbilical imposition upon the breathing rhythm, so I have seen reason to believe that the feelings of the mouth and of the eyes are strongly modulated by the imposition upon them during infancy of this umbilical pattern. This is, I think, particularly demonstrable in the later act of weeping, which in its more violent forms is associated with that involuntary sucking of breath we call sobbing. Tears are not possible to the newborn child, but when later the tear-ducts begin to function, this umbilical excretory sense is imposed, I believe, upon them. Crying is, I think, essentially a product of the fetalization of the head, and the basis of it is a sense of longing for the womb, this being expressed in terms of the long-forgotten fantasy of sucking blood (expressed in sobbing) and in excreting blood through the eyes, expressed through the flow of tears.

This mouth and eye complex appears to be of short duration, for the head-as-fetus is not, in the feelings, left long upon the newborn shoulders. The act of suckling, because it also leads to the stimulation of the nerves of the gastrointestinal linings, seems to remove the fetal feelings from the head and to establish them in the gut itself. Inevitably, as a result of this sense of the down-sucking of the fetus-as-head, the older sense of the mouth and eyes as umbilical cord is lost. I cannot make it too plain that the fetal feelings do not seem to be sucked *out* of, or away from, the head

[1] See Appendix L.

into the gut, but that the head continues to be identified with the fetal feelings, so that the head feels to be the fetal self sucked down into the gut.

This sucking down of the head is felt at least partially in terms of a war between the breath and the movement of the gut. For whereas the breath moves in and out of the body through the same orifice, and so seems to suck down and to restore the head with each cycle of the breath, the influence of the gut is almost entirely downwards. Thus, whereas the act of breathing seems to restore the head as fast as it sucks it down, the gut does no such thing. Indeed, as we shall later see, it sucks the head right down and projects it, in feeling, at the bottom.

The reader may have noted that I referred to the influence of the gut as 'almost entirely downwards'. This slight reservation is rendered necessary by the fact that the gut also, like the windpipe, has an upward as well as a downward motion. True, the upthrust of the gut is only sporadic, and is caused by the phenomena of vomiting and belching. In dreams one finds a close identity of feeling between belching and the act of expiration, and also between vomiting and the outgoing breath. And just as the act of expiration seemed to restore the head to its normal place, so also do the acts of belching and vomiting. Both these somewhat abnormal acts are felt as an effort to restore the head to its proper place, as if they were a kind of ally of the upgoing breath. Indeed, when eventually the head is felt to be restored, after its journey down through the gut, those feelings always have an undertone of upbreathing, belching and regurgitation. One can understand this peculiar link only on the principle that the movement of fluids, gases and solids in the tubes of the body (especially of the very young infant) has a configurational significance almost entirely lacking from the feelings of the adult. Thus every movement in the respiratory and alimentary tubes is felt by the newborn infant to be invested with deep significance, a significance which ultimately comes into close association with our moral feelings. Ultimately, as it seems to me, this fact can be understood only on the grounds that the umbilical tubes and their opposed streams of blood evoke in the feelings the primary sense of meaning.

The Nature of the Self

Needless to say, the war in the feelings between the respiratory and the gastrointestinal rhythms is won by the latter. No doubt this is due to the fact that the internal surfaces of the gastrointestinal tract are very large, and that in consequence their neural excitation produces in the brain effects which outweigh those created by the neural excitation of the lungs, and indeed even by the excitation of the special senses. Thus the stimulation first felt on the fetal skin, and then felt in the orifices of the head, is overwhelmed by the feelings created by the food in the gut. And thus it comes about that the feelings of the fetal self, plus the feelings of the head, seem to be transferred to the gut, with the result that both fetus and head seem to be in the gut.[1] This is a strange logic which certainly affronts the logic of the waking conscious mind, but the story it tells is consistent and, with a little adjustment, entirely comprehensible. Moreover, it is a story which dominates the myths and *märchen*.

---

[1] Or, if you will, the gut seems to contain the fetal self as head, or the head as fetus.

Chapter Seven

THE GASTROINTESTINAL STAGE

WITHOUT APOLOGY, I begin this chapter with a mild recapitulation. As the infant begins to suckle, and as the gastrointestinal tract becomes thus irritated, there develops the distinct sense that the child has swallowed its own fetal self. This fantasy is no doubt produced by a situation similar to that which caused the switch of feeling from the fetal skin to the head. That is to say, the excitation of the nerves of the gastrointestinal tract is felt in terms of the fetal skin. The brain cannot yet distinguish between the different kinds of stimuli which it is asked to administrate. All it knows is that something which derived from the fetal skin was first switched to the head and then to the stomach. It fails to distinguish between these stimuli, so that the net effect is that the fetal skin feeling is added to the feelings of the head, and both are then added to the feelings of the stomach. This, at any rate, is the way I rationalize the fact that in human dreams and myths there is a distinct statement that the child feels to swallow its own head, and that this feeling of the head is in turn so identified with the fetal feeling that the child also feels to have swallowed his own unborn self. The excitation of the stomach thus becomes identified with the excitation of the nerves of the head and of the fetal skin, and the net subjective upshot is the creation of the fantasy that the fetal self is in the mother's womb, an organ which is now provided by the child's own stomach, his body being felt as his mother's.

This feeling that the trunk is his mother's body, and his stomach mother's womb, is not altogether without precedent in the feelings of the newborn child. This strange feeling-development was prepared and foreshadowed by the natal fantasy that the placenta had suddenly gone inside the body and become the lungs. This experience served to prime the feelings to accept the sense that the child's trunk is its own mother's body—since where the placenta is, there also is the womb and the mother. The reader is bound to find such assertions incredible. How is it possible that anyone could identify his own trunk with his mother's body, or feel his own stomach to be his mother's womb with him inside it? The reader could no doubt concede that this might be an occasional aberration of infancy, but he is being asked to believe that it is a universal infancy experience, and an integral part of the evolution of the individual mind. Yet no fact of the feeling-life is more emphatically stated in dreams, and none more fully asserted in myths and *märchen*. The reader will be familiar with that ubiquitous fairytale figure, the Wicked Stepmother who seeks her step-child's discomfort. She stands for the gastrointestinal tract in its false maternal role. The most explicit example of this is to be found in the story of *The Juniper Tree*, where the wicked stepmother actually causes the head of her small stepson to be cut off and eaten.

It is inevitable, however, that the adult should find such assertions incredible, because his feelings are now normally incapable of experiencing what the infant goes through. The situation can be explained most simply by saying that whereas the adult's feelings identify him with his whole body, those of the child do not. To the infant the body is an unexplored territory through which the uterine sense of pattern is still wandering. We adults tend to think of ourselves as related to our bodies as a whole. But the infant feels the "I" in its *original* sense, namely as the pattern of uterine feeling, and this entity does not become established in relation to the whole body for some years after birth. During infancy it wanders about the body and identifies itself with different organs as it goes. It is this journey and its transformations that we are studying here.[1]

I have already stated the principle that the uterine pattern is indivisible—that wherever the sense of the fetal body is, there also

[1] See Appendix J.

must appear the sense of the placenta and the umbilical cord The sense of the transfer of the fetus to the stomach through the swallowing of the head means that although the mouth can continue to act its umbilical role, the eyes no longer can. The milk taken in at the mouth still is felt as blood coming from the placenta, and it is passed down the esophagus, which takes on the character of the umbilical vein. *But the sense of the dual (arterial) outflow is transferred from the eyes to the legs.* The legs feel to be the umbilical arteries to the fetus in the stomach-as-womb. The feet feel to be passing out blood to the placenta.

Ideally, the placenta is *now* the mother's body, though the child will do what he can with a surrogate. Ideally, he feels that the mother's body is the placenta from which he takes blood through his mouth for the fetus in the stomach, and to which he returns blood through the legs. I think that most natural mothers have experienced this, although they may not have known consciously what was going on. They have felt how the child, as he suckles at the breast, kneads at his mother's body with his feet in a rhythmic manner. I have every reason to believe that this kneading motion is the direct product of the feeling that the legs are umbilical arteries pumping blood into the placenta.[1] Indeed, the feet themselves are felt as a placenta.

May I remind the reader why it is that the newborn legs take on this umbilical arterial feeling. Before birth the femoral arteries were but an offshoot from the umbilical arteries, and it is for this reason I believe that the newborn legs are all set and triggered to take on the umbilical arterial feelings if given the slightest chance to do so. This opportunity comes, I believe, because yet another complication is added to the fantasy of the fetus in the stomach, namely a temporary identification of the heart with the fetus in the stomach. One can easily see how the heart could become involved in this complex of feelings. Not only is the heart close to the stomach where the fetus is felt to be, but it also moves

---

[1] I have already indicated not only the original placenta but also three post-natal surrogates, the lungs, the breast and the mother's body generally. This seems to raise the question: 'How many fantasied placentas are there?' I have attempted to answer this question in Appendix C.

about in the body as the fetal self once moved in the mother. Moreover, before birth the heart drove blood through the umbilical arteries and their femoral associates, so that one might put it that the feelings are all primed to feel the heart as fetus and the legs as umbilical arteries, this fantasy requiring for its creation only a relatively minor adaptation of past experience.

This identity between the heart and the head-as-fetus often lingers on in the organism and causes elusive troubles. There is nothing better known to me than the dream symbolism which reveals lingering relics of this infancy feeling. Many people no doubt succeed in making a complete separation between the feeling of the heart and the fantasy of the fetus lying in the stomach. But, judging by my experience, there is a large number of people who do not succeed in completing this separation in the feelings.

The complex of feelings related to infancy sucking and kicking inevitably takes on the complex of feelings evoked in the umbilical cord. Thus, as the umbilical venous flow seemed to the fetus to make it hollow and to establish the placenta as an aggressor, so exactly the same feelings are engendered at the mouth in the act of suckling. The suckling baby senses that the inflow of milk (which he feels to be umbilical blood) is an aggressive act against him. It hollows him out and makes him no longer a solid entity but a hollow thing able to be occupied. He is, indeed, made hollow in feeling by the act of feeding. The rhythmic thrust of the legs is also felt by the child to assume the feelings generated in the umbilical arteries. The legs are felt to be excretory tubes, resulting in the excretion of an imaginary flow of blood at the feet. They are felt also to be instruments of aggression, and the kicking of the infant quickly expresses this inherent feeling.

This umbilical feeling in the legs is very near to the surface in many people, and is powerful in children. Many children feel a distinct relation between their legs or feet and mysterious snakes. I knew a child who was always concerned that snakes were after his feet. I knew another child who, under a light anesthetic felt that his legs were twisted together like snakes. These are only two specific and clear instances of a common feeling which I believe takes a collectivized form in the Greek myths of the snake-legged gods. Many of the Greek gods were evidently originally thought of as snakes, or as having twisted snake-tails in place of legs. This mythology should not be thought of as belonging only to an ancient time. It exists no less in the 'ancient time' of every modern man, to wit his own infancy.

The gastrointestinal stage apparently lasts until the infant has oriented his feelings of anal excretion. It may seem odd to the reader that any child needs to orient these feelings, since presumably such functions are automatic. The functions certainly are, but this is not to say that the *sense* of those functions is attained without some kind of effort. Indeed, the content of many dreams suggests very strongly that the infant has a considerable struggle to escape from the feeling that it is the *legs* which excrete, and not the rectal and urinary tubes.

This must indeed appear odd unless we keep firmly in mind that we are not dealing with the physical feelings attendant upon bodily function, but with the creation of a liaison between those physical feelings and the psychological feelings already created by the uterine organism.[1] Those psychological feelings are the very substance of the "I" which is busy getting oriented in the postnatal body. We must keep firmly in mind that the "I" is the complex of feelings which, originally physical in the womb, has been transformed into psychological feelings. Now, the original feelings of the uterine life were very much concerned, as we know, with the pattern of ingestion and excretion, for this is the root of the umbilical pattern. Therefore the "I" of the infant has a great affinity, as it were, for all that involves taking in and giving out. This is especially true in respect to the *legs*, since the legs, of all the bodily organs, have the closest original connection with the umbilical arteries, for reasons which I have shown.[2] The legs are not merely, like the eyes, *configurationally* involved with the umbilical arterial feelings, but they are *organically* involved from the earliest days of the uterine life. For this reason it is not only

---

[1] In a word, between the 'blood-feelings' and the nerve-feelings; see Chapter Three.
[2] And shall show again; see Figure Six.

Fig. 6.

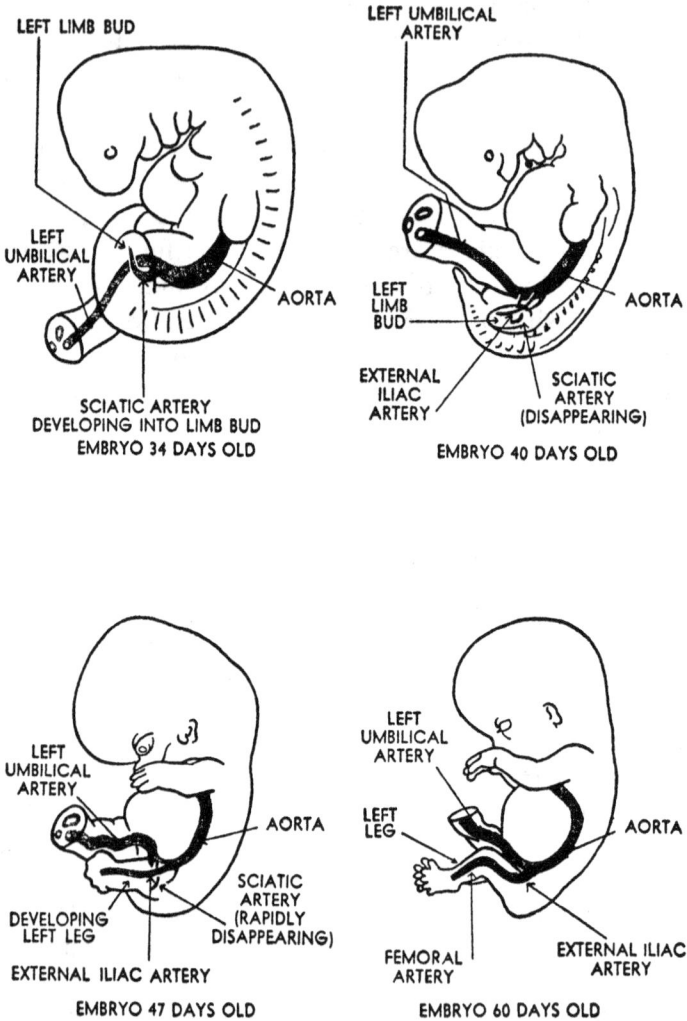

Schematic view of the development of the arteries of the human legs. These schemata show that the blood supply to the human legs is at first a minor offshoot from the umbilical arteries.

With acknowledgements to Professor J. D. Boyd and Messrs Heffer & Sons.

very easy for the legs to assume postnatally the old feelings of the umbilical arteries, but it is also exceedingly hard for the child to detach his excretory feelings from the legs.

This excretory umbilical element in the feelings of the legs is so important that I feel it cannot be over-emphasized. For this reason I have reproduced in Figure Six a series of drawings which were made for me by a competent artist under the supervision of a leading embryologist. These sketches show clearly that the arterial supply to the legs of the human embryo are at every stage second-ary to the umbilical arterial flow. In an embryo of thirty-four days there are no legs, only limb-buds in which very small sciatic vessels are present, these being mere offshoots from the umbilical arteries which already are well developed. In the embryo of sixty days the external iliac and femoral arteries are developed, the original sciatic arteries having disappeared. But these new arteries are still only a relatively minor offshoot from the umbilical arteries, and though they develop by term, yet the supply of blood to the fetal legs remains only a spillover, so to speak, from the umbilical arteries, which retain their primacy until birth suddenly brings their functions to an end. This relative poverty of the blood-supply to the femoral arteries is supposed to be at least one cause for the relatively poor development of the legs of the child at birth. The human baby at birth is, so to speak, the eternal cripple so far as its legs are concerned. Before birth the fetus might be described as a creature with vascular tubes in place of legs, and to be 'treading' upon the placenta with the rhythmic beat of the cord. I feel confident that this is why in dreams we find so strong a confusion between the legs and the umbilical arteries, and why in the myths we find Heroes with bleeding feet and with crippled legs who have also strong symbolic fetal indications.[1]

For a considerable period of its life, so my experiences suggest, the infant confuses its legs with its urinary and fecal ducts. And the reason for this confusion is that whereas the *physical* feelings are increasingly asserting that these ducts are the twin excretory

---

[1] In my unpublished work on the analysis of the myths and ancient symbolisms, I have drawn attention to the remarkable fact that the Hebrew language, with its strong feeling-content, out of six words for the legs, has four which link with the idea of flowing liquid.

tubes, the older *psychological* feelings are stubbornly asserting that it is the legs which carry out this function.[1] This struggle creates a powerful identity between the legs and the rectal and urethral passages. This identity is not felt merely as a vague confusion. On the contrary it is so definite and so precise that the left leg is felt to be the rectal passage, with the left foot as the anus, while the right leg and foot are felt to be the urethral passage. Nothing could be clearer and more insistent in dreams than the identity between the left leg and the rectum, which seems to be even more marked than the connection between the right leg and the urethra. The same identity is expressed in the myths and *märchen*.[2]

It might perhaps be well to add here that my conclusions as to this identity between the left leg and the rectal passage are not drawn only from dreams and myths. In addition, I have actually observed this confusion in being in the little child, and have on several occasions been able to assist the struggle in the child's feelings. I have observed strange complexes of behavior in little children which specifically have linked the rectum with the left leg, and I recall vividly one case in which a child was plagued by constipation and by a great concern for her left leg, being sent into wild paroxysms of grief because she fell and bumped her left knee. She also was morbidly concerned by the least little smear of mud upon her left shoe.[3] Her infantile prattle added its quota of evidence to these symptoms, and when at last I was able to play a little game with her, aimed at the ending of this confusion, all her symptoms, including persistent constipation, ended with impressive speed. I well recall the amazed amusement with which a mother reported to me that she discovered her little boy with his right foot over the edge of the toilet and heard him solemnly explain that he was making water from his foot.

[1] It has long been known that feet play a role in the feelings which has no obvious rational meaning. One thing I have noticed is the way in which 'smelly feet' figure in dreams. The context always suggests that this is really a reference to the excretory ducts, with which the feet are linked as shown above.

[2] See Appendix K.

[3] The reader may be interested to note that it was Cinderella's *left* foot from which the Golden (that is, fecal) Slipper slipped, and that the cause of its loss was pitch (another fecal symbol) smeared on the stairs.

I would like to add here that I believe that this confusion of the legs with the umbilical arteries and the excretory ducts is the indirect cause of two marked symptons found in pregnant women. The first of these is physical and the second emotional. Since we all carry over into adult life a strong 'unconscious' memory of this confusion, we may well imagine the way in which these memories could be remobilized by the experience of pregnancy. The woman now actually feels in her inside the presence of that very leaping fetus which as a child she had fantasied to be her own fetal self confused with her heart. I believe that this experience remobilizes the old infancy feelings that the legs are umbilical arteries, and I believe that this provides a psychosomatic basis for the common phenomenon of pregnancy, namely the appearance of varicose veins. These enlarged veins in the legs no doubt have also an obvious mechanical cause, but I have seen indications in dreams that the confusions here reviewed also play a definite part. The emotional symptom referred to above is that familiar pheno-menon of pregnancy, the perverted appetite. Pregnant women often do the most astonishing things to procure certain kinds of food. This also becomes understandable when we know that as an infant she herself lived through the feeling that she was sucking blood from her mother-as-placenta and returning it through her legs. I believe that the pregnant woman remobilizes this sense of sucking blood, and that deep under her conscious mind this is the root cause, however obscured, of her perverted appetite. She is trying, by heaven-knows-what obscure associations, to replay the fantasy that she is sucking blood from mother-as-placenta. My indications are that the special foods and almost ritualistic means of acquiring them possess subtle associational links with the sense of mother-as-placenta. The confusion between the left leg and the rectal passage has another consequence which is of the profoundest possible importance for the development of the feelings, and I could not stress it too powerfully. It is a consequence which dominates the whole of the subsequent feelings, for it brings about in us all a complete sense of identity between bone and feces. I propose now to explain this identity, but not until he has reached the end of this book will the reader realize how important it is.

The left leg, being linked in feeling with the rectal passage, acquires the sense that is is excreting feces. This, as will be obvious, must be a much more difficult confusion for the feelings to handle than those of the right leg, which are asked only to equate blood and urine. Both blood and urine are liquids, so that their confusion does not result in any great strain. But the left leg is linked with that much more difficult business, namely the excretion of feces, which is attended by far greater fuss and involves more external effect upon the senses. The bowel feels at times that it is filled with a hard substance, a feeling which the leg knows well, for is it not a kind of tube of flesh filled with hardening bone! For the left leg this has special significance, since that leg is identified with the feelings of the rectum. Both feel to be filled with a hard substance, and it is here that there is created the primary link between bone and feces which is never lost. It is a feeling which dominates the sense of the skeleton and especially of the skull, as I shall later show.

I need hardly say that both the legs and the excretory ducts assume the old umbilical arterial feelings, to which have now been super-added the postnatal feelings with which they have become associated. Thus we have both at the legs and more especially at the excretory ducts not only the sense of excretion, but also the sense of aggression and of loss of self. The infant feels that he is being constantly lost from his feet, to which must be added the subsequent feelings of his own 'loss' at birth.

There is another struggle which takes place in the feelings of the child concerning its legs. The spiral twist of the cord is imposed upon the feelings of the legs, which feel in consequence to be twisted together. This spiral twist is felt by the child to have some vital relation to life itself. The more conscious the child becomes of its legs as ambulatory instruments, the more this sense of spirality is depleted. Put simply: the more that the leg-bones harden, the less the infant can feel them as capable of assuming the spiral twist. This growing sense of the legs as 'walking sticks' is not unnaturally connected to the hardening of the leg-bones. Hence in this sense also the hardening bone appears in the light of a negation of life, which is to say as death. This is an added reason why the hard bone is felt to be the very instrument of death, and in part accounts for the death-symbolism of the skeleton.[1] The reader will see that the legs appear to be the locus of an important complex of feelings in which are to be seen the elements of feces, hard bone and death. The unraveling of this complex is a very important achievement in the evolution of the infancy feelings, and anyone who thinks that it is other than a universal problem would do well to ponder upon the ancient mystery of the Riddle of the Sphinx, which is concerned entirely with the nature of the legs. This solution of the 'riddle of the legs' is perhaps the most crucial event in the life of the infant.[2]

The eventual clearing of the confusion between the legs and the excretory ducts has a profound result. For one thing, it brings to an end the confusion between the feelings of the heart and the sense of the head-as-fetus-in-the-gut.[3] Since the confusion involving the heart also involves the sense of the legs as umbilical arteries, the drawing away of this sense from the legs relieves the heart of that confusion. At least, this is true in principle, though certain trying and often dangerous hangovers can remain. For another thing, the clearing up of the feelings of the rectum changes the entire gastrointestinal feelings. The child no longer feels that it is bearing its fetal head in its stomach. This feeling is replaced by another, namely that the head-as-fetus is born out of the anus.

Fortunately I am here upon somewhat more familiar ground, since it is quite well known in modern psychology that the child feels its excretions to be a form of birth. Indeed, for long after childhood the act of excretion is able to reawaken the old terrors experienced at birth. We all feel a little that to excrete is to give birth—not just to give any sort of birth, but to give birth to ourselves. This fact is not unrecognized by a number of psychologists but, apart from my own efforts, I do not know of the least attempt

---

[1] If the mere visibility of the skeleton after the decay of the body were the cause of its symbolic nature, then it might just as easily be the symbol of immortality as of death, since it persists when the rest of the body has disappeared.

[2] Riddles about legs are by no means confined to the familiar Sophoclean play about Oedipus, but exist in many forms and in many languages.

[3] See the Prologue to Part Two.

to explain the phenomenon. This sense of birth at the anus is not something which arises *de novo* there. It is due to the transfer to the anal excretions of the original feelings generated in the umbilical cord, namely that in the umbilical arteries we 'lost ourselves' perpetually. This feeling collected to itself the undertones of birth, and these it brings to the anal excretions. In this way also the sense of aggression first generated by the umbilical arterial flow is transferred to the anal motions.

The rectal extrusions evoke also the sense of death first evoked in the umbilical arteries. Again and again in dreams and allied associations there appears evidence of a basic feeling-relation between death and excretion, and the feces are frequently associated with, or even represented by dead bodies. This strange association is by no means a discovery of mine, and has been known in depth-psychology for a long time, but until now the principle governing the association has not been recognized, namely that the umbilical arterial flow seems to bear away the fetal nuclear sense and to destroy it in the placenta. This sense of death is carried to the rectal excretions along with the total umbilical complex.

The gastrointestinal stage may be said to come to an end when the umbilical arterial feelings are transferred from the legs to the urinary and rectal ducts. In this act the legs are discovered in their normal character, and the feelings of excretion oriented at their normal stations. With this discovery of the anal aperture (and the evolution in the feelings amounts to no less!) there dawns the sense of anal birth, so that the head-as-fetus feels to be extruded at the anus in a way that parodies the original birth of the child himself. At the same time, the heart is relieved of its connection with the sense of the fetal self in the stomach. The head is now able to feel 'born' at the lower end of the trunk. And here it seems to exist for a time in a strange and paradoxical form, as will be shown in Chapter Eight.

A very large part of the evolution of the feelings appears to take place in association with the development of a sense of direction and polarity in the fundamental orifice of the body. The long tract which stretches from the mouth to the anus, with its several ancillary passages, is the scene of something which far transcends the vital original functions of the nutritional organs. Strange as it may seem, the simple achievement of orientation of these two ends, the mouth and the anus, is in itself of vast importance to the child, and to the eventual adult of which he is the forerunner. Grave confusions exist in many people between the mouth and the anus, and lead to all manner of evils, physical, emotional and even moral. This is the reason why the 'pot training' of the infant is of such importance, and why the feelings of the anus are the source of character-elements. The polarization of the fundamental tube is aided as well as complicated by the development of the voice and the related act of speech, which serves to relegate the anal thrust to an inferior position in the feelings. The relation between speech and the anus, however, is preserved in the feelings, where one finds constant evidence of a direct link between the sound of the voice and the sound of flatus. Another vital factor is the development of the teeth, an organic experience which also plays a large part in the polarization of the gut. It is a well known fact that there is a very close relation between the development of teeth and the mental processes of the child, and I believe that the root of this link is to be found in the fact that the growth of the teeth, and especially of the second teeth, gives enormous emphasis to the polarity of the fundamental tube.

Later on, when I come to deal with the development of a sense of upthrust in the spine, see Chapter Ten, the reader will see that the whole gastrointestinal tract comes to bear a relation to the spine which is foreshadowed by the relation of the umbilical arteries to the umbilical vein. He will see that, in a broad sense, the gastrointestinal tract feels to be the analogue of the umbilical arteries while the spine assumes the feelings of the umbilical vein. And for this role also the gut is fitted since, like the umbilical arteries, it is the organ of excretion, and it assumes the elements of death and aggression first generated by the umbilical arteries.

Chapter Eight

THE MOCK HEAD AT THE BOTTOM

Is ANAL BIRTH felt just once only, namely at that moment when the infant first discovers his anal orifice in his feelings, or does it take place over and over again? This is a question I cannot certainly answer, but I incline to the second view. At any rate, one of the peculiar results of this strange fantasy is that the bottom acquires the sense of the head. I mean this very literally, namely that for a period the buttocks and associated parts take on the sense of a distorted head and face that have been extruded from (that is, given birth to at) the anus.

It is as if the head had been sucked down through the oesophagus into the stomach, and after a period there had been projected out at the other end, where the feelings sought to find some kind of likeness in the organs there available. Thus the two cheeks of the buttocks do surrogate duty for the cheeks of the face, the anus doing duty for the mouth. This much is absolutely certain. Pubic hairs very frequently are confused in the deep feelings with a beard or a moustache. This also is not in doubt. As to the accommodation of the other facial organs at the bottom I am in some doubt. There is no doubt that such accommodations are made, but I am uncertain as to whether these are specific, as is the case with the link between the buttocks and the cheeks of the face. Sometimes the legs, due no doubt to their pre-existing link with the eyes, take on an ophthalmic role. The penis or the clitoris seem to do duty for the nose, and no doubt this explains why one finds in women dreams and associations dealing with a mutilated nose.[1]

This feeling of a mock head at the bottom is well represented in symbolic form by the figure of Bottom in *A Midsummer Night's Dream*. The words themselves explain the meaning if they are taken literally, for a Bottom is a bottom even if spelled with a capital B, and the ass is of old an anal symbol, while the very word 'ass' is used today in America for the backside. Bottom with the ass's head is an apt way of referring to the mock head which is felt by the infant to exist at his bottom, a head which has been sucked down from its high estate, held for a time in the stomach and then extruded in a highly battered and distorted form.[2]

In spite of the persistence of the cephalic elements in these feelings, the fetal feelings remain in evidence. It is not just the head that has been sucked down and reproduced at the bottom: it is the fetus himself. It is the 'head as fetus'. Indeed, it seems certain that the only reason why the head is felt to undergo these odd experiences is because it acquired the fetal status in the first place. Apart from that I see no logic in the events here outlined. The head is the fetus to the child's feelings, and as such it carries on the process imprinted deep into its nature by the remorseless beat of the cord. This calls for it to be sucked down and destroyed in order to be renewed and restored. The migration of the head down the gastrointestinal tract is simply the accommodation of the first part of this process. The cycle of restoration we shall consider later.[3] This movement of the head down to the lower end of the trunk is the way in which the postnatal body accommodates the configurational feelings generated by the uterine organs from the cosmos. It is only by this strange series of organic fantasies that the configuration survives in us and in the end can emerge as our sense of self.

---

[1] Consider the nursery tale that the Queen was in the parlor EATING bread and honey, and the King was COUNTING OUT HIS MONEY (excretions): and that with this activity there is associated the maid, who, while hanging out the clothes, got her nose pecked off.

[2] I have analyzed the tale of Bottom the Weaver in detail in my book on mythology.

[3] See especially Chapters Ten and Eleven.

In this process I think that the mock head at the bottom is simply a side-product. I do not think it is an essential part of the process at all, but rather a complication brought about by the fact that there is a rough simlarity between the two ends of the tube. At the top end the tube culminates in the sphincter of the mouth, set roughly between two cheeks and lying beneath a nose. At the lower end the tube culminates in the sphincter of the anus, set roughly between the two cheeks of the bottom and lying somewhere near the penis or the clitoris. It is this rough basis of feeling-association which, I think, gives rise to the sense of the mock head at the bottom. What really is important, however, is that the head at the bottom is still felt to be the fetal self.

The reader will by now have learned to expect that wherever the fetal feelings appear in the body, there also will the related feelings of the placenta and of the umbilical cord be found. This is true of the feeling of the fetus at the lower end of the trunk. Once the sense of the 'fetus at the bottom' appears, the earth itself begins to be felt by the child as the placenta. The two newly-discovered excretory ducts, the anus and the urethra, are now felt as the umbilical arteries. As to the sense of a back-flow from the placenta (the surrogate of the original umbilical vein), this is now related to a mysterious upthrust from the earth which the child begins to feel. I shall outline this new development in the following chapter.

Chapter Nine

THE EARTH AS THE PLACENTA

WHEN I FIRST began to detect symbolic indications that the child feels the earth in placental terms, I took the view that this must surely be a pure and unadulterated fancy. Certainly it is true that the earlier infancy feelings already discussed are also in a sense fancies. That is to say, they do not correspond to any evident physical reality. But they do at least all take place inside the body of the child and in relation to his own personal functions. At least we can see a connection between, let us say, the cheeks of the face and the buttocks. Even if the connection be unusual and unsuspected, there is at least the connection of the living flesh and blood. But the idea that the earth becomes the placenta projects the drama of the feelings outside the body. Since I could not at first detect, or even surmise, the existence of any mechanism for linking the feelings of the child to the earth, I assumed that this must be the point at which pure fantasy, bereft of any physical mechanism, took over in the feelings.

I held this view for a long time. I simply could not see how the infant could gain any sense that his fecal and urinary excretions make a relation with the earth. And yet this is what dreams and associated symbolisms plainly asserted. They asserted again and again that the infant thrusts umbilical blood into the earth from his rectal and urinary tubes. In other words, the fetus at the bottom felt the earth as the placenta, and into it he was making a dual thrust of excretion as once he did in the womb through the umbilical arteries.

I could more easily have understood the evidence before me if my patients and subjects had been living in primitive conditions, taught from earliest infancy to perform their excretions direct upon the ground. But to a race of people living cut off from contact with the earth by buildings, pavements and the most elaborate and often exotic toilet arrangements—to such a people I felt this intimacy with the earth could not apply. Yet I was in the end compelled to see that the relation between the body and the earth through the excretions is an absolutely concrete one. I have analyzed a few people who may be said to have been reared in relatively farmyard conditions. If there was any difference between their excretory feelings and those of a city-bred person, it was quite imperceptible to me.

I do not know at what period of the child's life this sense of the earth as placenta develops. It seems to have some connection with the act of standing, in which act the child for the first time develops a specific personal relation to the gravitational pull of the earth. Since I can offer no real information as to the chronology of these events, I will content myself with stating as briefly as possible what I know.

The child comes to feel that his fecal and urinary excretions are the umbilical arterial thrust, and that the earth is the placenta. He feels that in response to this excretory thrust the earth replies with a backthrust which he must accommodate. And he feels that all the old elements which were generated in the umbilical arteries *vis-à-vis* the placenta are now evoked in his excrementory relation with the earth.

The infant senses that the earth is the surrogate of the mother's body, which in its turn had assumed the role of the placenta. Possibly this may be the reason behind the phrase 'Mother Earth', which carries on in vague and general terms a specific feeling which the ancient Greeks made concrete in the figure of the Earth Mother. It is interesting to observe how the earth plays a placental-type role to the animal. It receives the animal excretions and, partly from the effect of these excretions, is able every year to yield an upthrust of vegetation. This in itself is an absolute analogue of what the fetus feels in respect to the placenta, namely that it receives his excretions and in return yields alimentation.

Food and the Dead

At first I was inclined to suppose that in some way the human being senses this relation at quite an early age, and by linking its own ordure with the annual rising of the vegetation, equates the total cycle with its umbilical 'memories'. But eventually I was compelled to see that such a view is superficial and not in accordance with the facts in the deep feelings. I was compelled to admit that the infant senses a concrete relation with the earth, and a concrete backthrust from it—a backthrust which, though it may be related to the rise of the vegetation, is certainly not known to the infant in that connection.

The infant senses that just as the placenta received its excretions through the umbilical arteries, so the earth now receives its urinary and fecal excretions. This alone would serve no doubt to identify the earth as the new placenta. But just as the placenta felt to be the place of death and destruction, so now the earth is felt to play that dread role. In communities where the idea of interment of the dead is familiar, this sense of the earth as the place of death receives a kind of collective emphasis from external experience. Indeed, one may see in primitive ideas, and even in modern fantasies, the way in which the two sets of experience interweave. The child is aware that the earth is the recipient of his 'dead self', so that his feelings are all primed to accommodate, with varying degrees of horror, the external evidence offered by the interment of the dead.

There is not wanting evidence to show that the idea of agriculture may have arisen first through the burial of grains of corn with the dead. If this be so, then we can hardly escape the possibility suggested by my new discoveries, namely that there lies in us all the deep knowledge, umbilically generated, that the place of the dead (the placenta) is also the place of food. Therefore, the original observation that these buried seeds (corn) gave rise to an 'upthrust' of new plants for food, accommodated at once the umbilical experience that excretion of the dead into the earth would result in a 'backthrust' of food. This fact every fetus experiences, and if it had no part in the first dim idea of agriculture, at least it endowed agriculture with the cosmic overtones which agricultural religion acquired. It is a fact that all agricultural societies possess the cult of the dying and rising god. The origins of this cosmic overtone in agriculture are, in my opinion, to be found in the fact that our feelings focus in the uterine memory of the fetal Shining One who constantly was lost in the depths of the placenta and as constantly restored.

Thus in our feeding it is true that after birth we continue, both indirectly and directly, to feed from the place of death and of excretion, just as before birth we felt to do. But I cannot make it too clear that the backthrust from the earth, felt as a response to the urinary and fecal downthrusts, is not a mere symbolic overtone of the fact that we feed upon the plant. It is something much more concrete than that, and it is experienced by the infant long before it is in a position to comprehend the relation of the earth to food and to manure. *A direct upthrust from the earth is felt. This upthrust impinges upon the infant body and seeks to enter it.*

Just what this upthrust is I have no certain idea. I am sure that it is a real thing, and not due to any unsupported fantasy. Apart from asserting this as indubitable fact which I can demonstrate, I can only offer what I believe to be a plausible theory. It seems highly likely that there is a circulation of energy between the earth and its surrounding atmosphere.[1] Just what this energy may be I cannot assert. It is my suggestion that the excretory processes of the infant somehow become linked with the downward half of this cycle of energy, and become in some way influenced by it. It is as if something that the child does when it excretes links its body with a flow of energy going down into the earth. I cannot help feeling that there must be some such link because, as I shall presently show, the very organs which are involved in the downflow (the anus and the urinary organs) are those which are first tempted to respond to the backthrust from the earth.

This backthrust from the earth (like that from the placenta through the umbilical vein) is felt as a threatening and aggressive act. It feels to the child as if something from the earth is seeking to penetrate its body and to hollow it out. All the fears engendered in the fetus by the umbilical venous flow are remobilized by this

[1] For the sake of brevity I shall in future refer to this circulation of energy either as 'an earth current' or as 'earth currents'.

sense of the earth's upthrust. This thrust is also felt to carry up to the infant a kind of information. The infant definitely feels that down in the earth there resides a being or beings who have the power to influence his feelings. This is entirely akin to the experience of the fetus in respect to the placenta, namely that the placenta transmits to the fetus certain deep knowledge from the past—an experience which I have interpreted in terms of the placenta as one of the instruments of heredity.[1] I have every reason to believe that this feeling of the infant for the earth is not due only to the superimposition of placental 'memories' upon the earth. There actually is something down in the depths of the earth which affects the infant by exporting into its nervous system mental elements belonging to the human past on this earth. How these mental elements get into the earth in the first place, and are stored there, it is beyond me to say for certain, but I am quite sure that they are there. It is as if the infant passes from its body, in the act of excretion, something other than mere waste material. This mysterious something connects with the downgoing cycle of the earth-currents and passes into the earth, where it makes connection with earlier influences in the earth, and then returns to the child's body bearing the effect of these influences.[2]

No doubt the reader will be tempted to assume that I am making wild guesses. I can assure him that my basic material is drawn from the observation of persistent indications registered in the deep feelings of men, women and children. But since my assurances can count for little to those who have not shared my analytical experiences, I can only draw attention to the fact that there are hallowed conventions and stories and legends which point to something of the kind. We have the old convention that the Devil is down below in the earth, and that he can influence human

[1] See the second half of Chapter Three.
[2] I believe, in fact, that the act of excretion serves to carry away from the organism not only waste chemical elements, but also unwanted (repressed) mental elements. Thus I find evidence that the placenta is the first instrument of the so-called Unconscious, and that the earth itself is the second instrument. In both cases the organism 'represses' into the organ of the Unconscious by means of the act of excretion. This is another instance of the concrete nature of my psychology, which finds referents for its concepts in the physical forms of the body and of its environment.

beings. This might be dismissed as a mere superstition save for the fact that the Devil is associated in folklore with powerful umbilical elements. Anyone who cares to study the Grimm tale of *The Devil and the Three Golden Hairs* will see at once that it is a representation of explicit umbilical and placental elements transferred to the earth.[1] The ancient Greeks had a class of gods known as the *chthonian* gods, who lived in the earth and were related both to the dead and to snakes—a symbol of the umbilical feelings in the earth![2]

The upthrust from the earth is also felt by the infant to restore to him something that was formerly lost in the earth. This feeling echoes the original feeling of the fetus for the placenta, namely that it not only sucked his very self from him and destroyed it, but also restored it again. The infant feels that his fetal self has been sucked down into the earth, destroyed and restored again.

Finally, though this ought in one sense to stand first, the infant feels that he is nourished by the upthrust from the earth. This feeling is, I believe, an absolute imposition of the umbilical feelings upon the earth circulation, since it has no support in fact. But it is important to note that the infant seems to confuse this upthrust from the earth in some degree with the thrust of his mother's nipple into his mouth. So that it seems that the earth thrusts up a sort of nipple. And in this connection there is a great struggle in the feelings to overcome the sense that the anus is the mouth. There is a distinct feeling in the infant which would identify the earth's upthrust with an alimentary thrust designed for the mouth. I shall presently show that it is important for the infant to overcome this sense that the anus is a mouth suckling to the earth. For this sense, if it is not overcome, tends to reverse the polarity of the trunk, at least in part, so that the feelings do not fully and clearly register the proper distinction between the two ends of the gut. It may seem to the adult reader negligible that an infant should fail in this distinction, but it has a powerful moral aftermath. For I am convinced by my experience that the basic human *feeling* for morality, as distinct from reasoned acceptance of moral

---

[1] See Appendix F for an analysis of this tale.
[2] This brief hint is, of course, expanded in my unpublished book on the myths.

rules, has to do with the primary feeling of the 'right-way-up' of the gastrointestinal tract.[1]

In this connection I would like to recount an experience of my own which, though it proves nothing, vividly illustrates what I mean. A little boy just turned three went on a stormy voyage in the course of which he was violently sick. This was a new experience for him, as he had been known in his family as a child who had been peculiarly free from all regurgitation. After the voyage was over, and he was being fed after a lapse of some hours, he looked at his mother and said: 'Mummy, I know the difference between the right and the wrong'. His mother was touched and startled by so adult a declaration, and it made a deep impression upon her. When she related it to me I could not help but see the probable connection between the moral feelings of the child and the opposing movements which he had just experienced in the gastrointestinal tract, namely the difference between eating and being violently sick for the first time in his life.

Those who feel that these statements are extreme, may do well to ponder the fact that the ancient Greeks regarded it as natural to suppose that Ge, the Earth Mother, should produce a child. There are a number of ancient illustrations of this event, which show Ge rising from the earth and handing a child to a waiting nurse or guardian. This has been regarded as an instance of 'giving birth upward', a concept which has distinct meaning in the terms here outlined. For indeed the earth, having assumed the placental characters, becomes not only the monster who destroys, but also the one who 'gives birth upward' as, deep in the feelings, we all know that the placenta did long before.

[1] Perhaps the reader has already surmised that this fantasy that the earth is mother, and the anus a mouth suckling at her, is related to the painful subject of homosexual behavior in males.

Chapter Ten

TRUE AND FALSE ACCOMMODATIONS OF
THE EARTH'S UPTHRUST

LET ME STATE at once, if dogmatically, that the proper accommodation of the earth's upthrust by the infant body is into the spine. This is true of both the boy and the girl. In the case of the boy, the upthrust is also partly accepted by the penis in erection. Having said this, let me now first mention three specific errors of acceptance which lead to various mental, moral and physical evils.

There is a strong inclination on the part of every infant to accept the earth's inthrust into the anus. I have already hinted at one reason for this tendency, namely that the child finds difficulty in distinguishing its anus from its mouth. I have seen dream after dream in which something stirring in the earth is felt to be mysteriously related to mother's breast. The infant is inclined to feel that this mammary element arising from the earth must be accommodated by his anus. Along with these feelings one always finds traces that the child has not yet properly polarized the feelings of his gastrointestinal tract, so that mouth and anus are indeed confused. I have already shown that this feeling of the anus as mouth is implied in the feeling of the mock head at the bottom.

In the case of the girl infant, as one might readily suspect, there is a tendency to feel that the thrust up from the earth threatens also the vagina. The girl child therefore has a double struggle in respect to the accommodation of the upthrust from the earth, a struggle which is further compounded by the fact that the girl feels that her clitoris can accommodate it in the same way that the boy's penis does. This matter I shall revert to later.

It is quite impossible for me to render any detailed account of the evils which result from the false accommodation of the earth's upthrust. Each case must be dealt with *de novo*, since the evils which result from false accommodation of the upthrust are numerous and varied. However, when I come to deal with the development of the sexual feelings, I shall revert to this subject in more concrete terms.

If the earth's upthrust be successfully excluded from both anus and vagina, yet another possibility arises. Prevented from entering these lower orifices of the body, the earth's upthrust may be in part accommodated all over the skin surfaces. It will be remembered that the sense of self originates in the feelings of the skin, so that there is a lingering sense that the skin may be the proper accommodation of the self which has been down into the earth and back. One often finds in dreams indications that the mysterious 'energy' which was excreted from the lower orifices, and which went down into the earth and back, has been restored not inside the body, but onto the skin. This is represented in dreams in terms of a dirty cloak which in some mysterious manner has been drawn up from the earth to cover at least part of the body. It is as if the original fetal skin feeling, with its sense of pristine purity and nuclear significance, has been 'dirtied' by its association with the feces and with the earth, and in this impure form has come back from the earth to cover the body wholly or in part.

I must hasten to add that I have never yet met a case where the infant feels that all the earth's upthrust is accommodated in this way. Indeed, were all of it so accommodated, or even a large part of it, nothing but disaster could result. Since I am not a doctor, it has never been my privilege to try to help the insane, but I notice that certain cases of insanity are accompanied by a strong urge to smear the body with feces. I have met with several cases in psychiatric literature where the patient has greeted the psychiatrist with his or her body covered in this revolting manner. And I feel certain that this is simply the expression of the fact that in infancy the luckless individual actually felt the earth's upthrust to be its own excretions which had been down into the earth and upon return had been allowed to flow up over the skin.

Here I feel it necessary to digress for a moment to state that what I have written above seems to suggest that this thrust from the earth is a real and concrete energy. Otherwise, how could it penetrate the body or flow up over the body? One gets the impression almost as if the child were standing over a jet of some intangible fluid which, deprived of a point of entry into the lower end of the body, sprayed out and flowed up over the skin. I am fully aware of the apparent contradiction here, since we are presumably dealing with configurational feelings, and not with fluids, however intangible.[1] No purpose would be served by my trying to solve this problem at this juncture, since I have not sufficient knowledge. I can only report the facts as I know them.

The proper accommodation for both males and females is 'in the spine'. I place these words in quotation marks because I have no proper idea of the actual physical mechanism of such an accommodation. Yet the facts of the feelings are not the least in doubt: the infant who properly accommodates the earth's up-thrust, feels that it neither enters the anus nor the vagina, nor floods up over the skin, but that it enters the body and becomes the spine and, in degree, the whole skeleton.[2]

The proper accommodation of this mysterious upthrust from the earth leads to the sense that it has penetrated the lower *part* of the body (but not any *physical orifice* of the body) and has given rise to the skeleton. I have already explained in Chapter Seven the origins of the link between the bones and the feces. This is due entirely to the fact that the left leg and the bowel are identified in the feelings, so that the bone in the former and the feces in the latter become also identified. Therefore the child feels that he is excreting *bone* into the earth. It is not only fecal matter but *bone* that seems to go down into the earth and to return again. And when this upthrust from the earth penetrates the infant body, it

---

[1] See the Epilogue.
[2] This statement requires the qualification that the little boy takes a part of this upthrust into the feelings of the erect penis.

seems to carry up with it the mixture of feelings in which bone and feces are not merely confused but identified.

Yet not only the feelings of bone and feces are associated with this downthrust into the earth and the return therefrom. The very fetal self is associated with it. Just as the umbilical arterial flow seemed to carry the nuclear sense away, to destroy it and to restore it, so now the excrementory flow seems to carry the nuclear feelings into the earth, associated with bone and feces, and to return them again. The upthrust from the earth thus seems to carry with it the wretched self, battered and distorted, compounded with feelings of blood, bone and feces, and to restore it again to the body of the infant. When this energy is felt to be assumed into the infant body, it seems to fill that body with the self in the form of the bony structure, which in turn is felt as fecal matter. The trunk now becomes a desperate sort of mother, penetrated by the upthrust from the earth and charged with the self as fecalized skeleton.

It is for these reasons, I believe, that the skeleton has so universally become accepted as the natural symbol of death. This insight came as a great surprise to me, since I had assumed, as I suppose we all have, that the skeleton is associated with death for quite superficial and obvious reasons.[1] But there seem clear indications, both in the deep feelings of the individual and also in certain otherwise meaningless folk-material, that the human being actually feels his skeleton to represent the thing that has been down into the earth and back.

In the female infant this spinal and skeletal accommodation of the earth's upthrust is the sole proper accommodation. In the boy, part of the upthrust is taken into the feelings of the erect penis. The little girl actually goes through a crucial experience of trying to accommodate this upthrust in the feelings of the clitoris. But she normally realizes that this is impossible. Where, however, the girl resists and seeks by some feeling-device to persist in this clitoral accommodation, grave troubles seem likely to occur. The Freudian idea of the 'castration' experience in the girl is, I feel sure, not sexual at all in the narrow sense, but is the product of

[1] See Chapter Seven for some additional remarks on this point.

this crucial experience in trying to accept the earth's upthrust into the clitoris or its feelings, and the realization that there *is* no proper accommodation.

The boy's penis accepts a part of the upthrust from the earth, and this gives rise to a very definite confusion between the penis and the spine. I have come upon a great number of cases where this confusion has led to mental or even physical difficulties. In extreme cases, the feelings seem to have completely failed to distinguish between the penis and the body as a whole. This may lead to a feeling that the body is a penis, with the head as the glans penis, or to the feeling that the penis is a miniature self, or very likely a little of both. Indeed, I have seen so many signs of this confusion that I incline to the belief that it must be universal in men, and that this may be why the penis is so universally referred to in terms which either directly or obliquely serve to identify it with a miniature man.

I have actually encountered several instances in which the penis is felt to be the spine that is connected with the head through the mouth. That is, there is a deep feeling that instead of the spine entering the skull at the occipital base, it enters the skull at the mouth in the form of the penis. I have in mind the case of a man who confessed to a complete lack of interest in sexual matters, and who yet had indulged a lifelong habit of masturbation. The odd thing about this masturbatory performance was its complete lack of any sexual associations. The fantasies which accompanied it were strong, but were entirely asexual. It required many months of analysis to bring me to the point where I could see what the patient was trying to tell me. His penis had, in fact, never become a sexual organ at all. It was entirely a cervical substitute. It was felt to enter the head through the mouth instead of through the base of the skull.[1] The patient satisfied (or acted out) this confusion in a very subtle way. It involved a personal ritual that required a handkerchief for its performance. Save for the masturbatory act, which the patient deplored, it

---

[1] I realize that the cervical stem does not 'enter' the skull at all, but the fact that it subserves something which is felt to enter the skull confers upon it this false sense.

was an entirely inoffensive ritual, but in the final analysis its purport stood out clearly: it had the aim of making an indirect and highly obscure connection between the penis and the mouth, so that the feelings were satisfied that the head actually was affixed to the top of the penis via the mouth, and not at all in the normal fashion.

The infant, then, feels that the earth's upthrust is accommodated in his spine specifically, and in his skeleton generally. The internal skeleton of the trunk is felt to be molded of fecal matter which has been extruded from the anus, passed down into the earth and back into the trunk again. I do not understand the full mechanism of this odd achievement; I simply report what I know. But the reader must not lose sight of the fact that although it is feces which have been thus involved, these really are still the fetal self and the head. Indeed, they are still identified with the head-as-fetus. It is not just feces that have thus been involved, nor even the head, but both as surrogates of that fetal self whose essence must be kept alive in the body if the sense of the self as a cosmic impress is to survive. This is the link with our humanity. Without it we are either insane or dangerously ahuman. Like a snake, we are then only a mass of neural mechanisms with a social amplification, without true link with the creative pattern that alone gives us spiritual value.[1]

Another stage of this remarkable 'journey' now opens up. The trunk which felt to extrude the feces as head-fetus, to receive back that element from the earth, and to accommodate it in the skeleton, now feels to extrude the same element from the neck in the form of the skull. The skull is felt as a ball of fecal matter which has been extruded up through the neck and hollowed out. This is the report which I find in the deep feelings. I can only state it as a fact which I can demonstrate, and try to give some idea of the mechanism by which this odd feeling is evoked.

There is no doubt that the head which the human adult is consciously aware of, and which physically has been on his

---

[1] It is demonstrable that the value of the Christian teaching is largely attributable to the fact that it 'keeps alive' this link in the feelings between the postnatal self and the old uterine pattern with its cosmic intimations.

shoulders from its formation, is not *felt* at all in this simple fashion. It is *felt* to be the fetus, which has been sucked down into the stomach, extruded as feces, reproduced in mock form at the bottom, sent down into the earth and back, readmitted into the trunk as skeleton, and then extruded again through the neck. I am fully aware that this sounds wild in the extreme, and my sympathies are all with the reader in his bewilderment. But these are the facts which dreams tell when they are patiently analyzed by my methods, and not guessed at with a prejudicial theory in mind. Moreover, myths and fairy-tales support my assertions. There is plenty of evidence in these old symbolic statements to show that the human head has, in the feelings, gone through an evolution which bears no relation to the ordinary anatomical facts. One of the very best instances of this type of symbolism is to be found in the Grimm story of *The Goose Girl*. If this is read carefully, in the original version, the underlying content can easily be seen. The story tells of a princess who falls from her high estate (and her horse) in the act of drinking from a stream which carries away her power. It tells how the head of her horse is cut off and pinned upon an exit (symbol of the bottom), and how at last through certain events connected with her hair (symbol of the head) her identity is guessed, whereupon she is induced to climb into a stove (the hollow skull) and so is restored to her place.[1]

Here I must mention the strange fact that the upthrust of the head from the trunk seems to be powerfully connected in the feelings with the outthrust of the arms. Whether this is due or not to the original experience of the average child in the lifting of its head I do not know. Certainly there is a tendency for the child first to approximate to the standing position in the act of crawling, in which his head comes up in close relation to the thrust of his arms. I do not know if this is the actual cause of the feeling that the head's upthrust is related to the downthrust of the two arms, but I do know that in the feelings it attracts to it the configurational sense of the umbilical cord, namely that of two thrusts in one

---

[1] Naturally this is but a rough outline of the story and its interpretation. It is condensed from my book on the analysis of the myths and *märchen*.

direction versus one thrust in the other.[1] In this connection the reader's attention may be drawn to the story of the blessing of Jacob by his father, for the achievement of which the mother placed fur upon the boy's hands and neck. When we consider that the act of blessing involves the head, this story may appear to have great significance in the present terms.[2]

With the advent of this new sense of the head there is remobilized all the old feelings which have been involved from the outset, namely the old uterine feelings plus those acquired by them in the course of their postnatal evolution. Indeed, I can liken the movement of these feelings through the body to the movement of a mass of water which, starting from a source in a pristine state, moves along a well-defined course, gathering certain elements as it goes, until at last it arrives at a destination where it piles all its contents into a heap. The mass of water represents the uterine feelings; the river-channel represents the gastrointestinal tract, the earth and the spine; while the ultimate destination is the head. In the feelings associated with this 'restoration of the head' are to be found summed up all the past experiences of the feelings. And here I feel it advisable to repeat what I have said before, namely that this analogy of the flow of water is so persuasively like the reality it represents, that one is tempted to regard the whole process as an actual flow of some subtle energy. But since the term 'energy' properly connotes a physical energy, and since no such energy ever appears to have been detected, I can only suppose that what is really involved is a constant serial transformation of the feelings, which gradually exert upon the nervous system a configurational significance derived as I have shown.

The restored head feels to be not only a ball of fecal matter that has been extruded from between the shoulders and blown or hollowed out, but it feels also to be the lost and restored fetal

---

[1] The fact that the thrust of the two arms assumes the affect of the umbilical arterial flow leads to a feeling that the two arms are connected to a placenta at the hands, and that the hands are bleeding. Thus what has been true of the feet is also true of the hands, namely that they are felt to be bleeding.

[2] As, indeed, I have shown it to be in my larger work on the subject of the myths, in which I have demonstrated that the whole myth of Jacob and Esau is an almost serial account of the processes described in this book.

self. Everything points to the fact that at first, though passingly, the fetal self is identified not with the head as a whole, but specifically with the skull. In the next chapter I shall show how this is swiftly changed to something quite different. But the first result of the sense of the new emergence of the head from the trunk is that the skull itself feels to be the fetal self which, identified with the original postnatal sense of the head, has gone through so many damaging and bewildering transformations.

The skull feels to be a very battered and distorted fetal self, which after becoming identified with the postnatal head, was sucked down into the gut, reborn at the anus, projected into the earth, drawn back from the earth, accommodated anew as the skeleton, and then extruded from the trunk as skull. That is the short sequence of events, the complexities of which I have already set down.[1]

With the skull established as the fetus, the original uterine pattern swiftly re-establishes itself. The trunk now feels to be the placenta, while the neck feels to be the umbilical cord. *In assessing the significance of this statement, the reader should remember that what the feelings are apparently trying to do is to preserve the memory of the cosmic impress gained by the uterine organism.* If this is lost, or gravely impaired, then the result is a creature who is little more than a 'zombie'—a creature without a soul. The pernicious modern theory seems to be that a human child, raised according to the rational ideas of our time, ought to be a true human being. This theory, which ought to be the monopoly of the Communists, who believe that the mind is only the brain in neural action, is tacitly accepted by a vast number of well-disposed but secularly-minded people. It is persistently held in spite of all evidence to the contrary, which plainly shows that little children, unless they are given some means of preserving alive their original uterine sense, can grow up into well-fed, well-educated and powerful menaces. The Christian religion seeks to keep this original uterine pattern of the cosmos alive by means of its rites and doctrine. Does it not keep alive the sense of a divine Man, one with the Father, who went through a series of struggles only to die on the Cross and to

[1] See also the Prologue to Part Two, and the sketches given there.

be restored to God—a Man whose memory is kept fresh by the rite of eating his body and drinking his blood? Surely anyone but the most biased individual can see that this rite and imagery is entirely in accord with what I have written in this book! For that in us which is divine is the cosmic impress made upon us *in utero* by the Universal Design of creation. This it was that created the divine spark which became associated at birth with the head, was eaten and destroyed, and descended into the earth and rose again, and suffered in the skull (golgotha), as I shall presently show.

To revert to the narrative: the skull feels to be the lost and restored fetus; the trunk feels to be the placenta; the neck feels to be the umbilical cord. On the surface it is evident that the identities and relationships are apt. As the fetal body felt to be the core of the self, with the placenta as a supporting and feeding twin, so the head feels to the trunk. The head feels to be the seat of the self, and the trunk is the organism which maintains the head, supplying it with refreshed blood and taking away the waste. The trunk is the place of respiration, alimentation and excretion. The older feelings are primed to accord this configurational nature to the head, trunk and neck long before now, for the feelings still remember that at birth the head stood in fetal relationship to the trunk through the neck in the act of breathing.[1] They remember also that the oesophagus was the umbilical vein to the fetus-in-the-stomach. Therefore the head had of old a fetal status that is remembered in the feelings. Similarly the trunk of old had a placental status; the neck an umbilical one. All these old feelings are now remobilized in the new sense of the skull as fetus and the placenta as trunk, the two being joined together by the neck as umbilical cord.

In this connection I would like to point out something rather remarkable concerning the neck: all placental mammals without exception have *seven* cervical vertebrae. That is to say, put into plain language, every creature that *in utero* has an umbilical cord has *seven* bones in its neck. Indeed, all mammals, with two remote exceptions, have seven cervical vertebrae. This circumstance may appear a little extraordinary when we realize that the giraffe

[1] See Chapter Six.

with its enormous neck, and the whale with its virtually non-existent one, both have these seven cervical vertebrae. These facts are rendered specially intriguing to me because I find that the deep feelings invest these cervical vertebrae with special significance for the feelings. I shall in a later chapter suggest their relevance to the seven notes of music.

I must make it plain that the configurational feelings of the human being, when they reach the passing stage of development here indicated, seem to sense the architecture of the skeleton. How this can be I have no means of suggesting. But there appears in human dreams a very consistent memory of the skeleton as a sort of structure which the "I" must 'climb' in order to reach the head. I cannot even begin to account for this in any satisfactory way, but the facts are incontestable to anyone who has had experience of my analytic methods. *In this complex of feelings the seven cervical vertebrae tend to figure with great and intriguing frequency.*[1]

These seven cervical vertebrae appear to offer to the feelings an accommodation for the periodic sense evoked in the beat of the blood in the umbilical cord. Even as I write this, I very naturally wonder just how the skeleton can accommodate any feelings of any kind. I very naturally wonder if I ought not to write rather of the nerves which use the spinal column as their fortified cable-sheath. Perhaps so, but I must insist upon the bare facts, namely that it is the *bone* which appears to be remembered. The symbolism is always of a bony character, and sometimes in the course of associations it comes right out into consciousness in the form of direct references to the skeletal structure.

The reader will remember that I showed how the umbilical beat generates a sense of the structure of space-time. This structure is essentially fourfold, being related to the elements of point, line, plane and solid.[2] This fourfold character is translated by the umbilical cycle into a sevenfold pattern, which is essentially due to a complex created of two fourfold series. It is significant, I feel, that the cervical stem of the human being, composed as it is of

[1] See Appendix Q.
[2] My meaning can perhaps be grasped more easily after referring to Figure Three.

seven vertebrae, is divided into two separate fours in the feelings by a peculiar circumstance of the nervous structure. It is a fact that the nerve-supply which operates the diaphragm derives from a point in the neck closely related to the fourth cervical bone. Since the diaphragm separates the trunk into two parts, and controls not only all excretions, but also all breathing, it can be seen that there is a distinct possibility that the central point of the neck feels to be a point of *division* of the whole organism. The respiratory cycle, moreover, is thus related to the neck in such a way that it offers a distinct possible accommodation for the umbilical sense of back-and-forth flow in the neck in terms of breathing. This possibility, I may add, is not mere guesswork. I have seen persistent symbolisms in dreams which lend themselves to the explanation that the central focus of the breath is directly linked to the midpoint of the seven bones of the neck.

I have earlier shown that the umbilical arterial feelings become closely associated with the legs. I find this fact significant in my effort to explain why it is that dreams frequently represent the head as if it were a deformed self walking upon the top of the trunk by means of the neck as a kind of leg. Frequently one finds the head represented as a sort of mannikin who hops about on one leg. Pending the hoped-for publication of my book on the myths and *märchen*, the reader may care to read the Grimm story of *Rumpelstiltskin* in the light of the above. The fantasy of the head as a creature standing on a neck-leg is complicated by another in which not the neck but the lower jaw is felt as a leg. Indeed, in some cases the lower jaw is felt as if it were two bowed legs joined at the feet. In such fantasies there are not wanting indications that the teeth of the lower jaw are felt as toes. It seems that the basis of this peculiar fantasy lies in the fact that when the infant suckles he not only then begins the first rhythmic movements of his lower jaw, but also (as indicated in Chapter Seven) at the same time the first rhythmic motions of his legs. Thus it appears that the legs and the lower jaw gain a certain association in the feelings. It is worth noting that each side of the infant jaw bears five teeth, just as each foot bears five toes, but as to the basis of the fantasy which specifically links them I know nothing more. I can only say that an exactly analogous fantasy is not infrequently found between the hands (or arms) and the upper jaw, and that in this fantasy the ten upper teeth of the infant are associated with the ten fingers. The reader may feel that such fantasies are of no conceivable importance, but I should add that I believe certain bodily distortions of a supposedly 'rheumatic' character to be the psychosomatic symptom of an unconscious effort to make the body conform to the distorted picture of the self as a head walking on its neck or jaws, with its hands as upper jaw. Naturally the actual conformation to such a fantasy can be but small, but the tiniest approximation would be crippling.

*   *   *

The sense of the skull as a piece of feces extruded from the trunk also brings with it the sense of birth. For as the anal excretions earlier assumed the still older feelings of birth, so now the extrusion of the new head from the trunk also assumes both sets of feelings. That is, the head feels not only to be a piece of feces extruded from the neck, but to be also the self in the act of being born upwards out of the trunk. Now, however, there dawns the feeling of a still wider cycle. For now the head feels to have been the fetal self which went down the gut, into the earth, back into the trunk and up again as the 'new head' and the 'reborn self'. Now the whole trunk begins to feel as if it were a sort of umbilical cord in which there takes place a two-way flow. The head is felt to be constantly in process of being sucked down and restored. What at first was felt as a single unique journey, now becomes felt as a continuing cycle. There is a constant sense that the head is sucked down into the gut through eating, and excreted into the earth and then restored again as skeleton and as head.

How long this total overall process lasts I cannot say. So far as I know for certain it may be active in degree all our lives. But on this point I must plead relative ignorance. I know the process is felt, but I am not sure quite when it begins to be felt or for how long it lasts. This is one of the many problems waiting more research by my methods.

The Relation of Head to Trunk

All the old feelings once evoked by the flow of blood in the umbilical cord now are evoked in the feelings of the relation of the head to the trunk. The elements of aggression and destruction, restoration and alimentation are all there. And all are overlaid or underlaid with the additional feelings which have been evoked in the body in the course of the journey outlined in the foregoing pages.

Chapter Eleven

THE SKULL AS WOMB, TOMB AND THINKING BOX

THE DEVELOPMENT described in the previous chapter is so unlike anything one could imagine of a child's experiences that I offer no apologies for recapitulating it. The trunk of the infant, having seemed to swallow the head and to excrete it at the anus, now seems to swallow it at the lower end and to excrete it at the top. Owing to confusions between the two ends of the trunk, as well as to a primary confusion between bone and feces, the newly-restored head is felt in terms of a ball of fecal matter. However, it is not now as a solid ball that the head is felt, but as a blown-out or hollowed-out ball. It is, in fact, not with the head as a whole that the child is involved at this stage, but with the skull only. On top of all this, it must be remembered that the child's own sense of self is identified at this stage with this hollowed-out ball of bone-feces. The nuclear sense of the child is now identified with its own bony skull. That is the situation at which the infant had arrived in the stage described in the previous chapter. It is a situation so bizarre as to confound the imagination, and I trust that the reader understands that its discovery and confirmation astonished me as much as my description of it must now be astonishing him.

The next stage, which is the subject of this chapter, takes place through a complete reversal of this identity of the nuclear sense with the skull. Suddenly, so it appears, the nuclear sense quits the skull and identifies itself instead with the *contents* of the skull. What had formerly been attached to the *outside* of the head now attaches itself to the *inside* of the head. It is a complete reversal in the feelings of the head. Such a reversal of polarity is beginning to be a familar theme in these pages. The most impressive instance is that which takes place at birth.[1] Before birth the body (the fetal body) feels to be nuclear to the womb, and that sense of nuclear feeling is directly related to the skin—to the periphery of the body. At birth the body loses its nuclear status and, indeed, very swiftly assumes the peripheral role, feeling that the fetal self has gone inside it. This is a simple instance of the reversal of polarity in the feelings as between nuclear and peripheral. It is this kind of reversal which now seems to assail the feelings of the head: at one moment the skull feels to be invested with nuclear feeling, and at the next it feels peripheral, with the nuclear sense inside it, attached to the brain.

What is so extraordinary is that this new condition of the head actually is felt as if it were a restoration of the uterine life. The thalamus now feels to be the fetal nuclear self, and the cortex of the brain is felt as the placenta. But this restoration is by no means an unmixed blessing in the feelings, for the skull is not that gentle and pliant mother which the fetus knew *in utero*. It is a hard and bony mother from which all *physical* escape is impossible. I shall deal with the problem of this 'escape from the skull' in the following chapter. I must confess that I do not understand why this latest stage of development should appear as an entirely new one. That is to say, it is hard to understand why it is only now, at this advanced stage, that the infant feels his fetal self to be inside his skull. It is hard to understand precisely because from the very beginning, as we have seen, the thalamus appears to have been identified with the fetal body. As I showed in Chapter One, the fetal skin feeling appears to have been generated because the thalamus was bombarded with neural impulses from the skin,

---

[1] Chapter Two shows, however, that the umbilical flow evokes a continuous series of reversals of feeling in the fetus. Even before there was an umbilical cord the embryo underwent what may be regarded as a reversal of polarity, part of its ectoderm (skin) being quite suddenly folded inside, to become the source of the nervous system. Thus it is true that the skin which evokes the first sense of the 'ego' and the brain which inherits and develops that sense, both derive from the primal skin of the embryo. See also pages 216 and 217, and especially Figure Sixteen.

impulses which it had no means of releasing through cortical action. Why, then, should the head have to wait for this new stage in order to feel that the thalamus is the fetal body lying inside it? This is a problem I cannot yet answer.

Almost the identical problem faces us when we consider the assertion that now, at this present stage, the cortex of the brain suddenly feels itself to be the placental twin to the 'thalamic fetus'. For the cortex of the brain was first charged with that feeling right at the time of birth, as I have already indicated.[1] When the first breath was taken, two reactions were immediately evoked in the cortex. The first was a sort of great 'lighting up' of the brain caused by the greater oxygenation permitted by the action of the lungs. I have seen this represented again and again in dreams in the most precise terms, and I feel sure that it is not directly related to the new sense of 'light in the eyes', though it may be indirectly related. The brain cortex is specially sensitive to oxygen. The fetus never gets enough of it, and it has been suggested that the fetal brain exists on the border of mild epilepsy because of this oxygen starvation. Suddenly, as the first breath is taken, the brain cortex for the first time gets enough oxygen, or *begins* to get enough. And this fact, I believe, inseparably links the sense of the cortex to the lungs. But there is another reason, perhaps even more telling, why the act of breathing links the lungs to the cortex of the brain. This is a purely mechanical link, and exists in the fact that the cortices of the brain expand and contract slightly in entire synchronization with the expansion and contraction of the lungs. As the lungs fill, so blood is forced very slightly into the skull, causing the brain to shrink a little. As the lungs empty, blood pressure in the chest cavity drops slightly, and there is a flow of blood from the brain, which causes the hemispheres to expand. This lung-induced rhythm in the brain is quite miniscule, but it is observable, and it is enough to create (or perhaps to confirm and to amplify) a sense of identity between the lungs and the cerebral cortices. Now, as we have already seen the lungs at birth assume the sense of the placenta, creating the the following equation in the feelings: cortex = lungs = placenta.

[1] See Prologue to Part Two and also Chapter Six.

The Meaning of Hysteria

Thus it is that the identity between the cortex of the brain and the placenta is established *at* birth, just as the identity between the thalamus and the fetal body was established *before* birth. This makes it very hard to understand why these identities should remain, as it were, latent and quiescent until the feelings have been through the strange maneuvers outlined in the preceding chapters. Yet this seems to be the case, for not until the stages outlined in the previous chapters have been fulfilled, does the skull actually feel to be the mother's womb with the 'fetal-thalamus' and the 'placental-cortex' inside it. This is a mystery which I can at this time only indicate. I do so because to leave it unindicated might lead to unnecessary criticism, and leave the discerning reader to assume that I had not even considered what is, in fact, a very pressing and ever-present problem in my mind.

This mystery does not, however, in any way alter the facts as known to me and constantly confirmed by experience. The infant, in due time, comes to the stage where he feels that his skull is mother's bony womb, and that in that bony womb he lies as fetus, the role being played by his thalamus. And with him there in that joyous-fearful place is the faithful placenta, its role being played by the cerebral cortices. That is the fact which not only dreams but also myths reveal. It is testified to by the strange confusion which has existed in the medical world concerning the condition known as hysteria. The word 'hysteria' is derived from a Greek word for the uterus, and means something like 'the wandering of the womb'. For this reason it was long supposed to be an affection of the womb, though the famous Willis insisted that it was an affection of the brain. However, we read that even the youthful Freud got into trouble in Vienna for referring to hysteria in a man, being told by a senior physician that hysteria referred to an affection of the uterus, and so was not possible in a man. But in the light of this book we can clearly see that the womb (though not indeed its physical form) *can* wander through the feelings, and that it *does* at last land up in the skull. Did the same percipient men who coined this term also coin the terms which describe the coverings of the brain as the 'hard mother' and the 'tender mother'?

The Nature of the Self

It will be evident that, quite apart from any of the considerations outlined above, the structure of the brain is eminently suited to act as the recipient of the configurational impress, for the thalamus is undoubtedly the nuclear center of the brain in a neurological sense, with the cortex as the periphery. Moreover, the 'umbilical' two-way link between them is not wanting, for they are joined by a constant two-way flow of neural energy, which is called the thalamocortical circulation, of which I shall say more later. There is, indeed, plenty of evidence to show that the brain actually receives a direct cosmic impress of the universal design, in addition to that 'secondhand' one which it receives from the uterine state, and this I propose to deal with in the next chapter, in the context of which it properly belongs.

Apart from the structure of the brain, however, its functions show a configuration which is entirely suited to the evocation of the uterine pattern. This, I hasten to add, is no mere theoretical assumption, for the evidence is to be found in dreams. Or perhaps I had better say that evidence constantly appearing in dreams is fully satisfied by the explanation offered here, and does not readily suggest any alternative theory. I shall try now to describe this relevance of the brain's functions to the uterine pattern.

The human thalamus comprises two small kidneylike organs, the thalami, into which pour almost the whole of the affector impulses reaching the brain. A great number of these impulses pass up the spinal column, though the impulses from eyes and ears naturally do not. (Only the sensations of smell seem to be uncertainly conveyed to the thalamus.) Having reached the thalamus, the incoming impulses are sorted out and the related impulses are carried out to the cortex where they receive spatial orientation. Here also, on the cortices, lie the motor centers which drive the voluntary muscles of the body. These motor impulses do not pass out to the muscles through the thalamus, but go direct from the cortices to the motor system. Thus in a very crude, overall fashion, as roughly illustrated in Figure Seven, the brain may be said to experience a sense of ONE-IN and TWO-OUT, a pattern which I have already shown to have the most profound umbilical significance for the feelings. Indeed, I have seen in dreams many signs that the brain feels that it receives inthrusts of energy up through the neck, and responds to them by a dual backthrust made by the arms. The legs also play a similar part, but it would appear that the thrust of the arms is the most important to this complex of feelings. This is very natural, since the hands and the arms of man are developed to an extraordinary degree by conscious use, whereas the use of the legs is much more automatic. The legs walk without thought, but the arms and hands tend to be lost and aimless unless they are being used for the conscious purposes of the mind. It is for this reason, I suppose, that the sense of the umbilical arterial thrust is strongly imposed upon the arms and hands. This comes out in all manner of peculiar forms, but it may be seen very powerfully in the symbol of the bleeding hands, which appears not infrequently in both dreams and myths. And many dreams reveal the unconscious sense that the placenta is attached to the ends of the hands.[1] To some degree this may arise from the fact that the hands and the feet are so similar that the configurational elements attaching to the one may transfer to the other. But I do not think this is the main reason why the strong sense exists that the placenta is attached to the ends of the hands. Many a very sensible secretary would be surprised to find what feelings her typewriter evokes, and many a pianist shocked to discover how his piano takes on placental significance. The rhythm of piano-playing, with the constant relation between the thrust of the two hands and the stimulation of the thalamus by the music, evokes a powerful pattern of feelings in terms of Figure Seven—a pattern which the umbilical feelings immediately invest with their own significance.

One often hears of 'thought in action' and of the experience of being stimulated in thought by the rhythm of walking, or of thinking best when the hands are engaged in some purely automatic rhythm. I think it is highly probable that the reason for this experience (which is undoubtedly not purely imaginary) lies in the fact that all these things set up a circulation of neural energy from the thalamus out to the cortex, and so through the motor system into spatial action, by means of which in turn new

[1] See Appendix C.

sensations are generated that flow back to the thalamus, and so set up a wide circuit of energy between the focus of the brain and the external world. The thalamus might thus be regarded as a veritable point from which are sent thrusts of energy to the peripheral cortex, wherefrom again, now greatly amplified and modulated, muscular thrusts are generated. These thrust out against the spatial environment, contact with which gives rise to stimulations that cause afferent impulses to flow up the spine and to impinge upon the thalamus. Here we get a complete, if limited, back and forth flow of neural energy between the peripheral organs of the body and the focal nucleus of the brain. The reader will remember that I have suggested the principle that wherever a living point is linked to a periphery by a back-and-forth flow, then a form of mind appears. I think that here we have an instance of this, and that it accounts for the phenomenon of 'thought in action'.

In Figure Seven I depict the circulation of neural energy which goes on in the course of the use of the arms and legs. This shows how afferent impulses a travel up the spine into the thalami b-b', as a result of which impulses c-c' radiate out to the cortices d-d', culminating in efferent impulses e-e'. This is, however, by no means a satisfactory depiction of the total situation, since the radiations c-c' from the thalamus are not, as is suggested in Figure Seven, a one-way flow. They are, in fact, an absolutely two-way affair at every point. There is between thalamus and cortex a point-to-point relationship. It is said that when a wave of neural energy spreads over the cortex, it does not do so in a direct fashion, but does so only by referring back again and again at each point to the thalamus. Therefore the relation between the thalamus and the cortex must be regarded as something absolutely and intimately two-way at all times. So intimate is this connection that the neurosurgeons and the neurologists have found it quite impossible to study the thalamus and the cortex in functional isolation, since when cells of the thalamus are destroyed, their opposite numbers in the cortex immediately begin to degenerate. Similarly, when cortical cells are destroyed, their related thalamic cells also at once begin to atrophy.

The Thalamocortical Circulation

Figure Seven therefore evidently stands in need of modification. No impulse from the external world is ever communicated from the thalamus to the cortex in the manner shown therein. Rather is it achieved in the manner depicted in Figure Eight. The thalamus and the cortex have their own intimate circulation, and it is evidently into this internal circulation that the external circulation of 'thinking in action' is geared.

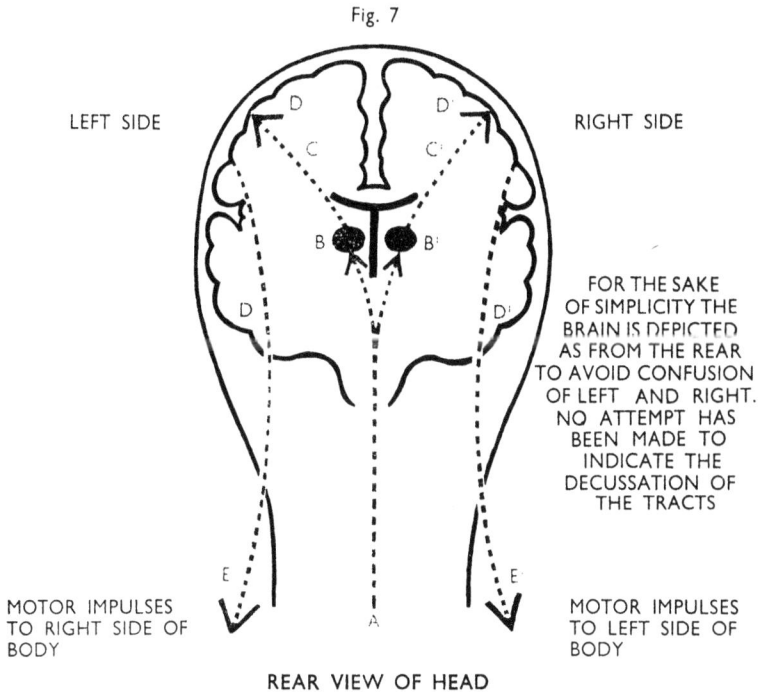

Fig. 7

LEFT SIDE

RIGHT SIDE

FOR THE SAKE OF SIMPLICITY THE BRAIN IS DEPICTED AS FROM THE REAR TO AVOID CONFUSION OF LEFT AND RIGHT. NO ATTEMPT HAS BEEN MADE TO INDICATE THE DECUSSATION OF THE TRACTS

MOTOR IMPULSES TO RIGHT SIDE OF BODY

MOTOR IMPULSES TO LEFT SIDE OF BODY

REAR VIEW OF HEAD

In Figure Eight I have tried to show a very rough distinction between the external neuromuscular circulation and the internal neural circulation. My intent is to show that although the latter originally was evolved to serve the former, it has in man acquired a configurational life of its own, just as the umbilical circulation of blood, formed for an organic purpose, has come to serve the purposes of mind. In man the thalamocortical circulation of neural energy still serves the external circulation of neuromuscular

147

energy. This it does by providing a pathway between the thalamus and the cortex. But this is no longer its sole function. It has now gone off on an entirely new line, namely the evocation of mind. I have tried to depict this situation in Figure Eight, which can best be understood by contrasting it with Figure Seven. In Figure Seven the thalamocortical circulation (*c-c'*) is depicted only as a one-way link conveying impulses from thalamus to cortex and so completing the total external neuromuscular circuit. In Figure Eight I have shown this thalamocortical circulation by means

Fig. 8

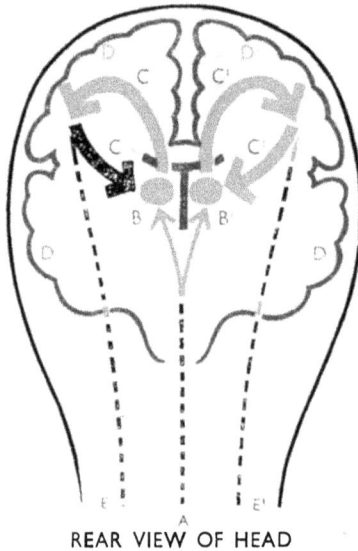

REAR VIEW OF HEAD

of two sets of heavy red arrows. It is my belief (based upon the testimony of dreams) that it is this circulation which links together thalamus and cortex in such a way that they become the configurational analogues not only of the universal design but of the fetus and placenta. I may add that, to the best of my knowledge, it is now generally recognized by neurologists that this thalamocortical circulation of neural energy is crucial to the act of thought.

Thinking and the Uterine Pattern

We can understand how this can be if we consider for a moment what thinking is. Thinking is an act of interplay between concepts, and each concept may be regarded as an integrated cluster of 'particles' of feeling or memory. Every concept consists of a collection of memories which has been drawn together by affinity of association, and identified by that label we call a word.[1] The mind as we ordinarily know it consists very largely of these integrated entities called concepts and their interplay. To this interplay we give the name of thought. Every act of thinking requires the existence of two concepts standing in opposition, a relationship which we designate by calling the one 'subject' and the other 'object'. Thinking appears when the two are permitted to interact by means of a verb. A verb is simply the name for that condition of mind which sets two opposed concepts into interaction, resulting in a new concept. As I see it, concepts may be likened to molecules, and thought may be likened to the chemical action which takes place between molecules, resulting in the rearrangement of their constituent atoms. Concepts interchange and rearrange their constituent feeling-parts (or memory-parts) during the act of thinking.

Has the concept, then, a structure? I think it has. I think that the structure of a concept reflects that pattern with which the reader will now be familiar—the pattern of the universal design; the pattern of the nucleus within the periphery. The nucleus of every concept is, so to say, a little piece of the thinker's own 'ego'. This little nucleus is the focus around which the memory-pieces or feeling-pieces integrate. It is precisely this structure, I believe, which is served by the structure of the brain. Or perhaps I had better put it in another way: I think the structure of the concept is a reflection of the structure of the brain that thinks it. I believe the thalamus is the agent of the nucleus of every concept, and the cortex the agent of the peripheral memories. The thalamocortical circulation is the means whereby a kaleidoscopic series of conceptual images is formed. For in the course of this constant electrical dance concepts are formed and dissolved, integrated,

[1] Which serves to explain why the brain's capacity to think is so largely dependent upon the social environment and its inherited vocabulary.

149

opposed and brought to synthesis in the establishment of new ones. A concept is, as it were, the subjective sense of the thalamus and the cortex in dynamic interrelation.

This configurational process in the brain is not, however, as I see it, evoked *de novo* in the brain as a purely neural phenomenon. It is imposed upon the neural process by the feelings first generated in the womb. That is to say, because the uterine feelings are imposed upon the brain, and because these feelings represent the first evocation of mind, the brain becomes the instrument of thought. As once the primary power of thought arose in the umbilical flow between the fetal nucleus and the placental periphery, so now that power is extended and amplified in the neural flow between the thalamus and the cortex of the brain.

The reader may object that such a statement makes it appear that thought as we know it is generated in the umbilical cord. I do not believe that this is so, nor that I have ever implied it. Consciousness certainly is evoked between the fetus and the placenta, for consciousness appears whenever a nucleus and a periphery are linked by a two-way flow. But on each level of the establishment of this pattern there appears a form of thought appropriate to that level. In the case of the uterine organism that thinking is extremely limited. I have already shown what the single proposition is that occupies the uterine consciousness. It is simply this: *The nucleus is forever being drawn into the periphery, destroyed there, renewed and restored.* This is the basic thought of man, upon which his whole power to think is erected. The fetal nuclear feeling might be called the first subject, the placenta the first object, and the umbilical flow the first verb. It is for this reason, I believe, that every act of thinking is permeated with the original uterine sense, so that it is possible for the Christian to say that behind all the appearance of this world there stands the figure of the Son who is also Father, and who entered the Mother, was destroyed, renewed and restored. This is the basic concept not only of man but of the universe itself.

Anyone who inclines to think that this is a mere newfangled interpretation of Christian meaning twisted to serve the end of this book, might do well to consider the strange myth of Prometheus. This mighty figure stole fire from heaven in a hollow reed, and afterwards was chained to a rock in the Caucasus. His name means 'the fore-thinker'. I have examined this myth in detail in my unpublished work on the myths, but here I mention only the barest outline as it relates to the present discourse. Is it not the fetus who 'steals the fire from heaven' (the nuclear feeling) in the 'hollow reed' at his navel? Is it not he who afterwards feels to be bound and chained in the rocky skull? As to his name, I do not believe that it means simply 'the one who thinks ahead', but that it means the fetus as the one who thought before there were thoughts in the brain.

In my view, a concept at root is a little replay of the primary design of the womb, and it is made possible by the same kind of pattern at work in the neural currents of the thalamocortical circulation. In a sense then, every concept is a representation of the original drama of the fetal nuclear self struggling with the placental periphery. Every act of thinking is a replay of the struggle of the nuclear feeling to overmaster the periphery. The thalamus is the great juggler, seeking to master an ever more varied periphery of memory and to make it respond to his nuclear powers.

The fact that the thalamocortical circulation has umbilical undertones accounts, I believe, for the existence of the senses of color and of musical sound. It will be recalled that I showed the umbilical cord to evoke in us the first sense of periodicity.[1] The fetus does not feel the beats of blood in the cord as an endless and undifferentiated sequence, but as an endless series of sevenfold patterns. I believe that it is this sense of sevenfold sequence, imposed upon the thalamocortical circulation of neural energy, which causes the brain to integrate the perception of light into the forms of the color spectrum, and likewise to give musical form to the perception of sound. It is for this reason, I believe, that there exists a tantalizing analogy between the musical scale and the color spectrum—an analogy which, to my best knowledge, has never been satisfactorily explained.

The reader will, I hope, understand that it would be quite impossible for me to set down here the evidence for these assertions,

[1] See Chapter Two.

for it is drawn from a great number of separate analyses, few of which, taken one by one, would seem conclusive.[1] But anyone who understands the symbolic nature of the myths and their value, will see plenty of evidence to show that the ancient people knew that the sense of music (if indeed not of color) had an umbilical source. I will mention here but one of these pieces of symbolism, namely that of Cheiron the centaur, who taught so many of the Heroes of Greece in a cave. The placental nature of this centaur is overwhelmingly evidenced by the symbolic nature of his doings, and it is significant that he invariably seems to teach the Hero to play on the pipes. It is my belief that this is a symbolic manner of stating the 'feeling fact' that the sense of periodicity generated in that first umbilical 'pipe' in the 'womb-cave' is the basis upon which the brain creates its tendency to integrate sounds into musical notes.[2]

Here I may be allowed to digress for a moment to point out another strange link between the umbilical cord and the musical sense. The reader will recall that I have shown the neck to assume the umbilical feelings, and have shown how the seven cervical vertebrae seem in some way to become involved in this situation.[3] I have said that it is as if the neck somehow links the existence of its seven cervical vertebrae with the sevenfold periodicity evoked in the umbilical cord. Now, this has a sequel which it seems appropriate to mention here, namely that dreams frequently reveal a direct link between the sense of music and the seven cervical vertebrae. Again and again I have seen very clear indications which link the keys of a piano with the cervical vertebrae. This piano symbolism is by far the most frequent in my experience, but I have seen the same thing expressed in terms of the playing of a flute, while a 'cello is sometimes used to represent the trunk and its neck, with the sense that the notes picked out on that long 'neck' are really a representation of the seven cervical vertebrae. Now, of course, I do not know if the cervical vertebrae actually

[1] Appendices H and P may give the reader some idea as to the nature of my methods, and explain why the evidence is difficult to set down in any reasonable space.
[2] See Chapter Three.
[3] See Chapter Ten.

play any specific part in developing the musical sense. I should doubt it very much. I should suppose that the most likely cause of the link is the fact that in making music with our own bodies through singing (and perhaps in some degree also by whistling), we employ the throat and the beat of the air in that tube, and thus invoke the peculiar relations already noted between the act of breathing and the cervical stem.[1]

*   *   *

Now I must mention a complication which arises in the feelings of the brain's action.[2] As everyone knows, there is a general tendency among human beings to use the right hand where precision of movement is concerned. Since the right side of the body is supplied neurally from the left cortex of the brain, this means that a righthanded person may be said to be leftbrained. It is true that in the average (righthanded) person the left side of the cerebral cortex is of enormous importance, while the right cortex seems hardly to count at all in the mental function of that person. The right cortex of such a person may be severely damaged without seriously affecting his mental capacities. By contrast, a relatively minor damage to the left cortex can cause serious disability.

Since, as I have shown, the cerebral cortex is *par excellence* the instrument of spatial orientation, this seems to suggest that the left cerebral cortex of the average person is specially concerned with space, the right cortex not being so involved. The right cortex (in the righthanded person) seems to be in some way negative. Purely on the basis of my own observations, I feel able to suggest very strongly that the right cortex is dominated by the thalamus, while the left cortex dominates the thalamus. I will give my reasons for making this assertion.

Dreams have shown me again and again that the left side of the

---

[1] See Chapter Ten for some notes on the relation of the diaphragm to the neck. See also Appendix Q.
[2] The reader will remember that I use the term 'feeling' often in a special sense. That there is no ordinary feeling in the cerebral cortices I am well aware.

brain (of the ordinary average person) is specifically related in the feelings with the placenta. Thus I must modify my earlier assertion that the cortex of the brain feels to be the placental surrogate. It is specifically the *left* side which feels to be so identified. On the other hand, I have found that the right side of the brain feels to be the fetus, a circumstance which I link with the relatively inoperative nature of the right cerebral cortex. This modification does not really alter my previous assertion that the cortex is the placental surrogate, and the thalamus the fetal surrogate, but it demands the qualification that since the left cortex is dominant, then the left side of the brain feels cortical and placental, while the right cortex being relatively negative, the right side of the brain is dominated by the thalamus, and so is felt as the fetal side.

Whether these indications throw any light upon the problem of human 'handedness' I cannot say. I can hardly suppose that they are in any sense the disposing factor, since I presume that the formation of Broca's mechanism is determined before birth. While I do not think that the creation of 'handedness' in the human being is determined by the uterine elements, I think that my discoveries throw a great deal of new light upon the strange superstitions which from ancient time have attached to the use of the hands, leading to all manner of rites and conventions concerning their employment.

There are, however, other factors involved in the creation of superstitions concerning the use of the hands. Some superstitions concerning the hands seem to derive rather from the fact that both hands have taken on not only umbilical feelings but also the feelings of the legs with their umbilical undertone. Thus, just as the left leg feels to be linked with the rectal tube, so the left arm also feels to be linked, though in a lesser degree. And for this reason the left hand is often felt as the 'dirty hand' and the 'inferior hand' and even today is used by some peoples as the only appropriate hand for the performance of certain lowly human acts. The right hand, on the contrary, is the noble hand. However, there are other aspects of hand superstition which plainly reflect the sense that the left hand is the more 'fetal' hand and the right hand more 'placental'. The left hand is frequently employed as the active human symbol of all that is unconscious and dangerous, while the right hand signifies more the conscious relation with space. It will be seen that this accords fairly well with what we know of the feelings imposed upon the brain by the primary uterine sense.

*   *   *

The reader will by this time be a little reconciled, I hope, to the strange conclusions to which feeling-logic gives rise. The time has come to brace himself to meet the strangest so far mentioned. I will give the logical origins of the feeling first, although it was not discovered in this order, but was met with in fact long before it was explained. Given the facts that at one stage the head feels to be the fetus, and the trunk feels to be the placenta, and given also the fact that both fetus and placenta feel to be located in the skull, we get the following rough equations:

Trunk = Placenta; Placenta is in Skull ∴ Trunk is in Skull.

Head = Fetus; Fetus is in Skull ∴ Head is in Skull.

Do these odd equations have any representation in the actual feelings of the child? Indeed they do! Time and time again I have seen in dreams records of the moment of horror when the whole self suddenly felt to have been caught up and enclosed in the skull. We all go through this experience, which is very clearly represented in the myths. Perhaps the best known instance of this is the solemn burial of Jesus in the rocky tomb miraculously ready for that purpose upon Golgotha, a name which in Hebrew means 'place of a skull'.

I have found that people suffering from claustrophobia and from migraine tend to reveal that the source of their sufferings lies in this very fact, namely that they still, in their deep feelings, have not overcome or lived through the shocking infancy experience of being suddenly sucked up and imprisoned in their own skull. This fact, as I have explained, goes hand in hand with the sense that the skull is the womb with their own selves inside. But this womb is no longer merely the mother—it is also a tomb.

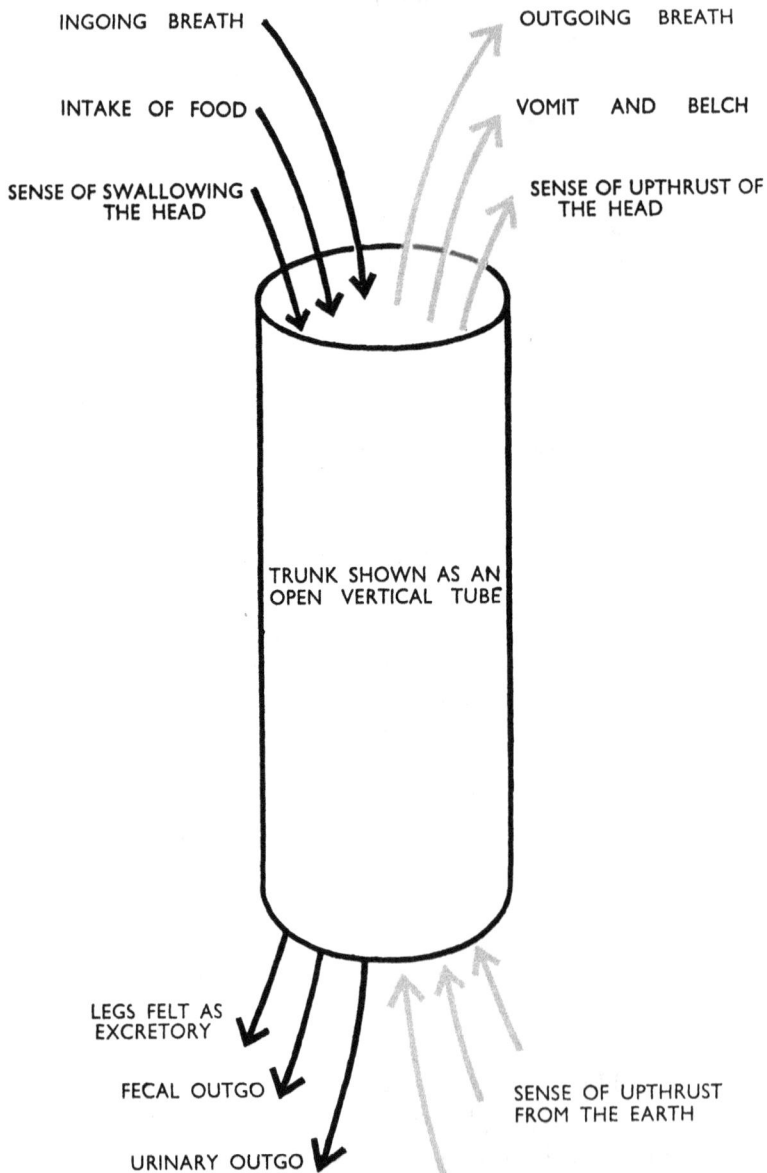

Fig. 9

INGOING BREATH

INTAKE OF FOOD

SENSE OF SWALLOWING
THE HEAD

OUTGOING BREATH

VOMIT AND BELCH

SENSE OF UPTHRUST OF
THE HEAD

TRUNK SHOWN AS AN
OPEN VERTICAL TUBE

LEGS FELT AS
EXCRETORY

FECAL OUTGO

URINARY OUTGO

SENSE OF UPTHRUST
FROM THE EARTH

Spine and Gut as Opposing Pathways

Very often one is handed horror dreams in which there figures a little mannikin, a deformed and compressed little creature who fills the dreamer with natural fear and foreboding. Upon analysis this little creature invariably turns out to be the representation of that moment when the feelings went through the experience of seeming to suffer the whole self to be sucked up and imprisoned in one's own skull.

*   *   *

A whole series of lesser confusions concerning the head and the brain derives from a confusion between the spine and the gastrointestinal tract. The reason for this confusion seems clear: the trunk is felt as a two-way tube through which impulses pass in both directions. The agent of the downward passage is the gut, for very obvious reasons. The agent of the upward passage (for less obvious reasons) is the spine. Therefore, spine and gut have this in common, that they represent the opposing sense of movement through the trunk. Whether or not this is the sole basis for their similarity in the feelings I do not know. But there is no doubt at all that they are felt to be related, and that this relation leads to confusion. The major outcome of this confusion is that the child does not 'know which way up he is', a condition which appears utterly meaningless until we remember that the sense of self in the infant is not identified with the whole body, but is felt to be moving inside the body itself. This self 'has no eyes' and cannot check up what it feels. To understand what is going on, we must think of the self at that stage as a fluid entity that is seeking to orient itself in the internal tubes of the body.[1]

I think the easiest way to present the facts of spine-gut confusion is to offer a sketch of the trunk as if it were a two-way tube through which various elements pass in both directions. Having given this preliminary schema (see Figure Nine), I can then more easily show some of the more common and more emphatic confusions and identities which arise in the feelings. Treated in piecemeal fashion, these confusions would sound like utter lunacy.

[1] See Appendix J.

But once the principle is seen, then each individual instance of confusion can be judged in its natural setting.[1]

All things entering the mouth and going down into the body tend to become identified in the feelings. The same is true of all that leaves the body at the lower end.[2] All that is felt to move up through the trunk and to emerge at the top end is likewise susceptible of confusion. Thus, for example, as I have mentioned earlier, the 'rebirth' of the head is felt to be associated with the acts of belching and vomiting.

In addition to the above, however, the two ends of the trunk are confused, so that what goes in at one end may become mistaken for what goes in at the other. Similarly, what goes out at the top may be felt to be going out of the bottom. Thus, for instance, there is a very powerful confusion in the infant between flatus and speaking or singing, and many a dream represents the bottom as a man with a deep voice. We are already familiar with another instance of the same thing, namely the fact that the upthrust of the 'new head' is felt in terms of an anal excretion.

I hope the reader will forgive the reminder that in this sense the trunk, in feeling, is simply responding to the basic configuration of all feelings, namely that a nucleus is always seeking a hollow into which it can enter and from which it can escape again. In this sense the human trunk might be likened to a sort of gun, with strong maternal undertones. It is a gun that can be filled, as it were, from either end and shot in either direction. The

---

[1] The reader will begin to understand something of my methods of feeling analysis. Once I grasped the logical principle of the feelings I was able to formulate possibilities just as a mathematician creates possible equations. And just as these equations are submitted to experimental test by the physicist, so I submitted my formulae to the test of continuous dream observation. The only difference being that I could not set my experiments at will. Rather like an astronomer, I have to wait for the phenomena to appear though, unlike an astronomer, I cannot predict them—cannot predict what kind of dreams will come.

[2] It is not entirely a matter of what actually leaves the lower end of the trunk, for all that is appended thereto also feels to be confused with the excretions. Thus the legs feel to be excretions or to be related to excretion. This is a rather special case, as Figure Six indicates. Yet the same sort of identification is felt between the genital appendages of the male and the excretions. Hidden deep in every male human being is an infancy horror of having felt that the genitals were fecal and were falling away.

basis of this strange feeling is undoubtedly the umbilical cord. The trunk-tube shown in Figure Nine is simply carrying out, in its feelings, the pattern imposed upon the organism by the original umbilical flow. Some of the more common confusions are:

1. The spine feels itself to be a sort of gastrointestinal tract that sucks down from the head-end to the bottom, just as the gut does. The result of this confusion is that the spine figures in the feelings *partly* as a sort of bony serpent which threatens to suck down the brains and to eject them at the lower end.

2. The spine feels itself to be a sort of gastrointestinal tract, but acting in the reverse direction. The result of this is that the spine is felt as a sort of bony gut which excretes into the skull. Indeed, I have seen a great number of dreams in which the indications plainly say that the skull is felt as a chamber pot with the brains lying in it in the form of excrementa, with urine playing the role of the cerebrospinal fluid.

3. The whole of the lower parts and their functions are felt to have been sucked up into the skull and identified there with various cephalic and cerebral organs. Thus it is not only true that there is, as stated in Chapter Eight, a 'head at the bottom', but there is in varying degree also 'a bottom in the head'. This results in various forms of confusion which can only *a priori* be given in principle, since the elements of confusion are subject to almost endless permutation and combination. The main elements seem to be:

a. The two hemispheres of the brain seem to be confused with the buttocks. And since the buttocks had already been confused with the still earlier feelings of the newborn cheeks, the brain's hemispheres also inherit a faint sense of being the cheeks of the face turned inside the skull.

b. The thalami of the brain appear to be confused with the genitals. But since the genitals have already been confused earlier with the nose, the thalami also inherit a faint sense that they are the nose that has dived into the skull.

c. The sense of being locked inside the skull is linked with an odd sense of constipation, and may be related to an actual nervous constipation. For whereas the child felt that he could excrete (himself) through the anus and so escape, he cannot escape in this fashion through the skull. There appears in dreams a familiar theme about trying to find a back door that once existed and no longer does. The dream is generally evocative of great fear, and the room in which the dreamer finds himself thus enclosed always shows signs of being the symbol of the skull—in which there is, of course no back (anal) door!

d. The lifting up of the bottom parts into the skull by no means excludes the feet. There are plenty of indications that some people (if not indeed all) suffer a confusion between the feet and the hemispheres of the brain. The confusion is represented in terms of a mysterious somersault, in the course of which the feet are caught up and enclosed in a rigid shoe or box. This shoe, when sufficiently analyzed, turns out to have strong associations with the skull. In such dreams there often appears also the experience of the legs being bound together and enclosed in a rigid tube.

e. Another strange confusion between the upper and the lower parts seems to be as between the jawbones and the pelvic bones. I have often seen in dreams symbolisms which responded (both as to inner nature and also context) to the idea of such confusion. This confusion seems to be related to the confusion between the mouth and the anus. For if the mouth is a downsucking organ related to the jaws, then the anus is frequently (if improperly) felt as an upsucking organ related to the pelvic bones. This confusion is probably related to another, and recognized, confusion between the mouth and the female organ, which latter is often felt to be a mouth with teeth in it. The 'vagina dentata' is quite a common fantasy, and even Swedenborg confessed to a dream in which it appeared. This confusion is recognized as being a cause of some male impotence, produced by the fear that the woman's organ is equipped with teeth that will bite off the penis. I have never seen this fear linked by psychologists with the confusion between the jaws and the pelvic bones, but I have myself often seen good cause for suspecting this extension of the general confusion.

f. Confusion in the deep feelings between jaws and legs give rise to a fantasy that the jaws, like the legs, are excreting blood. I have shown in Figure Six why the *legs* should feel this, and I now assert that this is transferred to the jaws. The sucking child feels, therefore, not only that he is sucking in blood and excreting it through his eyes, but also in fainter degree, through his jaws. I have seen indications which suggest that as a result of this the teeth are sometimes felt as if they were excretions, and that this is not unconnected with dental decay. Because excretion is associated with the sense of birth, the falling out of a tooth, or its extraction, often awakens birth echoes in the feelings—a fact which is not unknown to psychology, but which I have never before seen adequately explained.

The reader will naturally incline to exclaim that nothing so absurd has ever before been alleged of the human being. Truly I know of no previous statement in plain language. But this is not to say that it has not in earlier times been stated in symbolic language. Let me remind the reader of the remarkable myth of Jason and his quest for the Golden Fleece. I cannot demonstrate here that the Golden Fleece is the fetal skin feeling, though I have done so in my unpublished work on the myths. Yet if we assume that this be so, the meaning of the main outline of the discovery and retrieval of the Fleece becomes plain. Jason finds it hung upon a tree guarded by a fearful snake. His task is to slay the snake and to sow its teeth, whereupon a crop of armed heads arises. This snake on the tree is, of course, the symbol of the umbilical arteries twined upon the vein, but it is in this context transposed upon the gut and the spine. The tortuous gut itself has become the umbilical arterial serpent, and the spine has become the umbilical vein. Hung on this spinal tree is the Golden

Fleece, namely the fetal skin feeling in the brain. In this light the sowing of the snake's teeth and its strange crop of heads at once becomes clear: the snake's teeth are the excretions of the gut which must be made to go down into the earth, whereupon there will be felt a backthrust from the earth that will lift the sense of the head. In other words, the human being, if he is to get the clear and unconfused sense of his head as new self, must ensure that the gut is felt to thrust *down*, and the spine and head to thrust *up*. Once the clear directional sense is achieved, then the 'Golden Fleece' will be gained. Man will have controled his development by conscious means.

*   *   *

I trust that now, in spite of its several complications, the present narrative yields some light upon the relation of mind to the brain. The brain was created to be the central exchange for the integration of the bodily parts into a single whole and for the orientation of that whole to space and to its objects and events. It still performs this original purpose, though it is plain that its neuromuscular co-ordinations have been interfered with by the tendency of the head to become caught in a life of its own, wherein the play of social forces, through words and ideas, has upset the automatic operation of the nervous system.[1]

But the most mysterious aspect of the brain is the way in which it has become the seat of a sense of the self which transcends the bounds of neural mechanics or electronics. This fact the present book explains by showing that the sense of self is not *produced* by the brain at all, but has been *imposed* upon it. It is not, evidently, a sudden imposition. It is not a mystical one in the sense that an angelic or ghostly soul suddenly descends and takes possession of the brain. It is a relatively slow process by means of which the cosmic imprint received by the fetus is retrieved from the wreckage of birth, and then evolved through a series of most unexpected

---

[1] Those interested in this aspect of the brain should read the works of the late Dr Trigant Burrow of New York, and also might consider the writings of F. Matthias Alexander.

organs and processes, and finally imposed upon the brain. But very naturally this imposition comes to the brain in a very battered and cluttered state. It is no longer its own original glorious sense of cosmic nuclearity, able to stand represented by the Coat of Joseph and the sense of being focal to the very universe. It is rather a weary traveler, battered by its many transformations, soiled with most unpleasant associations. Yet we know how often in fairy tales the glorious prince comes to meet his beloved in the shape of a loathsome thing bewitched, but how in the end he is restored to glory. This restoration is, indeed, the ultimate purpose of all such efforts as this present book.

However, even this is not the end of the story presented here. For the brain *does* seem to receive a direct 'cosmic imprint' as well as the indirect one which we have studied above. Two imprints of the cosmos seem to struggle in the brain. It will be the task of the following chapter to give some indications of the nature and meaning of this direct cosmic impress in the depths of the skull.

Chapter Twelve

A DIRECT LINK FELT BETWEEN
THE BRAIN AND THE SKY

PLAIN EVIDENCE is to be found in dreams that at some time in the past a strange connection has been felt between the top of the head and the sky. As far as I can judge, this experience takes place somewhere between the ages of five and seven. I am able to make this attempt at fixing the time because of the remarkable evidence offered to the observant parent by children of that age. I have myself observed not only in my own children, but in the children of others, a period of great concern for the sky and even a great fear of it. One mother told me how her son of five was for a time always talking about putting a ladder up to a hole in the sky and climbing through. This at once brings to mind, of course, such stories as that of Jacob's Ladder and of Jack and the Beanstalk. Indeed, myths and legends of this order are quite numerous, and Sir John G. Frazer gives several instances of mysterious vines, ladders and trees which permitted men and gods to commune.[1]

It is through this experience, I believe, that the human brain receives that direct imprint of the cosmos mentioned in the previous chapter. It is by this means also, I believe, that the child gains relief from the terrible feeling that he is entombed in his own skull.[2] The suitability of the brain to receive this direct impress from the sky will be obvious to anyone who has followed the narrative to this point. For if the flow of blood in the umbilical cord, back and forth between the fetal body and the placenta, can

---

[1] Frazer, Sir John G.: *Folklore in the Old Testament.*
[2] See Chapter Eleven.

acquire a mysterious sense of the cosmos, then it is fairly obvious that the much more delicate neural circulation of the thalamo-cortical system should be able to register a similar influence. For the configuration of the thalamocortical circulation of neural energy is in many respects very similar to that of the umbilical circulation of blood. Both represent the back and forth play of energies between a focal nucleus and a periphery. Both therefore supply reasonable configurational analogues of the universal design.[1]

One is compelled to wonder if there is not a close connection between this head-sky relationship and the upright posture gained so completely by man. One wonders also whether the strange phenomenon of trepanning among certain Neolithic peoples is not related to some primitive awareness of this link between the head and the sky. Certainly in religion we get the distinct sugges-tion that there are two selves at war in us, and in the Bible we find a passage which without violence fits this concept like a glove upon a hand. I refer to the well-known passage in the First Epistle to the Corinthians, in which it is asserted that we are each involved, as it were, with two men, the first of whom is 'of the earth earthy' and the second of whom is the 'Lord from heaven'. This passage becomes even more telling when we look into it a little. For instance, the phrase 'of the earth earthy' does not convey to us quite what the Greek words do. The word for 'earth' used in the Greek testament is *ge*, and we at once recall that this is the name of the Great Mother who 'gave birth upwards'. This brings us to remember that in this Bible passage we come into an atmosphere very far from Christianity. It comes from a back-ground where this birth upwards from the Earth Mother, *Ge*, was an accepted fact, so that it can hardly help but echo the old feeling that this first man, who is 'of the earth earthy' is he who went down into the depths and was born upwards again. More-over, if we examine the word used in the Greek for 'earthy', we shall find that it is *choikos*, which has the significance of 'a poured out heap'. There is not wanting thus some evidence to show that this first man is not merely of *Ge*, but that he is also a dirty and

[1] My theme is that configurational similarities evoke the universal pattern.

poured-out one, namely a fecal man. This dirty man of the earth well represents the original uterine self who was felt to be poured out from the gut and sent down into the earth, to be 'born upwards'. The second man as 'the Lord from heaven' may more properly be described as 'the man from the sky' (*ouranos*).

The idea that we are compounded of a higher and a lower self is to be met with in almost every religion, mysticism and psychology. Even Freud was compelled by his observations to postulate a super-ego in addition to the ego. Jung's categories include the Wise One and the Shadow. Christianity invokes God and Devil. Even so abstract a concept as Christian Science sets mortal mind (disapprovingly uncapitalized) in opposition to Divine Mind. I think that all these things are merely approximations to the simple reality which I have tried to outline in terms of a direct and an indirect cosmic impress upon the brain. I may as well say at once that I am strongly of the opinion that the understanding of this lost link between the head and the sky, and its re-establishment as a living experience, is the next step in the evolution of the individual human being.

What is the specific nature of this link between the human head, or brain, and the sky?[1] What are the mechanics of it? I confess freely that I do not know. But I would say that I do not for one moment suggest that the mechanism of this link is 'spiritual', if I may use that loose term for want of a better. I should say that there is some subtle circulation of energy between the earth and something beyond the earth. It may, for all I know, be an electrical or electromagnetic circulation. It may be related to gravity. It may take place between the earth and the sun, or between the earth and some ionized or magnetic environment of the earth. Whatever it is, it evidently uses the human body as a sort of link, or perhaps it would be better to say that the human body uses the circulation. All these things are purely speculative. I mention them not so much for what they affirm as for what they

---

[1] I employ the word 'sky' simply for want of a better. Since I do not know the source of the influence 'from above', I prefer to use a neutral sort of term until I am in possession of more precise information on the subject. Moreover, I have good warrant for it from ancient thought.

avoid, namely any suggestion that this circulation, because it serves the ends of consciousness, must in itself be some mystical flux. I do not think that any such view is warranted. This book is indeed testimony to the very reverse, since it shows that the lowly physiological functions of the umbilical vessels, which surely are in no sense mystical, are the roots of mind in man. The circulation between earth and 'sky' need be no more 'mystical' than the circulation of the blood in the cord. If the circulation of blood in the umbilical cord can evoke consciousness, then a circulation of electrical energies can most certainly do so. The key lies in the configurations created.

What I *do* know about this earth-sky circulation is that it is felt by the human being in absolutely umbilical terms. It is so represented in dreams, and in ancient and primitive myths the umbilical elements are but lightly veiled. What are these umbilical elements which are manifested by the head-sky circulation? First of all there is the numerical pattern of two-versus-one. The circulation of energy between the head and the sky, when it appears in dreams, is hardly ever represented as a simple back-and-forth flow, but as *two* currents flowing in *one* direction, with a *single* current flowing in the *opposite* direction. What is more, the two currents are frequently represented as moving helically around the single opposing current. As if this were not enough, there are frequent confusions between this flow of energy and blood. Blood is felt to be rising and falling between the head and the sky. Moreover, both the head and the sky are frequently represented in either fetal or placental terms. So constant is this symbolism that I am compelled to the conclusion that our reaction to the head-sky feeling is dominated by the original uterine experience. The old uterine patterns have persisted unchanged in essence, and as they dominate the intra-organic feelings of configuration, so they also inform the extra-organic experiences. In a word, the deep feelings project upon the head-sky circulation the pattern of the fetus, the placenta and the cord in vascular interaction, just as they did at an earlier stage upon the relation of the trunk to the earth.[1]

[1] See Chapter Nine.

The Nature of the Self

I think it can be satisfactorily demonstrated that the Christian representation of the Crucifixion contains a powerful symbolic picture of the head-sky relation in markedly umbilical terms. Christ is crucified upon Golgotha, a name which means 'the place of a skull', and which therefore openly relates itself to the human head. However, not one cross, but three crosses are raised there, on the central one of which Christ is nailed, while on each side is nailed a robber. The picture presented is therefore of a central stem related to something destined to be lifted up to the sky, while on each side is something doomed to descend into the depths. Here we have the umbilical pattern perfectly represented, but set upon the skull. It would hardly be possible to create a more impressive picture for the stirring of the feelings. Yet, as we shall later discover,[1] this is the pattern of the *man's* head. It is the *man* and not the woman who feels the head-sky circulation in terms of ONE-UP and TWO-DOWN. The woman feels it in reverse, namely TWO-UP and ONE-DOWN. Are the woman's feelings therefore offered no catharsis by the Gospels? On the contrary, in the Gospel of St Luke, the picture is altered in a dramatic way, for Christ turns to one of the robbers and tells him that he, too, shall ascend. The picture in Luke is thus changed to represent TWO who go UP, and only ONE who goes DOWN. It is a picture of the meta-umbilical pattern of flow as it is felt by the woman in terms of her head-sky relationship.

Strong umbilical and uterine elements generally may be discerned in the symbolic representation which certain primitive Australian tribes have inherited. There is among these people a widespread belief in a mysterious rainbow serpent, concerning which a number of stories are told. The rainbow is apparently linked with a serpent because it is believed that it sucks up water. This, incidentally, is a belief which has been found in European folklore. This 'rainbow serpent' is related in primitive Australian thought with the 'milky way', which in turn appears to be related with the sense of a mother and a child stuck together. There is also a distinct sense of the relation between this 'rainbow serpent' and blood, and at least one Australian tribe believes that the serpent's

[1] See Chapter Thirteen.

totem place is the source of mankind's blood-supply. Moreover, as I have shown in my analysis of the myths, this rainbow serpent is linked direct with the rainbow which God set in the cloud after the Flood, and with the rainbow of Iris, both of which I can demonstrate to be unequivocally umbilical.[1]

The old legend of Jacob's Ladder, upon which Jacob saw the angels ascending and descending, and above which he saw God, is in my view an effort to symbolize this 'super-umbilical' circulation between the human head and the sky. Unfortunately the idea has grown up that 'God is at the top of the ladder' in the sense that the head-sky circulation is 'divine', whereas the trunk-earth circulation is 'bad'. I think this is an unfortunate legend which has served to bring the whole idea into contempt. The truth of the matter is, I believe, that there is nothing 'good' or 'bad' about these opposed circulations. They constitute a potential function of synthesis between two poles, the one in 'the sky' and the other in the earth, just as the umbilical flow provided a function of synthesis between the polar opposition of the fetus and the placenta. Moreover, indications are not wanting to show that these two states of opposition are of the same order. The placenta acts as the storehouse of past impressions, to which the fetus responds as an integrating center.[2] Similarly, it appears, the earth acts as the storehouse of past impressions,[3] while 'the sky' acts as the source of purpose and integrative meaning. In acting as a link between these two poles, the human being is involved in a cosmic process far wider than his personal ends and aims. Moreover, I believe that when the individual clears away the confusions which inhibit the operation of this process in his organism, a new level of consciousness manifests. The concept of 'cosmic consciousness' has been the subject of a great deal of confused mysticism, but I think that it has really a very concrete meaning. This becomes clear once we grasp the idea that consciousness is simply a condition of specific configuration. Consciousness appears whenever

---

[1] See Appendix P.
[2] See Chapter Three for comments on the placenta as storehouse of old knowledge or memory.
[3] See Chapter Nine.

a living point is brought into a two-way linkage with a related periphery. This is made abundantly clear by the discovery that the uterine organism, by the provision of this condition, becomes the source of the human self and the engine of the primary state of consciousness. If we suppose that the brain is the organ of consciousness *sui generis*, then any talk of 'cosmic consciousness' is rendered difficult of comprehension. The fact is, as I have shown, that the brain becomes involved in consciousness (in the human sense) because it also provides a polarity between thalamus and cortex that is mediated by the thalamocortical circulation. But once the human organism becomes the instrument of a circulation between earth and 'sky', then a new level of consciousness is inevitable.

If this be the case, why does this 'cosmic consciousness' fail to develop in us all? Why is it that we all seem to experience the head-sky link fleetingly in childhood, and then to lose it and even the memory of it? It is, I think, because the polarity of the human body becomes confused. That is what dreams suggest. They suggest that we do not, in the deep feelings, know which way up we are. The various thrusts shown in Figure Nine tend to become confused together, and these confusions not only serve to destroy the sharp polarity of the body, but they become transferred to the feeling of the head-sky circulation. Thus one finds clear indications in dreams that we have felt the flow of energy from the head to the sky in terms not only of defecation and urination, but also in terms of legs thrust up into the sky from the head, complete also with the allied sense of the legs as umbilical arteries 'bleeding' to the sky. The reciprocal downflow of energy from 'the sky' to the head is accordingly felt in terms of the earth's backthrust, which seems to threaten the head with dangerous invasion. All the fear and guilt which we have acquired from the umbilical stage on through the postnatal stages outlined above become transferred to the feeling of the head-sky circulation.

To all of these confusions, guilts and fears there must, however, be added an important component to which so far I have made little or no reference. This is the genital component, to a discussion of which the following chapter is devoted. It is this component which, perhaps, plays the largest role in the inhibition of the head-sky link, and hence is the greatest enemy of the development of the new stage of consciousness which seems to be potential in the head-sky circulation.

N.B. Indications are found in dreams to suggest that at some time in our lives we feel that we suddenly turn upside down. The indications are that this is related to the suckling act. It is true that the neural connections to the brain are, so to say, upside down, inasmuch as the neural connections from the feet are made at the top of the brain, with those of the head related to the lower parts of the brain. I have shown that the infant feels his feet to lie up in his skull [160-d], but whether this is related to the fact noted above I do not know. Certainly part of the fantasy is due to the operation of the sense of smell. The whole brain is peculiarly related to smell, since the cerebral cortices are derived from the original smell-organs. Now, I have shown that the first breath causes the brain to feel placental [96], but with breath comes smell, so that the brain in its placental associations is related to smell. The child very early associates smell with its excretory functions, and we know that the placenta is the first excretory pot [29]. Here, then, is another link between brain and placenta. But the feet also feel to be placental [105], and they also become linked in feeling with the excretions [107], so that the brain is linked to the feet also in this roundabout way through the sense of smell. This comes out very markedly in dreams in which feet and smell are linked [110].

Chapter Thirteen

THE AWAKENING OF THE GENITAL FEELINGS

I HAVE ALREADY shown that when the earth's upthrust is felt, it feels to associate itself with the boy's erect penis and also makes an attempt at association with the girl's clitoris.[1] I am not sure of the physical basis of this association, nor do I know if this represents the first awakening of the genital feelings. I should rather think it does not. Indeed, experience suggests that the awakening of the genital feelings takes place by a succession of stages, each of which brings its ebb and flow of sexual feeling, until puberty brings in the full flood.

What is quite certain is that as the sense of sex develops, so it colors all that exists already in the feelings for, as I shall show, the awareness of sex is simply the awareness of the *division*[2] between the male and the female, which is to say the division between the nucleus and the periphery. A male is inseparable from a nucleus. A female is equally inseparable from a periphery. The male sperm is simply a nucleus from which the surround has been modified to form the propellent tail.[3] The female egg is an enlarged cellular periphery. In the higher animals these fundamental elements are repeated in the very structure of the male and female bodies. The male body is designed not only to specialize the cell-nucleus (the sperm) but also to ensure its penetration into the female body. The female body is designed to be a sort of super egg. It is not too much to say that the penis is a super sperm, the uterus being a

[1] See Chapter Ten.
[2] The very word 'sex' is alleged to derive from the latin word 'to cut'.
[3] This is a rough and ready description, and ignores the centrosome, but it is true enough for the present purpose.

super ovum. Male *means* nuclear, solid and penetrant. Female *means* peripheral, hollow and receptive.

That this is no accidental division, but one rooted in some common principle, is argued by the fact that both plants and animals have in their different ways embodied substantially the same kind of configuration. It is perfectly possible to say that the very distinction we call male and female is simply another variation of the basic pattern of the relation between the point and the sphere. The attraction of male for female, and the mating urge, is therefore to be seen in terms of the quest of the nucleus for the periphery, and *vice versa*. Perhaps it is no more than an analogy to say that the force which drives the animal and plant worlds is thus configurationally identical with the force of electricity in all its forms. But the analogy is sound—both drives represent the chase of a nucleus to secure a periphery.

Male and female together represent the universal design of all creation: alone they are biological halves, whence comes the deep sense of the importance of marriage. If we incline to think of this as newfangled, we might recall that the first chapter of Genesis contains the statement that God made man in *his own* image and likeness, and that that image was male and female. God the Creator, thus says the Bible, is male and female, which is to say Father and Mother, which is to say Nucleus and Periphery. I mention this not because it proves anything, but because it shows that there is nothing 'newfangled' about my view. It is at least as old as the book of Genesis.

Indeed, it is much older than the book of Genesis in the history of the human mind, for there is powerful evidence in both dream and myth that every human being identifies everything nuclear with a male and with Father,[1] while at the same time identifying everything peripheral with a female and with Mother. These categories in turn stem back to the nuclear sense of the fetus (the first male) and to the placenta (the first female), and to their relations by means of the umbilical cord. The failure to realize this simple but fundamental fact has resulted in the over-sexualization of dream interpretation and of psychology generally.

[1] See Chapter Four.

The Nature of the Self

If male means only nucleus and female means only periphery, why should the distinction of gender be used at all? The answer surely stares us in the face: we are ourselves, each one of us, divided beings from whom one part has been taken away. What could be more evident than that each one of us must therefore suffer from a sense of incompletion. The sense of being an incomplete organism is rooted in our very flesh. The male is the point-creature ever seeking for the sphere. The female is the sphere-creature ever seeking for the point. This division and this longing we know in our very bones. We know the longing of the point for the sphere and of the sphere for the point, because it is our most emphatic single feeling. We may repress it, pervert it, sublimate it or indulge it, but it never leaves us. All that is male takes on the feelings once associated with the fetus and its subsequent accommodations in the postnatal body. All that is female takes on the feelings once associated with the placenta and its similar postnatal accommodations. For this reason the genital organs, as their feelings awaken and their purposes become clear, take on the feelings first generated in the umbilical cord.

Marriage and, indeed, all sexual experience, are thus dominated by the original uterine feelings. The husband is felt by the wife in terms of her own fetal self. The wife is felt by the husband to be the restored placenta. The human penis is sensed by both in terms of the back and forth thrust of the blood in the umbilical cord. It is in the stress of our sexual tensions that we experience the nearest and most poignant conscious relation with our original umbilical feelings. At the root of all our intuitions of maleness lies the primal feeling of our fetal body as the nuclear occupant of the womb, and of its related power to pierce and to occupy the placenta. Conversely, at the root of all our intuitions of femaleness lies our equally primal sense of the placenta as a pierceable and occupiable hollow. The fetus and the placenta are the first male and female in the human feelings, a fact which in the myth of Adam and Eve has been given a false anthropological connotation.

Need I say that the fetus knows nothing of these male and female categories as such! All he knows is that he possesses *par excellence* the sense of being solid and nuclear, and the allied power of being able to thrust out through the umbilical arteries to penetrate the placenta. Solid and hollow are all he knows! Penetrative and penetrable are his sole categories! But it is upon this basic stock that he will after birth graft his experiences of external gender, first in terms of father and mother, and then in terms of man and woman, male and female. We may express this by saying that while the fetus as such knows nothing of sex, he intuits through his relations with the placenta the categories of feeling from which the postnatal sense of sex will develop.

There is a very direct link between the male feelings after birth and the original fetal skin feeling. I believe that the postnatal feelings of maleness are added back to this primary nuclear sense. Similarly, I believe that the postnatal female feelings are added back to the original feelings of the fetus for the ambient womb and the placenta. It is a fact that in dreams the fetal skin feeling (and indeed the fetus as a whole) is invariably represented as a male. *In this special sense there are no female fetuses: every fetus is male, not genitally, of course, but over his skin.* In general one may say that in dreams the placenta is represented as female, but it is also true that the placenta is frequently represented as a masculine woman or a feminine man, this being a reference to the fact that the placenta, though primarily female (hollow) also becomes felt in degree as male (nuclear) through the venous umbilical flow.[1]

A male is nuclear, solid, penetrating, occupying and by definition impenetrable. The female is peripheral, hollow, penetrable and occupiable. This fact the reader may ascertain for himself to be a logical categorization. The external facts argue the correctness of the definitions. But I cannot make it too clear that I have derived these categories not by means of any sort of philosophic speculation based upon the physical facts, but from the testimony of the deep feelings. We all know, deep in ourselves, at the very root and core of ourselves, that male means nuclear and that female means peripheral. I cannot make this point too clear, for I want the reader to appreciate that I am not trying to impose upon him some intellectual creation of my own. I am seeking to report to him what I know to be at the core of his own

[1] See reference to the dual feelings of the placenta in Appendix G.

self. You yourself know, with a knowledge as deep as the cosmos, that male means nuclear and that nuclear means male. You yourself know, as your first item of knowing, that female means peripheral and that peripheral means female.

Nor is this deep knowledge merely of academic interest as a museum relic of the fetal life. For wherever in the postnatal organism there arises a sense of solidity, there will tend to be aroused the sense of maleness. And wherever this sense of maleness is evoked, there also will appear the simulacrum of the fetal skin feeling and, indeed, of the fetus itself. Since I cannot make this statement too clear or emphatic, let me mention a simple but typical instance of this postnatal evocation of the fetal feelings. I have had several patients suffering from subtle forms of eye-trouble. In almost every one of these cases dreams have reported that the eyeball moving in the socket had evoked the sense of the fetal self moving in the mother's womb accompanied by deep sexual elements. That is to say, in the deep feelings, the solid sense of the eyeball moving in the hollow socket had evoked the feeling of the male in the female and, at the same time, of the fetus in the womb. This same example can be used to illustrate the converse fact, namely that wherever in the postnatal organism there arises a sense of hollowness, there will tend to be aroused the sense of femaleness, and then at once the simulacrum of the womb and the placenta will appear. Thus, in the above example, the eye-socket tends to become the womb to the fetalized eyeball. I have even known several cases where the tear-glands played the role of the placenta in this context, and the tear-ducts played the part of the umbilical cord. These examples of the genitalization or sexualization of the non-sexual organs are by no means extraordinary. Everything in the body that can play a role approximating to the nuclear, is susceptible to the male (fetal) feelings. Everything in the body that can play a role approximating to the peripheral, is susceptible to the female (placental) feelings. And when such a mock-male and a mock-female organ are in some way related (as, for instance, the head is related to the lungs by the breath[1]), then that which relates them feels to be not only

[1] See Chapter Six.

the umbilical cord but also the male organ in action. Thus it is that every back-and-forth movement in the body, whether of gas, liquid or solid, takes on eventually a coital overtone as well as an umbilical one. This is the principle behind the facts which caused Freud to state the erotogenic character of the non-genital organs.

It will be obvious that if the non-genital organs are able to accommodate the uterine patterns of feeling, then the genital organs are by their nature even more susceptible. It is a fact, to which I have already alluded, that every husband feels himself to be playing the fetal role, while every wife links her sexual role with her own deep memories of how, as a fetus, she felt about the placenta. The rhythmic feeling of penetration and counter-penetration first experienced in the umbilical cord is the stem upon which all later coital feelings are grafted. When the male seeks to penetrate the female, the biological urge is informed and inspired, modified or amplified by undertones derived from the umbilical experience. The female, thus approached, evokes from her depths no less the memories of the umbilical pulse. To the postnatal desire of the male to penetrate the female, flock by affinity of pattern the feelings originally evoked by the thrust of blood from the fetal body into the placenta. The female urge to permit sexual intrusion receives no less a flock of memories evoked from the uterine life. What is true of the coital rhythm is true no less of those pseudo-coital rhythms which arise in the postnatal organism. For instance, the neurotic twitching of a nose, the jerking of a head, and even a stammer may be simply the effect of the imposition of a pseudo-coital (and equally pseudo-umbilical) rhythm upon a non-genital organ.

The sexual feelings graft themselves back upon the original umbilical feelings or, conversely stated, the old umbilical feelings are remobilized by the sexual urge and act. Thus it is that every form of sexual relationship becomes for the feelings a latter-day version of the primal vascular interpenetration between the fetus and the placenta. The male is thus always the successor of the fetus, while the female is no less the successor to the placenta and the womb. In this context we may see that the penis is the successor to the umbilical cord which, retrospectively, can thus be regarded as a kind of two-way phallus. But so unconscious are the old umbilical elements, and so conscious and assertive are the new sexual feelings, that the New subordinates the Old and assumes it into itself.

It is for this reason that we cannot find in our ordinary conscious sense of things, nor even in our feelings without deep analysis, any awareness of the relation of our sexual polarity to the primal polarities of the umbilical cord. It takes deep probing to discover that at the root of all our intuitions of maleness lie the nuclear feelings of the fetal body lying in the womb, and that the primal sense of the womb and the placenta underlies all our adult feelings of femaleness. The two things have become so coalesced, with the later sexual feelings so predominant, that it is impossible for any human being, without benefit of scientific analysis, to discover the origins of gender in himself. Even in analysis it is not easy to convince the analysand of these primal umbilical origins, for the new feelings (of genital sex) have so far assumed the old (umbilical) feelings as to reverse the primacy of their relations, and even to hide that relation altogether. The analyst himself, unless he has some criterion to guide his enquiries, will find sexual images supplanting the original umbilical ones. The fetus is frequently represented by a man, the placenta by a woman, and the umbilical drama as an act of copulation. By accepting this symbolism at its face value the analyst will gain a deceptively simple representation of the underlying feelings. Unfortunately for precise knowledge, this spurious simplicity hides an un-recognized complexity, and this disposes the psychologist to think that my revelation of the umbilical facts is but a gratuitous compli-cation of the supposedly simple sexual facts.

The over-sexualization of dream material stems back to Freud himself, and this shows up very plainly in his bizarre concept of the primal scene and his even more bizarre (but abandoned) original theory that neuroses are due to the sexual interference with children by their parents. The theory of the primal scene held that an overwhelming emotional effect is caused in the child as a result of witnessing his parents in sexual embrace. While this assertion may contain a certain truth, it is a fact that underlying all representations of the 'primal scene' will be found the symbolic description of the fetus in umbilical 'copulation' with the placenta. We can see how naturally this fits the fact that the fetal skin feeling is universally equated with the father, and the placenta with the mother. It is because the sexual feelings and ideas have overmastered the original umbilical feelings that the uterine feelings find expression in these family sexual terms. No doubt indeed a child *would* be emotionally disturbed by witnessing parental copulation, but this would be so precisely because the scene would call up from the depths of his psyche the oldest and most intense feelings he possesses—would, in fact, temporarily and shockingly 'open up the ego' by providing a perfect externalization of its contents. Freud's abandoned theory of the sexual interference with children by their parents is of the same order as his theory of the primal scene. Everyone represents his fetal skin feeling as his father and very frequently the placenta is represented by a sister, so that the elements of incestuous guilt indeed lie in us all. The very source of the horror of incest lies in the 'incestuous' uterine events which take place between the fetus and the placenta.

The successful analysis of the deepest feelings is further complicated by the fact that consciousness and gender grow from the same primary root of feeling.[1] Since the umbilical pulse evokes the dynamic sense of both gender and consciousness, and since gender is swallowed up in sex, all the signs have pointed to the conclusion that consciousness and sex are almost if not quite identical. This difficulty may be seen reflected in the term 'libido' which Freud applied to the fundamental psychological energy. This starkly sexual term applied to the roots of consciousness caused Freud a good deal of later inconvenience, and he strove to mitigate the consequences of it. But the efforts to demonstrate that the libido is not necessarily libidinal have not solved the problem, and we can now see why. Consciousness is fundamentally the tension between a nucleus and a periphery. Gender is of precisely the same order. Both begin for us as a dynamic tension between the nuclear feelings of the fetus and the peripheral

[1] See Appendix I on the myth of Adam and Eve.

placenta, hence both are of the same order. That also is why the relation of the thalamus to the cortex is felt in sexual terms.

It is not possible to ignore the fact that since the original uterine sense of gender has been swallowed up by the sexual feelings, the origins of consciousness themselves have become sexualized. We have to face this fact if only because we shall not otherwise be able to understand the meaning of the avowedly sexual symbolism in which the fetal-placental relations are expressed in both dreams and myths. Again and again in the myths we shall find the origins of mind represented in the most flagrantly sexual forms. If we give these representations a superficial assessment we shall be led into the error of wanton sexualism which has brought a great deal of psychology into disrepute.

If we could look through the fetal end of the telescope we should be able to see how completely sexless the fetal life is, and we should be shocked to observe how its configurational experience had become subsumed by the genital feelings. But since we can only look back at the fetal life through our modern adult end of the telescope, from the standpoint of the present, the fetus inevitably appears, insofar as we can identify him at all, as knowing all about sex and living in a state of perpetual libidinousness. The only clear way to present the fetal feelings it seems to me is to state them in the frankly sexual context in which they appear in our dreams and in the myths, and at the same time to make the deliberate correction in our minds to account for this bizarre situation. If we make allowance for the postnatal sexualization of the uterine feelings, the following summary is permissible:

1. The unborn baby feels that he is overall male, and that the blood which pulses from his body into the placenta is a male sexual thrust. In accordance with this feeling the placenta is sensed as the primary female.

2. A complication arises, however, because the blood returning to the fetal body from the placenta is also felt in the same sexual terms. This gives rise to the fetal feeling that the placenta is partly male, and thus able to make him (the fetus) feel partly female.

3. The umbilical cord is thus sexualized and its pulse felt as a coital pulsation. The umbilical cord is felt as a two-way penis, the arteries being the 'fetal penis' and the vein being the 'placental penis'. The fetus and the placenta are the primary male and female, living together in a state of perpetual copulation. Owing to the partially male nature of the placenta, a definitely 'homosexual' element is present.[1]

When the primary fetal feelings[2] are amplified by the sexual component, then the fetal reactions to the placenta may be restated thus:

1. The placenta is felt to be the primary female as a result of the umbilical arterial flow, but this flow is also an excretion, whereby the placenta is felt as being a recipient of waste. The female is thus identified with an excretory pot.

2. The placenta is felt conversely in its venous pulse to be a feeder and life-giver, as also a male who can penetrate the fetus and render it female in feeling.

3. Not only is the placenta felt as a female, but as a victim able to be pierced, made hollow and occupied.

4. The placenta is felt partly as a male who is able to pierce the fetal body and make it in degree feel female, because hollow. In this sense the male role is felt by the fetus to be hateful and aggressive.

5. The fetus feels the placenta in part as a blood-sucking monster as well as a female. The female who is pierced and occupied is thus also the destroyer, the place of death and the tomb.

6. The placenta is felt not only as a female, as a recipient of waste, as a male, a feeder, a destroyer and a grave, but also as a female hollow from which the self is reborn again and again after every death—in short, the primal mother, the veritable Eve of mankind!

[1] See Appendix G.
[2] As listed in Chapter Two.

The Nature of the Self

The above tabulation offers us the rationale of various feeling-complexes which otherwise have no demonstrable principle whatsoever. I shall now attempt to state the most important of these complexes:

1. *A basic confusion between seminal emission and excretion and hence between the female and the toilet.*

Since the umbilical arterial flow is not only an excretion but also a male sexual thrust, it follows that the sexual emission of the male should evoke not only umbilical feelings, including a sense of blood, but also a sense of excretion. And since the postnatal excretions are principally associated in feeling with the anus, there is a link between anal excretions and seminal emissions. There is a powerful tendency to dismiss sexual things as 'filthy'. One is naturally inclined at first to think either that this is natural, if unfortunate, or that it is the product simply of repression and of parental fear. But the evidence dredged from the depths of the feelings suggests that the reason for the association between sex and filth is to be found in the primal feeling-link between excretion and male thrust forged in the umbilical cord. This link can bring into being a most unfortunate complex of feelings towards sex and the sexual act. The man may be disposed to regard women with contempt deriving from his unconscious sense that they are nothing but receptacles of filth. This may give rise to all manner of ambivalent and torturing reactions both to women and to the sexual act. The woman may in her turn develop a feeling of revulsion to coition because her deep feelings urge that in the course of it she becomes no more than a toilet. She will from this develop a peculiar sense of fear and hatred of the male as one who would use her in such a fashion, although naturally her conscious mind would frame quite different and plausibly logical reasons for her feelings. The attitude of such a man or woman towards pregnancy may well be imagined in one of its many variants. The child is born of excretions as a plant grows out of a manured soil! The child itself thus is a dirty and despicable thing! A thousand permutations of such feelings are possible. Moreover, since the man or woman caught in such feelings was himself once a child and, by the logic of the feelings, begotten in this 'dirty' fashion, either a very elaborate defence mechanism must be erected in the mind, or the very sense of self must be soiled and denigrated. Man is nothing but a piece of feces, the feelings would say. Against such a horror a mental barrier must be erected, lest self-depreciation tumble headlong into a condition of utter despair and even of suicidal desperation.[1]

2. *A basic confusion between male penetration and destruction.*

The thrust of umbilical arterial blood into the placenta is felt not only as a male thrust into a female, but also as a piercing of the placenta, and hence its destruction as a nucleus. This feeling is amplified by the fact that the fetus also, in turn, feels the placenta to be both an aggressive opponent and a male consort. In this way is created in the human male a postnatal link between the male sexual act and aggression. In this feeling-context the female is sensed not only as a 'hollow' but as a victim, from which may develop aggressive and even murderous attitudes towards the human female. Here is sown at least some of the seeds of those sadistic impulses which are an affront to any sense of human love.[2] From the same roots may derive at least part if not all of the female fear and dislike of the copulatory act, which is thus felt as an act of aggressive penetration calculated to destroy her. Also there may arise from this the woman's resentment of her female status, and the not-uncommon rage of the pregnant woman at being found 'hollow' and 'occupied' by a fetus. These feelings will, of course, not be accorded their true reason by the conscious mind, which will remain entirely ignorant of their source. Since both man and woman have had the same fetal experiences, both having felt to be nuclear-male to the uterus and the placenta, the original source of their feelings will be identical. The feelings themselves will have, however, received a different postnatal

---

[1] I have already indicated in Chapter Seven a link between anal excretions and birth. It is obvious that this will add itself to the above confusions by sheer affinity of feeling.

[2] These impulses are further supported and amplified by those detailed under section Three of this tabulation.

accommodation. Both will have felt *in utero* the nuclear pride of being able to pierce and to occupy the placenta. Both will have felt the fear and rage at being made hollow and 'female' by the placental counter-thrust through the umbilical vein. The normal man greatly reduces this fear because he has the genital structure with which to continue the fetal feelings of being able to penetrate. He may even use this genital power as a means of working off his fetal rage against the placental inthrust, and turn it against any luckless female who is subject to his sexual advances. One is unfortunately familiar with the fact that low types of men are prone to beat their wives. This always appears revoltingly strange to men who are by nature inclined, or by upbringing educated to regard a woman as a proper object of affection and care. But I think we may see in this unhappy male behavior a reflection of the fact that the fetus gains a sense of rage against the placenta, and feels it as an enemy which ought properly to be thrust at. These feelings seem to arise in men especially when they are drunk, so that the normal control of their emotions is in abeyance. While on this subject I would mention that I have frequently heard of women being kicked by their husbands and lovers. And although I have no direct evidence on this point, since an avowed wife-kicker has never been among my patients or subjects, I suspect that this wife-kicking is related to the fact that the feelings of the legs are deeply and prenatally related to the two umbilical arteries. Thus the act of kicking at a female (wife or lover) may stem from the fact that this is a very close approximation to the way in which the fetal self was felt to penetrate the placenta—the umbilical thrust and the kicking of the legs being closely related in the feelings.[1] The normal woman, although as a fetus she felt exactly the same as did her husband, has no reassuring genital equipment, though certain abnormal females will seek to adopt some artificial mechanism. Being constitutionally organized to be penetrated, the woman may become plagued by the primal fetal fear and rage against penetration, and thus become a great deal more susceptible than the man to this particular evocation of the uterine feelings.

[1] See Figure Six.

Placental Woman as the Vampire

3. *A basic confusion between the female and the placenta as blood-sucker, destroyer and place of death.*

The placenta is felt not only as a female but also as a destroyer, and thus as the implacable enemy not only of the fetal skin feeling but of the male. The female thus takes her place in the feelings as a monster akin to the female spider who devours the male after copulation. In the adult male this may give rise to a horror and fear of the female body as the engulfer and destroyer not only of the penis but of the whole self. The female body is felt as a place of death, and as a grave. The depths of this revulsion must be observed in order to be believed, for the ordinary person cannot conceive of the lengths to which it may drive the unfortunate man plagued by it. It sometimes takes quite explicit form, though its origins remain entirely unconscious. The man literally fears the female body, and especially the genitalia of the woman. Or it may drive him to acts of rage against the woman, and may form, conjoined perhaps with the elements of rage indicated in section Two of this tabulation, a murderous attitude towards the female. The human female may, on the other hand, develop a sadistic attitude towards the male and his sexual functions, and secretly delight in the exhaustion of the male by her coital activities. She becomes, in fact, at least in some degree, the blood-sucking vampire, and the seminal emissions of the male are for her a veiled form of the blood from the fetus, and a manner also of 'paying back' the placenta for its destruction of her own uterine maleness.

4. *The basis of the incest fear.*

The root of incestuous guilt is plainly seen in the umbilical reactions. It has already been shown that the fetus feels not merely that he thrusts out and penetrates the placenta, but that he himself is sucked down into the placenta and occupies it, being therein destroyed and renewed. When we add to this picture the contents of the present chapter, an astonishing complex of feelings emerges —a complex which is in no sense the product of my own cerebration, but which stares at us again and again not only from many a dream but also from many a myth. This complex may be described now as follows:

185

The Nature of the Self

The fetus feels not merely to penetrate the placenta as a male does a female, but actually himself to go into her and occupy her, and to be born from her as a new self.

It is easy to see how this strange feeling is composed through the superimposition of the postnatal genital feelings upon the entirely 'innocent' prenatal umbilical ones. The fetus does indeed feel, for the reasons shown earlier, that he penetrates the placenta as a hollow thing, and that in another aspect of his feelings he himself actually travels down the cord and occupies that hollow, from which in turn a restored nuclear selfhood is borne up the umbilical vein.[1] Here already is a complex of two entirely distinct fetal experiences. The sense of being able to thrust out blood and penetrate the hollow placenta is quite distinct in origin from the sense of being drawn into the placenta and occupying it. The two senses are indeed related, but they are not precisely the same. The first is that feeling which the fetus gains by being a nuclear and outthrusting entity. The second is the sense that the fetal skin feeling is itself being drawn away through the umbilical arteries. The two sets of feeling naturally coalesce.

When this complex of feelings becomes associated with the genital feelings, the result is a very complex sense that penetration into the female means entering her and becoming her baby, and being reborn. Now, therefore, since the placenta eventually becomes related in the feelings with the mother, it is easy to see how there can grow up a peculiar sense that we ourselves entered mother's body sexually and caused her to conceive us anew, and to bring us to new birth. This complex is amplified by the strange fact that the fetal skin feeling becomes identified with the father. The fetus feels to be not merely male but, in retrospect, to be its own father. Thus the entry of the male into the female, his destruction and his rebirth there, are felt in terms of the sexual entry of the father into the mother, his engulfment and destruction by her, and his reproduction as son. It is a fact, which I have seen presented symbolically again and again in dreams, that we all sense that we are somehow our own father who was taken into the mother, destroyed and reborn as ourself. Thus, in order that we may be

[1] See Chapter Two.

born, the father must be slain: here is one aspect of the root of the Oedipus Complex, concerning which I shall have more to say below.

At the risk of repetition, I want to make it clear that this umbilical-sexual-generative complex is universal. We all without exception feel that we have entered our mother sexually in the form of our own father; that in the mother we have 'slain' our father-self and have been reborn of our mother as child. Though I have seen this strange complex represented in dream after dream of modern human beings, I could hardly dare to formulate it so emphatically were I not supported on all hands by the great myths and religions. These offer the theme of constant rebirth in a form which permits the deep feelings to find an expression for what otherwise would prove an insufferable burden.

This complex of uterine and genital elements is the reason for the powerful appeal to the feelings of the Christian doctrine of the Virgin Birth. Everyone, whether boy or girl, feels that he has taken part (as father) in the act which destroyed father and begat him (the child) as son. This is the torturing complex of feeling which, when superheated by the genital feelings, grasps at the doctrine of the Virgin Birth as a symbolic means of catharsis. All Christian dogma, without exception, can be shown to be of this order. Theology as represented by the Christian dogmas is not direct knowledge of God, but is the image of God (the universal design) seen through a haze of uterine feelings. This can be demonstrated, for instance, of such things as the dogma that the Father and the Son are one. They indubitably are, for the nuclear sense, no matter how much scattered, is always unitary, even as the peripheral sense is always multiple. The fetus actually feels that he is both father and son, and that in the placenta (the mother) these two are separated, being reunited again upon the fetal skin.

5.   *The source of the so-called Oedipus Complex.*

The constant cycle of interpenetration between the fetus and the placenta is undoubtedly the root of that complex of feeling which Freud termed the Oedipus Complex. According to the Freudian concept, every boy harbors a desire to possess his mother, and a related death-wish against his father, while at the same time fearing death or castration at his father's hands. This peculiar complex of desire and fear we inherit, according to Freud, from remote ancestors who actually lived through such a struggle and, it is presumed, imprinted its elements deep in the human 'unconscious'. This fantastic Freudian approximation is brought down to concrete fact as soon as we see that the complex of feeling was inherited from no historically distant ancestor, but from that immediate 'ancestor' who was our own fetal self, who actually *did* live through this struggle. This 'fetal ancestor' (regardless of his genital anatomy) was felt as the primal male. He was both father and son, and his struggle against himself was centered in his relations with that uterine 'female', the placenta. This 'fetal ancestor' felt that every time he thrust into this uterine female the 'father' aspect of his feelings died. In this way the sexual act is directly related to the death of father. Moreover, with every thrust made into this uterine 'female', the fetal male felt a backthrust from the placenta through the umbilical vein—a thrust which made him in degree less male. The so-called Oedipus Complex in the postnatal feelings is but a pale simulacrum of this uterine drama. It is less true that the boy 'desires' to possess his mother than that he has *already* in the uterine feelings done so over and over again. It is not so much that he harbors a 'death-wish' against his father as that he already *in utero* learned to relate the 'death of the father' with the thrust into the female. As to his fear that his father may castrate him, each one of us before birth *knew* that with every thrust we made into the 'female placenta' we received back from it (in its male aspect) a counterthrust through the umbilical vein that made us seem relatively emasculate.

It is only after birth, when the genital component is added to the uterine feelings, that this prenatal drama takes on a sexual character. In the womb, naturally, the fetus knows nothing of father and mother as external objects, though in degree he may intuit the existence of father as a result of parental copulation during the period of his uterine life. All the fetus knows is 'solid' and 'hollow'. He knows that the mysterious 'partner' with whom he shares the womb is in turn both of these—both solid and hollow, pierceable and piercing. He knows that when he pierces the placenta in its hollow aspect, it immediately (or concurrently) thrusts back and pierces him. After birth this experience becomes gradually metamorphosed into the following complex: 'Every time I thrust into mother, father makes me less male'. To 'make less male' is, of course, in postnatal terms, to castrate. Hence arises the so-called Oedipus Complex. The boy may never get within a million miles of *thinking* it, but he cannot help *feeling* it, for the associations are ready made. We are dealing not with conscious associations but with unconscious associations made according to the logic of the feelings.

While I would not like to say that the creation (or even the stimulation) of the Oedipus Complex depends upon parental copulation during the gestation of the child, I am quite convinced, from the evidence before me, that the fetus is powerfully influenced by it. When a pregnant woman lies with a man, her child knows a great deal about it. I have discussed elsewhere the possible link between the mother's feelings and her unborn child's,[1] and will repeat here only that the fetus senses the pressure upon him through the abdomen, and links that pressure with the presence of the placenta. No doubt copulatory pressure tends to compress the placenta and so to drive extra blood into the fetal navel through the umbilical vein. I do not know in just what degree this is the cause for the appearance of a greater Oedipus Complex in some than in others, but I know that the fetus suffers 'configurationally' by parental copulation.

6. *A basic confusion between eating and the sense of rebirth.*

We have seen that the retroaction of the postnatal sense of sex upon the fetal feelings creates the strange complex that the self enters the placenta as father enters mother, and is reborn from that organ as son. This entry is felt as a sexual thrust, but it is also felt in terms of the actual entry of the self into the mother for rebirth—a rebirth which takes place through the return of the blood from the placenta into the fetal body. The self senses in this context to be reborn through its own navel into the fetal

[1] See second part of Chapter Three.

body. But since this ingoing blood is also felt as an eating, there arises the strange complex of feeling that we are reborn in the act of eating. We are reborn, so to speak, straight out of mother (placenta) into our own mouths (navel). To make this odd complex of primary feelings clear is not easy, so that I propose to try to illustrate it by examples from myth and rite. The Greek Kronos was said to devour his own children as soon as they were born, and this I believe to be an effort to externalize our own fetal experience. In the same light I see the mystical rite of the eating of the body of God or of the Son, whether in its Christian form or some pre-Christian context.

*   *   *

The so-called sexualization of the non-genital organs, to which Freud called attention, may now be very simply understood. The original umbilical pattern becomes caught up after birth into the sexual feelings, so that wherever the umbilical pattern migrates, there also migrate or are evoked absolutely gratuitous sexual elements. Freud stated that every organ of the body possesses a latent erotogenic significance in addition to its ordinary functional role. He further asserted that a great deal of illness can on this theory be traced to the fact that non-genital organs are behaving partially as if they were genitalia. At the time that this idea was propounded it inevitably evoked either scornful laughter or shocked accusations of wanton sexuality. We need hardly wonder at this, since the idea as propounded seems utterly without roots in any cause. Why should the heart or the lungs, the nose or the foot be inclined to behave like a genital organ? On the face of it, the statement is preposterous.

But as soon as the matter is restated in the terms of the present book, the claim is not so outrageous even on the surface. It may be badly put, but it is no worse than many a first approximation. The truth is that as the male and female feelings develop in the human being, they are so strong as to color every feeling with which they have an associative link. And with what feeling have they not such a link, since all feelings derive from the basic feeling of a nuclear body lying with a twin, whom he is constantly piercing with blood and who is in return as constantly piercing him. *The uterine pattern is essentially the same in configuration as the sexual pattern.* And since the non-genital organs of the postnatal body accommodate the uterine feelings, they also by definition are compelled to accommodate the sexual feelings. It is not really true that the bodily organs are trying to act as genitalia, but rather that they are trying to act like fetus and placenta in order to keep the cosmic pattern alive in the feelings, since it was between the fetus and the placenta that the pattern was first sensed. Because the sense of these relations has become genitalized, the organs which assume it also have become genitalized.

*   *   *

I have said above that the postnatal feelings of sex overwhelm the older umbilical feelings and, indeed, assume them. Therefore, wherever in the postnatal body the umbilical feelings appear, there also appear the sexual feelings. I shall now attempt to give instances of this confusion.

I have already shown how at birth the head becomes fetalized, while the lungs play the placental role, with the breath assuming the umbilical feelings. This must now be amplified by the contents of this chapter. Through the retroactive influences of sexual feeling, the head is felt to be male, the lungs female, and the breathing cycle is felt to be copulatory. The head feels to penetrate the lungs in a sexual sense, and to beget there the sense of the self, which is then 'reborn' in the upward breath. Since, as I have shown, the fetus feels not merely to penetrate the placenta, but actually to enter it as father and to be reborn from it as son, this is now inevitably imposed upon the breathing. There is a distinct sense in the early breathing that thereby the head is the father who is engulfed in the mother, destroyed and restored again as son, this whole process taking place with every complete cycle of the breath. This peculiar feeling-association is the source of a number of subtle respiratory difficulties and is, in my experience, very much involved in many cases of asthma.

The Nature of the Self

When through the act of sucking the infant feels to draw its head into its stomach, the same sexual feelings are awakened. The stomach is felt as female and the head, as formerly, is felt as male. The heart also, through its involvement with the sense of the head-in-the-stomach, becomes felt as male. The legs of the child feel to be male organs thrusting into the maternal body (or surrogate) as into a female. Through this thrust of the legs the child seems not only to thrust into the female (mother) but to enter her body. The fantasy-child thus begotten is felt to be reborn in the act of suckling. The relation of the legs to sexual action is well known, and it can be seen in such odd phenomena as the sexual fetishism associated with shoes and in the old phrase 'to tread' as a euphemism for the male act. The retroactive action of the sexual feelings thus converts the umbilical feelings in stomach, legs and mouth into a sexual drama. This does not mean, as I see it, that the infant feels the sucking and kicking experiences in sexual terms. What it means is that the feeling-imprint left by these experiences is colored by the later dawning of the sexual feelings. If we see this clearly, it will be much easier to see how the child's feelings may seem to 'remember' that in the act of sucking and kicking it became father, who thrust into and entered mother through the legs, and was reborn of her through the sucking act.

The next stage of development is no less sexualized retroactively. The fecal and urinary excretions, which take over the umbilical arterial feelings from the legs, in their turn become felt as male emissions. The earth is felt as the female, and the excretions are felt to penetrate her and to cause her to give birth. The male self (as father) is felt to descend into this earth-mother, and there to beget himself as son, who is then reborn from the earth as the new child. This feeling, as I have suggested earlier, is the root of that strange Greek concept that Ge was a mother who 'gave birth upwards'. It is interesting to note, in passing, that there was a rite of 'smiting the earth' in ancient Greek religion, which had the intent to bring up the underground folk. My discoveries suggest that this rite was a way of 'playing out' the feeling experienced when we as infants 'smote the earth' with our umbilically-amplified sense of excretion, and evoked a responding back-thrust.

Sexualization of Earth's Upthrust

This response from the earth is felt in terms of the original experience of the umbilical venous inflow. This inflow was felt not merely as a rebirth, but also as a thrust, the placenta having reversed its polarity from hollow to nuclear. Upon this relatively 'innocent' complex the sexual feelings impose a most lurid retroactive coloring. For now everything nuclear is made male, and everything male is identified with father. Conversely, everything peripheral is now made female, and everything female is identified with mother. Thus it is that the upthrust from the earth is felt to be a thrust from father's penis. This is perfect association-logic for the feelings, since the umbilical venous inflow = male thrust = father's sexual thrust. The identification of the earth with the placenta amplifies this odd equation to read: Earth's upthrust = placental thrust = father's sexual thrust.

Now, it is a fact of the most overwhelming importance that the retroaction of the sexual feelings actually leaves the infant with the impression that father has tried to thrust his penis into the anus or vagina or both. Nothing in the whole dictionary of Freudian ideas has seemed more forced and starkly revolting than that a child at some time in its life fears rape (anal or vaginal) by its own father. The imputation of such ideas to little children has seemed the zenith of overheated, even bestial sexuality. Yet the fact is that these feelings are constantly observable in the deep feelings of all manner of human beings. The upthrust from the earth, as it seeks to enter the anus or the vagina of the child, is in this odd roundabout fashion associated with the father's phallic thrust. And this actually can appear in the Freudian terms aforementioned.

Since the earth's upthrust feels to be taken both up the penis and up the spine, these organs of the body feel to be agents of father's phallic thrust. The association-logic of the feelings is not hard to analyze. The upthrust from the earth is felt as father's phallic thrust. The penis and the spine are felt to be its products. Therefore they are not only agents of father's penis; they *are* father's penis. It is for this reason, I believe, that the boy suffers so much struggle in his feelings with his father. *His penis is not his own—it is father's*. This odd feeling greatly amplifies the latent

Oedipal feelings already noted earlier in this chapter. It explains also, I think, why the girl feels that father is responsible for the failure of her clitoris to develop into an organ capable of assuming his phallic earth-thrust. If father is responsible for the girl's sense of phallic failure, it is the same thing to the feelings as if father had cut her penis off.

When the upthrust from the earth enters the infant body, it is felt as father entering mother. The infant trunk is well primed to feel to be mother, as I have shown. And now the little boy or girl can feel that father has entered mother's vagina in the form of his or her small anus, giving rise there to a new gastrointestinal self. This feeling reanimates the older gastrointestinal feelings of being one's own fetal self in one's own gut, but now instead of the mouth playing the role of 'vagina' to the nipple, it is the anus that plays this role to the earth's upthrust. The little girl may acquire similar feelings in respect to her vagina. Here lies the seed of endless and dangerous fantasies which could not possibly be catalogued *a priori*, but which are instantly recognizable *a posteriori*.

Even the *proper* accommodation of the earth's upthrust gives rise to similar peculiar feelings. The upthrust seems to enter the trunk and to create the sense of the skeleton. The skeleton thus is felt as a distorted and peculiar child created in the trunk (as mother) by the earth's upthrust (as father). It must be remembered, however, that at all times the father is not felt merely as a static individual who penetrates mother and begets a child. He is felt instead as a dynamic father-son who is always entering the mother as father and being reborn of her as son. Thus it is that the upthrust from the earth is felt both as father's phallic thrust and also as the 'upward birth' of the son from the earth. And it is thus this son who arises from the earth and seeks to enter the infant anus or vagina. It is this son who *becomes* the penis. It is this son who enters the body and *becomes* the skeleton.

Such statements must seem not only fantastic, but also impossibly complex. But if the reader will see that they are due to the unchecked process of feeling-logic at work in us all, and if he will take the little trouble required to understand the simple principle

194

of that feeling-logic, then these strange assertions will seem to him neither complex to understand nor, when understood, too ridiculous to accept. They are merely the interweaving of a complex of feeling governed by a simple original and persistently dominant configuration. This configuration is that of a point within a sphere, the two being linked together by a two-way flow. This pattern is derived from the cosmos in all simple purity. It is overlaid and complicated by the elements indicated in Chapter Two. It is imposed again and again upon level after level of organic functioning. But always the same simple set of elements appears. Each set of elements attracts to itself that which is its configurational analogue. The result is the setting up of a number of complexes which have never been directed by the 'brain consciousness' which we identify with ourselves.

The simplicity of the univeral design as translated into human sexual terms by our deep feelings, is so naive as to be hardly credible. These feelings know only one process, and it is the process whereby father enters mother and begets a child. That is how the deep feelings interpret the cosmic fact that the nuclear energy is forever seeking a sheath and a place of renewal. Therefore when the feelings sense the upthrust of the earth, and sense that this thrust enters the trunk and becomes associated with the skeleton, they interpret this in terms of father and mother. The earth-thrust *is* the father, and the child's trunk *is* the mother, and the skeleton *is* the child which ultimately is born through the neck as skull. It is for this reason that little children are so aware of their father and mother and the mysterious thing they do together. The child wants to know what gets into what and how. The depths of this feeling can be felt in the utterances of children. One small boy, having been told he came from inside his mother, asked her where he was before that. 'You were with God', she replied, whereupon like a flash came the answer: 'Why did I have to get into you, then? Wasn't I all right with God?' This childlike concern with the thing that 'gets inside' and causes birth is by no means childish. This is the ultimate concern of the highest philosophy. It is the ultimate concern of religion. How and why did the Son, who is one with the Father, hence Father, get into the Virgin and become man and then become restored again to the Father. The Christians did not initiate this supreme concern of the grown-up child called man. The Greeks before them were much concerned with how the sky-god Zeus entered the temple of Semele at Thebes, and there begat Dionysos in the flames of his heavenly fire, but snatched him from the burning and restored him to himself by sewing him up in his divine thigh.

The penis of the boy, then, is the father's phallic upthrust in terms of the boy's own flesh and blood. But yet it is not father so much as the boy's own self reborn from the earth. The penis is 'the little man'. It is the little boy himself. The clitoris of the girl is the 'fig tree that was withered': it is the organ that tried to be the father's penis and the little self, but which the 'naughty father' withered. The spine of the child, then, is also the father's phallic upthrust in terms of the child's own bone. The skeleton is the self reborn in the trunk-as-mother.

The next step in the development of the feelings receives also in its turn the retroactive overflow of sexual feelings. The 'new head' of the infant feels to be the son who is born out of the mother-trunk through the shoulders as a result of penetration by the father. The head is felt as the 'new fetal self', and as such it feels to be male, and as such it feels to be father. The head and the trunk are related as father to mother, as male to female. And the phallic link is the neck. The neck has assumed the umbilical feelings from the very first moments of birth. It became the umbilical surrogate at the time of the first breath.[1] The first sucking and belching cemented this feeling.[2] Now, as the new sense of the head develops, these old feelings are remobilized, reanimated and amplified by new elements. For between head and trunk there is a flow not only of breath, of food and drink, but also of blood running between the heart and the brain. There is moreover the delicate back-and-forth flow of the nervous energy which unites the whole body and makes it one. The neck takes on the umbilical feelings, and because these have become colored with the ubiquitous sexual feelings, it feels to be a phallic instrument. The

[1] See Chapter Six.
[2] See Chapter Seven.

196

neck feels to be a two-way penis joining mother and father. The feelings of the neck are highly sexualized.

Suddenly, as I have shown already, the skull seems to become the mother's womb. The infant feels that his whole trunk is of a sudden sucked up and incarcerated in the skull.[1] There in this skull-womb the thalamus feels to be the fetus, the cortex the placenta and the thalamocortical circulation feels to be the umbilical flow. This also becomes sexualized. As the fetus once felt to be the nucleus, and became eventually associated with maleness, and specifically with the father, so now the thalamus feels to be not only fetal and male, but father also. And as the placenta was felt as periphery, but became identified in feeling with femaleness and with mother, so the cortex now becomes mother. And as the two-way umbilical flow became associated with the copulatory activity between father and mother, so now the thalamocortical circulation. The very process of thought, through this strange feeling-association, becomes a refined copulatory process. We may hardly wonder that the Bible uses the phrase 'to know' a woman as a description of copulation. Knowing and copulation, in this extreme basic configurational sense, are identical. *What is more, they are felt as such. No straining of philosophical niceties brings me to this conclusion: it is in the record of the feelings of us all.*

Something else I must say at this point: the skull feels to be mother's womb and the brain feels to be the uterine organism— fetus, placenta and cord. This maternal womb is felt to have been made pregnant through the upthrust of the neck. The cervical stem is felt as a penis that is thrust by the trunk up into the skull to cause it to become pregnant with the brain. I can only suppose that this strange evolution of feeling must be created not only by the flow of blood up into the skull and back, but also by the nervous flow. On this point I speak with no certainty. I offer it as the outcome of my own cogitations on the subject. What I do know for certain is that there is a very close link in the feelings between the penis and the cervical stem. These two are frequently confused. We need hardly be surprised at this, since both the sense

[1] See Chapter Eleven.

197

of the erect penis and the sense of the erect spine are closely related to the upthrust from the earth.[1] Thus the penis, which can thrust up into a woman and beget a child in her womb, feels to be identified with the neck, which also has the power to thrust up (blood and neural energy?) into the female-feeling skull and 'beget' there a child—the brain. The whole point to be remembered here is the supreme dominance of the universal pattern. The penis and the sperm represent the point, the womb and the ovum the sphere, and their relationship creates an unfoldment of a new fetal being. Through the neck, in a configurationally similar manner, flow up the neural impulses which excite the thalamus and remind it of its original fetal feelings.[2] The thalamus unfolds energy to the cortex and receives back a counter-flow, and in this two-way flow a new emergence takes place, an emergence that is not physical at all in any direct sense, but which causes physical reactions and makes man the creative being on this planet. Every thrust of neuromuscular energy is felt to be a kind of birth.

At this point I should perhaps mention strong indications which I have seen concerning the differences of feeling aroused by the head of a man as contrasted with the head of a woman. Though both feel to be the mother's womb with the fetal self inside, yet there is a subtle difference in feeling which I believe is the cause of the basic mental difference between man and woman. I have every reason to interpret certain analytic findings in the following manner. The human head, emotionally speaking, is a reflection in reverse of the trunk. The woman feels to have a peripheral trunk. She contains in her trunk the hollow womb and the penetrable passage that leads to it. She feels that her nuclear male organ started to develop but shriveled away. But in her head she feels that her thalamus replaces the missing male organs.[3] I have again and again seen symbolic statements in dreams and associations which, so interpreted, fit the total context of their appearance like a glove upon a hand. The thalamus in the brain of the woman

[1] See Chapter Ten, also Figure Twentytwo.
[2] See Chapter One.
[3] Dreams reveal a strong feeling-association between the two thalamic bodies and the two testicles.

feels not only to be the fetal self and the father, but it feels to be the compensation for the loss of the male organs.

The man, on the other hand, feels that his thalamus is partly 'robbed' by his genital activity. Hence his thalamic feelings are not so strong as those in the woman. On the other hand, his cortical functions are stronger. Man has the smaller buttocks and the undeveloped mammary glands, but the slightly larger average brain cortices. It is a fact that there is a feeling both in man and woman that the two hemispheres of the brain are the analogue of the buttocks, the cheeks, and the breasts. Though the man's cerebral cortices may not, save on the average, be bigger than the woman's, yet I have seen plain indications which would suggest that the man feels his more emphatic cerebral cortices as the compensatory development for his lack of the larger female buttocks and the larger breasts.

If one contemplates the bilateral symmetry of the human being, which is found, indeed, in all save the lowliest animals, one is struck by the fact that it represents a three-dimensional extension of the pattern of the point in the sphere. The point is drawn out into a line marking the division between the two halves of the body. The sphere is represented by the swelling bilateral contours as they arise equally around the mid-line. If the body is looked at in these simple terms, it will be observed that all the nuclear organs tend to lie close to the line. In this way we may note how the two eyes, the two thalami, and the two testicles lie on the midline.

This may appear significant if we observe that the female trunk is distinguished from the male trunk by its relatively large peripheral development. The female tends to have a swelling bosom where the male has only their rudiments. The female bottom is larger than the male. On the other hand, the nuclear elements of the male trunk, principally the testicles, are more developed. At the head this tends to be reversed, though the actual physical differences are relatively small. My analyses show me that both men and women relate these different organs in their feelings. Evidence is strong that we all link the breasts, the buttocks and the cheeks of the face in the feelings, and that we also confuse them in degree with the cerebral cortices. It is as if some subtle chemistry is involved in all these protuberances which endows them with a common feeling. In the same way the two eyes, the two kidneys and the two testicles are linked in the feelings, and with them also the two thalami. There is little doubt in my mind that the woman feels the lack of testicles to be replaced less by her ovaries than by her thalami. I have tried to show these distinctions in the rough sketches in Figure Ten, and I hope it will not convey

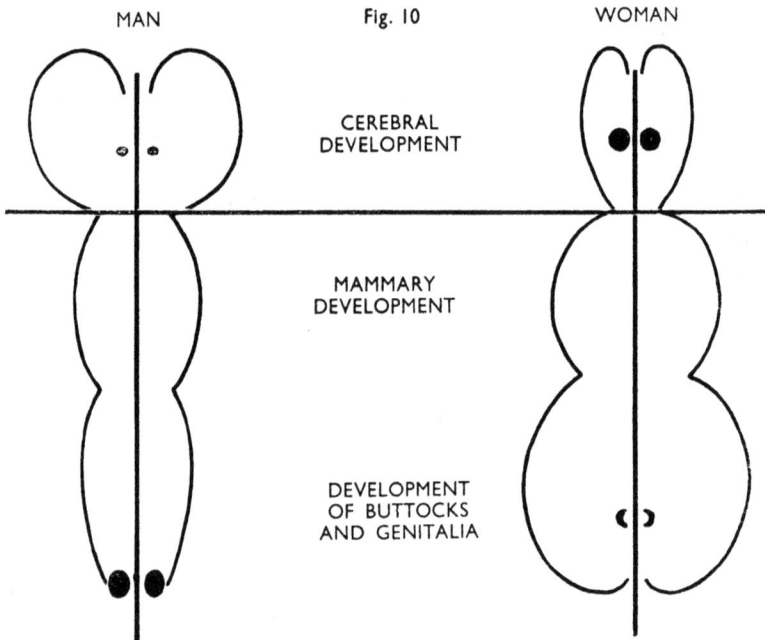

MAN   Fig. 10   WOMAN

CEREBRAL
DEVELOPMENT

MAMMARY
DEVELOPMENT

DEVELOPMENT
OF BUTTOCKS
AND GENITALIA

the idea that I suppose the female thalami to be physically larger than the male. The feelings are partly physical and partly psychological, and that is what the sketches attempt to suggest. Certain it is that the distinctions between the male and female ways of thought correspond fairly well to these configurational differences. It is commonly believed that the woman is more intuitive in her thinking. She is more to the *point*, without the use of *reason*. The man is often full of reason without ever getting to the point in the way that a woman does. I think this can be explained simply in the above terms: the woman has the more *nuclear*, the more thalamic, which is to say the more male brain. The man has the more peripheral, the more cortical, which is to say the more female brain.

The more male-feeling nature of the woman's head is not by any means always expressed in purely mental terms, but in subtle physical ways. One of these is in the use of the tongue. Although I do not wish to subscribe to the popular legend of the 'talking woman', I have had occasion to observe in women's dreams a very definite association between the tongue and the penis. The little member active in the mouth obviously makes a possible mock-penis even to the conscious mind, but in the feelings this is no mere pun, but an actual serious identity. It makes one look at the popular concepts of the 'strong, silent man' and the 'talkative woman' with new eyes, for there is no doubt at all in my mind that the woman often expresses her male thrusting and penetrating cephalic qualities with her tongue. This is, I may add, to my mind a false accommodation, since the real accommodation ought to be thalamic, and expressed in greater mental penetration and intuition. While on this subject, I should perhaps add that I have seen definite signs of even more grotesque, and quite painful, efforts of women to create a 'head penis'. I have helped cases of women with boils or other growths or swellings on noses and chins, and have found that their contemporary dreams contained strong indications that their symptoms were the psychosomatic outcome of trying 'to grow a penis' or, at any rate, to enlarge a convenient protuberance for the same (need I add unconscious!) end.

All that I have said above is supported to the hilt by what appears in dreams and associations concerning the link between the head and the sky. This also is felt not only in umbilical terms, but in the plainest sexual terms. The two-way flow between the head and the sky is felt not simply as a meta-umbilical act, but as a meta-sexual act. The polarity felt between the head and the sky, as between the trunk and the earth, and by extension between earth and sky, is felt definitely in sexual terms.

The Nature of the Self

Anyone who doubts this could with profit examine some of the primitive myths with an open mind, and some of the ancient legends also. The sky is Father and the earth is Mother. The falling rain or the falling lightning-bolt is a love-act. Out of this 'cosmic copulation' a child is felt to be born, as Dionysos was born out of Semele by the lightning-bolt of Zeus. This is what the human feelings have imposed upon the configurational facts of earth and sky.

Which, then, is male and which is female? Is the earth male or is the sky? It depends upon the polarity of the organs involved. When the trunk was felt to thrust by excretion into the earth, then the trunk was fetal and paternal, the earth being placental and maternal. But when the earth replied with a backthrust, then the trunk became maternal (female) and the earth paternal (male). So now it is with the sky. The man's head, since it feels to be more female than the woman's, feels the sky as male. The woman's head, being more male in feeling, senses the sky as female. *This is implied very powerfully by the fact that the deep feelings of men represent the head-sky link in terms of one upthrust and two downthrusts, while the deep feelings of women reveal the reverse.*[1]

In this the configurational domination of the umbilical pattern is seen. The fetus is the nuclear one who eventually assumes the male feelings, and it is he who makes two thrusts out and receives back a single thrust. So it is with the head of the normal woman, which seems to make two upthrusts to the sky and to receive back one. Conversely, the placenta is the peripheral one which becomes ultimately associated with female feelings, and the placenta receives two inthrusts and returns a single thrust. The man's head feels to do precisely the same *vis-à-vis* the sky.

*   *   *

The reader will see, I feel sure, that this sexualization of the non-genital organs, including the brain and its subtle relation with 'the sky', throws a great light upon an odd phrase that most people have uncomprehendingly heard, namely the phrase

[1] See Figure Twentynine.

'inner marriage'. This has been spoken of in the sonorous tones of mystery and superstition, and its real nature thus completely hidden. The character of this 'inner marriage' can now be grasped without undue subjectivism. It is the product of the fact that the cosmic pattern of nucleus and periphery, which is at work in our genital feelings and in our non-genital feelings alike, is also the nature of our consciousness. The constant interplay in us of these feelings on a non-genital level is therefore akin to a marriage, that is to say, to the interaction in us of male (nuclear) and female (peripheral) feelings.

Even the nature of our thinking processes has this 'marital' undertone. A thought, as I have shown, is the interaction between two concepts, each of which may be regarded as a cluster or integration of feelings and memories identified by that label we call a word.[1] Each concept has a core drawn from our own nuclear sense, a core of meaning—a veritable point which endows the cluster with an identity. The interaction between two concepts by means of the verb, causes an interchange of these feeling-units and the production of a new pattern. For this reason I have made an analogy between the process of thinking and the processes of chemical action, which consists of the interchange of electrons between atoms to form the molecule, but here I must now add that the conceptual processes are *configurationally* akin to those which take place in the interaction of sperm and egg. The very act of thought is a meta-sexual act.

To this sexualization of thinking must be added the fact that the relation of the head to the 'sky' is also sexualized. Therefore the ultimate step in human development is confused by all the elements which are at work in the deepest human feelings of sex and its pervading element of incest. As soon as the child senses the 'head-sky' relation, all the primary fears of incest swarm up to block it. How dare the presumptuous individual approach the sense of union with God if that union is already predestined in the feelings to be regarded in terms of marriage! It is at that point, I feel sure, that there begins to dawn the sense of 'original sin'

---

[1] This has profound significance for the understanding of dreams and their symbolism—see Appendix H.

as something which stands between man and his Source. The 'original sin' is that evoked in the umbilical cord, namely that we entered our mother as father and were born of her as self. In a word, original sin means incest, and our sense of it began in the womb.[1]

---

[1] See Appendix I.

Chapter Fourteen

PICTORIAL RECAPITULATION

In ORDER TO recapitulate without merely repeating, I propose to sum up the foregoing material by means of illustrations. The idea is that such a pictorial representation may enable a view of the whole process to be acquired, a view which otherwise tends to be obscured by the number of words required to describe it. It is not intended that this pictorial representation should add anything new to what has gone before, but that it should serve to make plain subtle processes which are extremely difficult to describe. It is hoped that the reader may also use this chapter as a rough index to the book, and to that end page-references have been given in brackets throughout the descriptive matter used here. In each instance the illustrations have been placed upon the righthand page, with the descriptive matter facing upon the left side. It is hoped that the reader may be persuaded to turn back again and again to the pages thus referenced and in this way link the details given in the body of the book to this pictorial summary. Only in this way can he gradually build up a fair idea of what is being described. This may sound rather a formidable undertaking, and it cannot be pretended that the meaning of this work can be grasped in a single straight reading. While every effort has been made to be simple and clear, even sometimes at the expense of a fully detailed account of the more complex matters, it cannot be denied that the material here offered requires study. Everything has been done to make such study as easy as possible, but there is no doubt that the work requires more than one reading to knit up the total picture in the mind.

It will be understood that these drawings represent an effort to achieve the next-to-impossible task of making pictures of things that have no spatial existence at all. Thus, for instance, the artist has been called upon to depict what goes on in the feelings when the baby first begins to suckle, at which time it feels that it sucks blood from the breast and passes blood back again through the eyes. The simple fact is that the baby does not do anything of the kind. He suckles milk and he passes out nothing through his eyes. The whole thing *exists* nowhere at all, using the word in its strict sense. The picture is wholly in the feelings—and how does one draw a feeling! The reader's active sympathy is certainly necessary in any effort to understand the present chapter. Perhaps this sympathy may be stimulated by the realization that we all are familiar with efforts to pictorialize the Unconscious, even though we have remained unaware of the nature of these efforts for the reason that they are presented as being something totally different. One of the best known of such representations is the Christian crucifix. This is represented as a sacred memorial of the divine being who came to save the world. In actual fact, as we can at once see when we awaken to the nature of the deep feelings, the crucifix represents an effort to hold before the eyes a memory of the strange feeling-events which constitute the very basis of the self. I do not wish to deny that it is a very remarkable achievement. Furthermore, I would not wish to deny that it does indeed represent something truly cosmic, for it represents the feeling-structure by means of which we are linked back to the original uterine pattern in which we all first received the imprint of the creative design, which we may certainly think of as divine in the widest sense of the term. It is a composite form in which many elements of the feelings are unified. I will mention but a single instance of the complex way in which the crucifix pictorializes the journey of the affect through the body. The wound in the side represents the navel blood, while the wounds in hands and feet represent the transfer of the umbilical feelings to those members. If we incline to the view that true art must at root concern itself with these deeper representations, then certainly the crucifix is one of the highest artistic achievements. It represents the human body caught in the throes of the configurational forces which distinguish the human from the ordinary animal body. The main architecture of the Christian church edifice is of the same order, except that it enables the individual to move through the building as once in his feelings his nuclear sense of self moved through the organs of his own body.[1]

Anyone who grasps this fact concerning the real nature of the Christian symbolisms referred to, will automatically absolve the following illustrations of being newfangled absurdities. They certainly are absurd inasmuch as they attempt the pictorial representation of the unpicturable. It is just as impossible to draw a feeling as it is to dig up a square root or prune a family tree. Yet the fact is that we all do unconsciously attempt to represent these strange things in our own bodies, especially when the feelings involved are for various reasons undeveloped or over-emphatic. Thus, for instance, a person whose feelings still have in them extremely strong memories of the sense of sucking blood and giving it out through the eyes may, as a result of this, try to 'play out' these fully unconscious feelings either in the mouth or the eyes or both. A good deal of eye trouble is demonstrable as being due to an unconscious need to carry on the infantile sense of the eyes as umbilical arteries. A good deal of subtle digestive trouble and food-faddishness is often found in people whose dreams show the mouth as a postnatal navel taking in blood. For this reason the illustrations given here are not merely useful as aids to the conscious understanding of the feelings, but also have a certain evocative power over the feelings, and an allied cathartic power also. For although I have not made any therapeutic claims for my work, it is a fact that a basic therapy inheres in it—a fact to which the medical profession gives unwitting testimony when it employs the 'sign of the umbilical cord' (and the Caduceus of Mercury is nothing else!) as its symbol. For the pattern generated in the umbilical beat is the structure of the self, and all therapy in the final analysis rests back upon the integration of the self.

[1] See Appendix J.

The Nature of the Self

ONE UNIVERSAL DESIGN governs all creation from atom to mind—that is the foundation upon which this book stands, and the idea represented pictorially by Figure Eleven. By its very nature the idea is impossible to illustrate convincingly, since it calls for the representation both of what is in space-time and what is not. The artist has sought to represent the distinction between these two categories by covering the Universal Design with a stipple that partly hides it from view, as on a stage a net curtain may divide the living actors and their drama from the ghostly forces behind the action. One may think of the Universal Design as a kind of invisible sun which 'shines upon the just and the unjust' in space-time. The Universal Design is in essence very simple. It consists of a focal and paternal nuclear quality linked by a constant back-and-forth flow with a peripheral and maternal quality. This simple pattern can be seen in various degrees of complexity in the created world. It is clearly seen in the basic pattern of the material world, namely the atom with its nucleus and its electronic sheaths. It lies at the root of all living forms, namely the unicell with its nucleus and its cytoplasmic surround. It underpins the very existence of the unicell in the form of the solar system, with its fiery nuclear sun and peripheral planets. For without that narrow temperature range which we call the state of warmth, which is produced simply by the relation of the earth to the sun, there could be no living cell. The very structure of space-time is permeated with it, since the essence of time is the point, and the essence of space is the expansive quality associated with every surround. All this might be deduced from a survey of the known facts of nature as revealed to our generation by modern science. But this book carries the concept into practical use by revealing it as the basis of mind. The human mind is the response of the human organism to the all-pervading influence which has guided the integration of all material forms. This response begins specifically in the uterine life, and is continued in the postnatal organs. The following pages will seek to show in pictorial form how the general creative process represented in Figure Eleven specifically acts to create the human self.

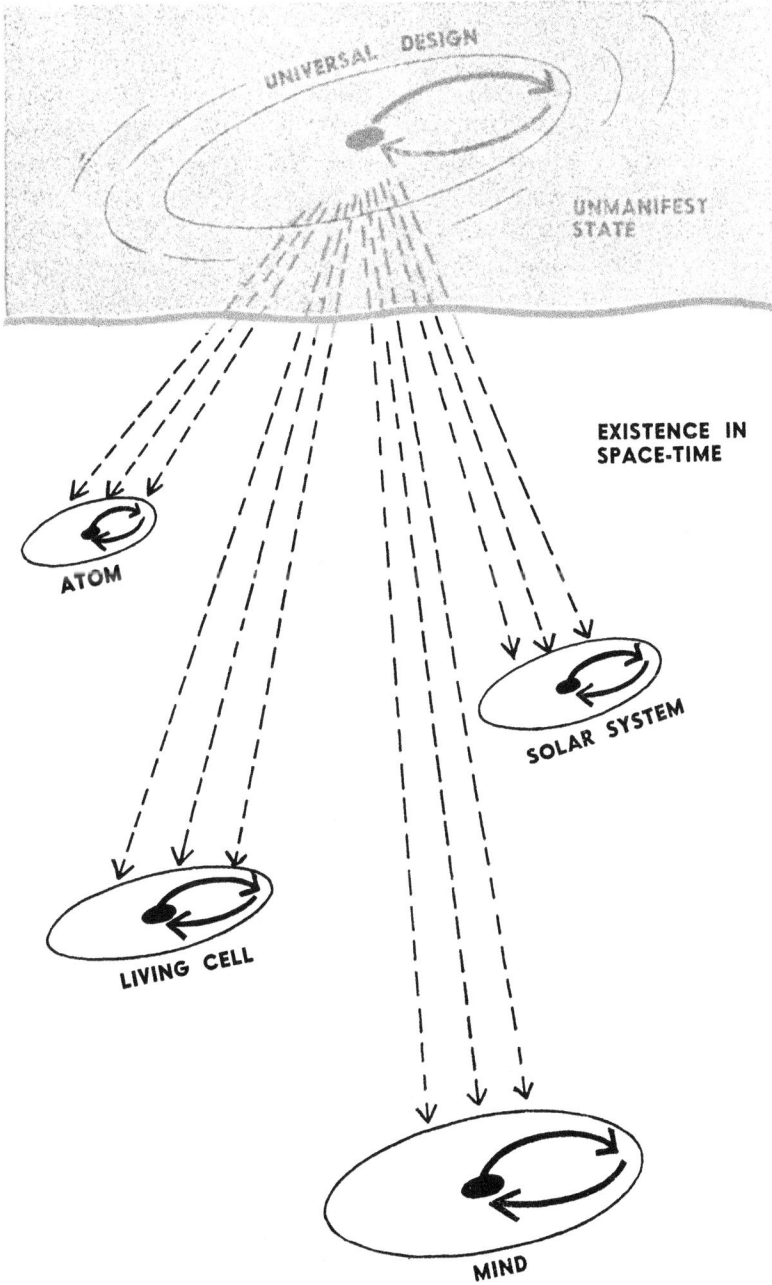

UNIVERSAL DESIGN

UNMANIFEST STATE

EXISTENCE IN SPACE-TIME

ATOM

SOLAR SYSTEM

LIVING CELL

MIND

The Nature of the Self

IF FIGURE ELEVEN represents the total process of creation, then Figure Twelve opposite represents that part of the process which ultimates in the making of the human self. The picture opposite is an attempt to show that the human self is composed of two cosmic imprints upon the human organism [165], one upon the uterine organism before birth, and another upon the brain after birth. These two separate cosmic imprints are represented in the picture opposite by the patch *e* in the human head. The Universal Design is shown as imprinting its nature upon the uterine organism [16] by means of some unknown mechanism [75] or emanation represented opposite by the arrow *a*, *a'*. The arrow marked *b* is simply a way of reminding the reader that the uterine imprint is displaced by birth [84], whereafter it travels through the human body, culminating in a movement into the skull [143] as represented opposite by the arrow *c*. Meantime the Universal Design has impressed its nature upon the postnatal head [164] by means of an unknown mechanism [166] represented opposite by the arrow *d*, *d'*. The human self is the outcome of the synthesis of these two distinct sets of impressions. Figure Twelve might be said to be a pictorial summation of the total process which will be illustrated by the remainder of this chapter. It is, of course, a great oversimplification, but it will enable the reader to remind himself of the essential simplicity of the pattern and the processes which go to make up the intense complexity of mind and personality. Omitted from Figure Twelve are all those elements of mental function which are related to the senses of sight, hearing, speaking and spatial and social orientation. These play an enormous part in the making of consciousness, and especially of the typical urban consciousness of our times. But hardly anyone would pretend that these elements of consciousness are fundamental. They are not the root of man. They do not have anything to do with the central nature of consciousness and of the self. Indeed, it seems to be a principle of spiritual development that this can take place only in isolation from all those factors which are most to the fore in the making of the typical modern urban consciousness. The illustration opposite represents schematically the basis of the self as a cosmic impress.

Pictorial Recapitulation
Fig. 12

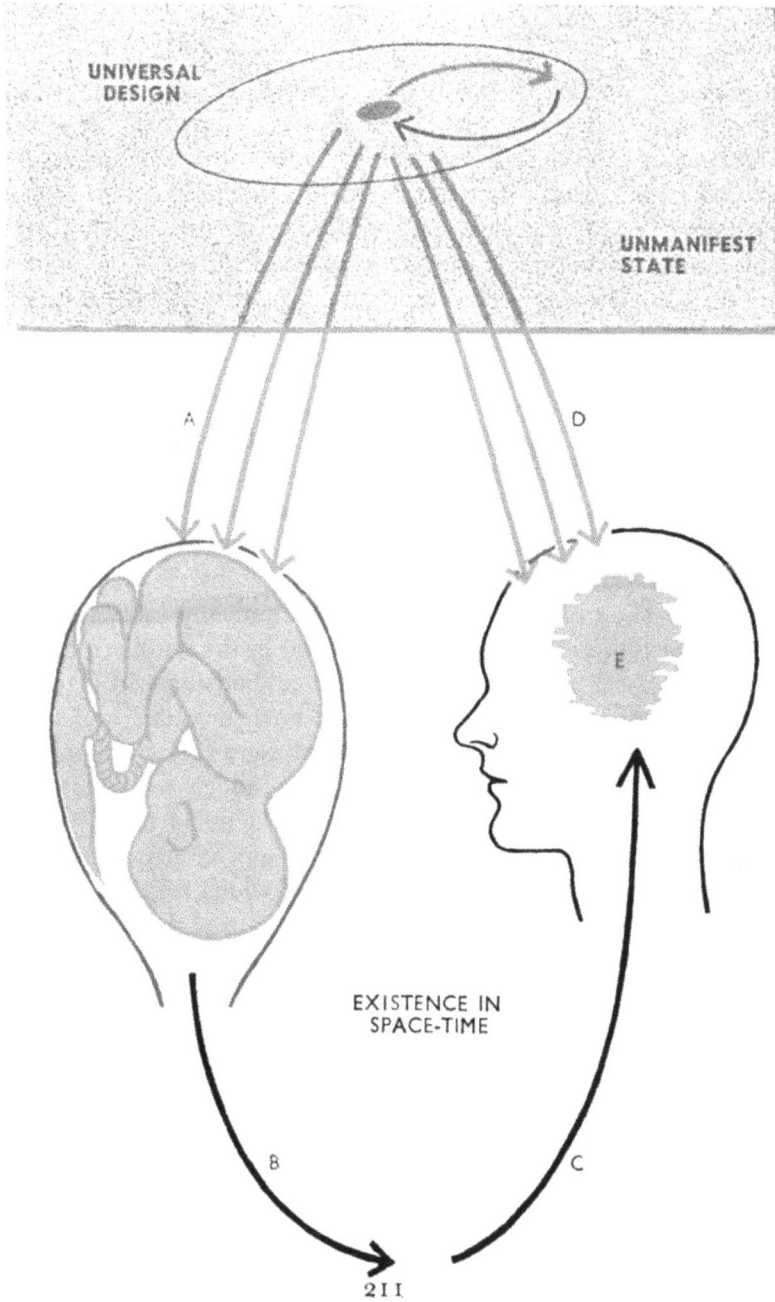

UNIVERSAL
DESIGN

UNMANIFEST
STATE

A

D

E

EXISTENCE IN
SPACE-TIME

B

C

211

The Nature of the Self

FIGURE THIRTEEN opposite shows the mechanism which brings into being on this planet that mysterious entity known as the human self. This is a purely empirical concept based upon information found in the depths of the human feelings, and though it is strange, it is a picture created by methods in the strict tradition of empirical science. It is distinct in nature from the picture presented by religion, theosophy and all forms of mysticism, which like to present vast and vague pictures which flatter the individual without stimulating him to evolution. This picture presents mind and soul as the outcome of elements which can be harnessed by biological mechanisms, and so raises the hope that man may evolve soul by the employment of similar mechanisms. The beginning of the self is to be found in the fact that the fetus feels himself to be a nucleus [15] as a result of the relation between his skin c and the womb [14]. In this way a basic orientation is created in the fetal feelings which matches the orientation of the cosmos [17] and permits a sympathetic resonance between the fetal feelings and the cosmos. This is amplified by the fact that the nuclear feeling of the fetal skin c is rhythmically increased and decreased [20, 21] by every beat of blood in the umbilical cord b as it passes back and forth between the fetal body and the placenta a. In this back-and-forth flow the fetal nuclear feeling undergoes a constant reversal of polarity [21] which shows certain signs that it might be electrical in origin [22, 23] though not in content. Because of this periodic relation between the nuclear fetal feeling and the peripheral placental feeling, the uterine organism tunes in the basic nature of the cosmos [42], of which it is a miniature imitation. This is the very first imprint upon us of the cosmos, and it forms the core of the self. The beat of blood in the umbilical cord gives rise in man to the first sense of space-time structure [37] which, in turn, evokes a sense of sevenfold periodicity [38] that ultimately conditions the brain to impose musical sound and color upon the physical perceptions. The very core of the self is this pattern created in the feelings by the fetus in its relation with the placenta through the cord and with the configurations of the wider cosmos. The uterine organism, originally a purely biological evolution, has become the instrument of soul-making.

Fig. 13

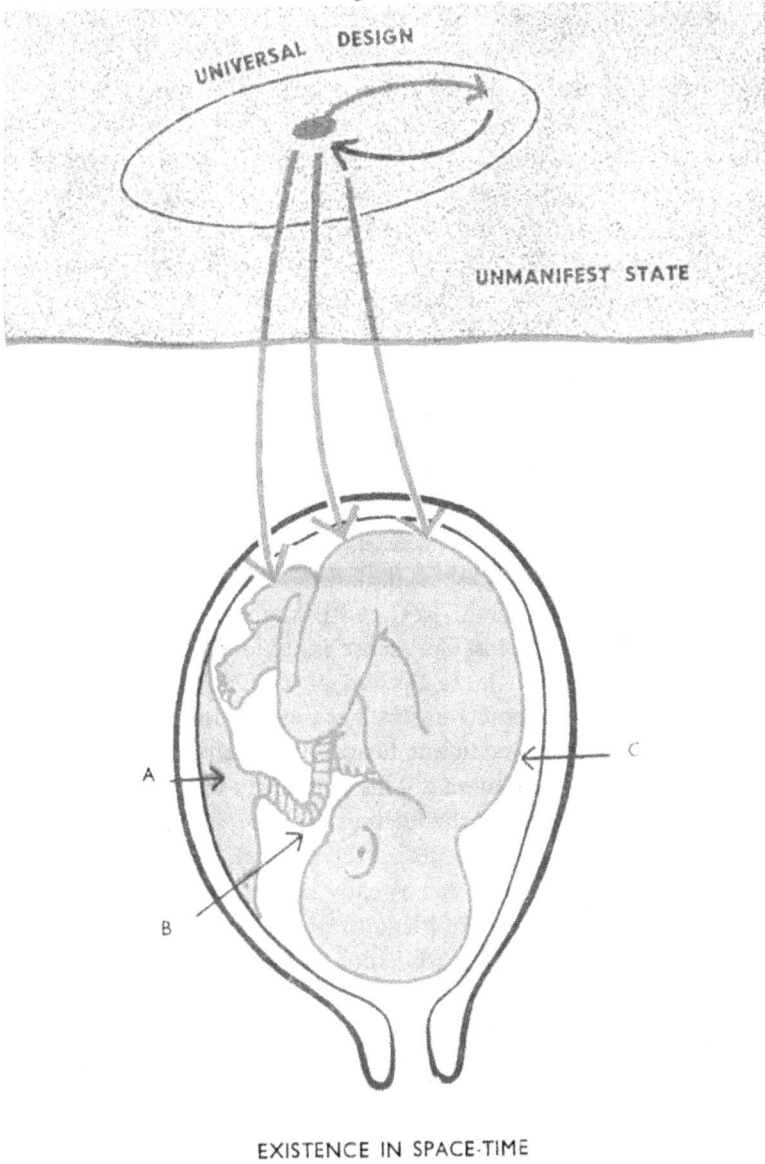

UNIVERSAL DESIGN

UNMANIFEST STATE

A

B

C

EXISTENCE IN SPACE-TIME

The Nature of the Self

IT IS OBVIOUS that birth revolutionizes the life of the baby, and a revolution in its sense of orientation might be assumed. But what is neither obvious nor subject to assumption is the strange sequence of events which takes place in the nervous system of the child, the occluded memories of which emerge in dreams and also in mythical material of all kinds. Figure Fourteen pictorializes the main feeling-changes caused by birth. The taking of the first breath is possibly the most shocking of all experiences at birth, and the lungs which had been 'solid' during their prior existence in the fetus are suddenly hollowed out, see Figure Fourteen-A. At this point the child tends to feel that the life-giving placenta is suddenly sucked inside his body and divided into two [96]. At the same time the eyes, ears, nose and mouth all become stimulated in a way that before birth had not been possible. The thalamus, long used to being activated by irritations from the fetal skin [14] cannot at first organize these new sensory experiences called seeing, hearing, smelling and tasting, and so it 'supposes' that these stimulations from the special senses are really from the fetal skin, with the result that the new-born child feels that his fetal sense is divided into several part-selves, each of which lurks [95] in an orifice of the head. This strange situation is depicted as well as possible in Figure Fourteen-B, which represents an infant head with a little fetus lurking in an eye and another in an ear. This is an early trick of the developing senses. But very soon the feelings of the special senses coalesce, and the whole head is felt to be the fetal self [96]. As shown in Figure Fourteen-A, the lungs already have taken on the placental feeling. Thus shortly after birth the head takes on the sense of being the fetal self, while the lungs play the role of placenta. Inevitably then the breath assumes the umbilical sense, and the back-and-forth of the breath is felt as umbilical blood [97] and evokes in the feelings all the old memories of the umbilical flow. This results in the situation roughly depicted opposite in Figure Fourteen-C, though it is impossible, save in a moving picture, to show the way in which the head is felt to move up and down the neck into the lungs and back [97] as once the fetus felt to go back and forth along the umbilical cord [22].

Fig. 14

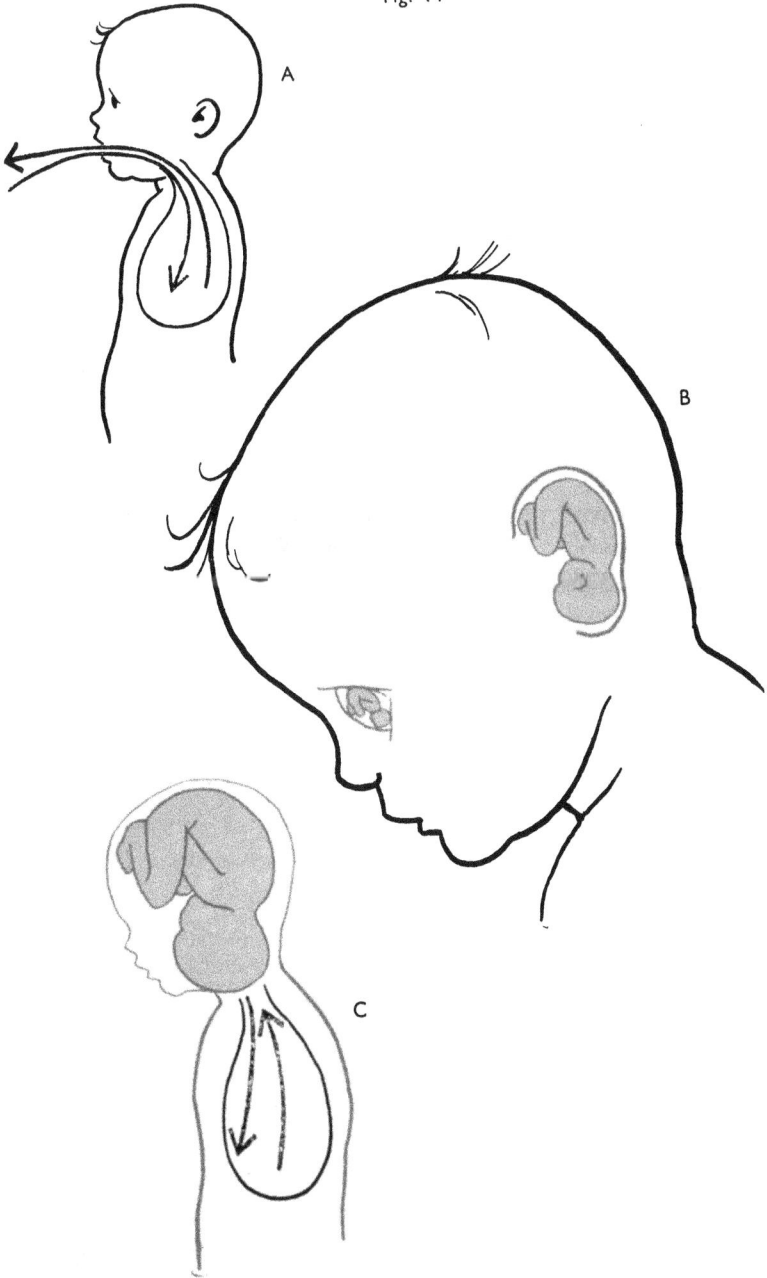

The Nature of the Self

THE FIRST REACTIONS created in the feelings by the act of suckling are illustrated by Figure Fifteen opposite. The infant feels that he sucks in blood and returns it to the mother through the eyes [100], which are felt as if they were the lost umbilical arteries. The stage is set for this strange reaction by the fact that the head has come to feel to be the fetal body [96], and by the fact that the primary core of feeling, which is the core of the self, demands a restoration of the original uterine set-up [87] in terms of the fetus, the placenta and the connecting cord. Only by this feeling can the newborn child retain his primary sense of his relation with the cosmos [16]. The first reactions to sucking are thus dominated by the recently-lost uterine state, and the mouth and eyes of the newborn child constitute a complex rehabilitation of the now-inactive navel, the mouth playing the role of the umbilical vein, with the eyes as the arteries. This strange feeling eventually gives place to another, equally strange, which is depicted opposite by Figure Sixteen. Now the infant feels still to suck blood from the nipple, but to return it *not* through the eyes but through the legs [105], which now become the agents for the rehabilitation of the feelings of the lost umbilical arteries. The legs are eminently suited for this role because their arterial supply is developed in close conjunction with the umbilical arteries [109], a fact which is made clear by Figure Six. An important concomitant of this new reaction to suckling is that the whole fetal self seems to be sucked down into the stomach, which now becomes felt as if it were the mother's womb. But since the whole head is felt as the fetal self, the reaction is as if the head itself (head as fetus) had been sucked down [103]. The reader will recall that, when *in utero*, the fetus felt that he himself was sucked into the placenta and restored cyclically [22, 28], and that this feeling became transposed upon the breathing [97]. But in the act of suckling, save for occasional belching and regurgitation [101], there is no backflow up the gut. The illusion that the fetal self is in the stomach in complemented by the matching illusion that the mother's whole body is now the placenta from which blood is sucked and into which it is discharged through the two legs. The mouth and the feet now take on the feeling-role of a complex navel.

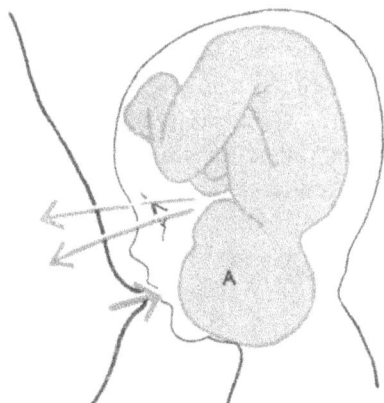

Fig. 15

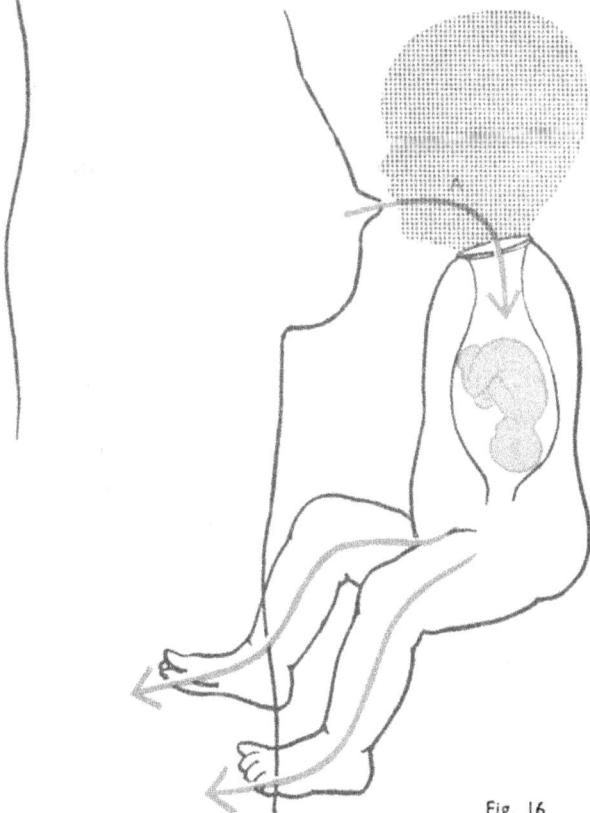

Fig. 16

The Nature of the Self

FIGURE SEVENTEEN opposite represents the artist's effort to portray a state of grave confusion in the feelings. The essential feeling-situation portrayed is basically that already indicated in Figure Sixteen, but elaborated by the fact that the infant feels that his heart is the strange head-as-fetus which he seems to have swallowed [105]. It must be understood that this confusion is not an occasional peculiarity of the developing feelings, but an experience shared by all human beings. I think we can understand it only in terms of a primary meeting of the subjective and the objective perceptions. That is to say, the child already *knows* that his fetal self (already identified with his head) is leaping in his body—*that* is the subjective component of his feelings. To this he now adds an objective component, namely that of the actual moving of his heart in the chest cavity. The two perceptions come into fantastical unity in this strange sense that the heart has become the fetal self leaping in the trunk—the trunk being felt as the lost maternal body [103]. The intake of milk *a* through the esophagus is felt as the intake of blood through the umbilical vein. The pulse of blood *b*, *b'* through the legs is felt as the outgo of blood through the umbilical arteries. It is relatively easy for the feelings associated with the heart to lend themselves to this fantastical association because in fetal life the heart pumped blood direct to the fetal legs in association with the umbilical arteries. Indeed, the vascular needs of the fetal legs are greatly overshadowed by the needs of the umbilical arteries, and the feelings retain the deep impress that in effect the umbilical arteries constitute the fetal legs, see Figure Six. See also Figure Nineteen-B. It is not suggested that the state depicted in Figure Seventeen is essentially different from that already shown in Figure Sixteen, and it may be assumed for practical purposes that they are one and the same state, and that they have been shown distinctly here only because their combined state is relatively complex to understand unless the components are presented separately. When considering Figures Fifteen, Sixteen and Seventeen with a single eye, the reader will be able to appreciate the existence of a subtle connection between the human eyes and feet—a connection having no ordinary physiological or anatomical basis.

Pictorial Recapitulation

Fig. 17

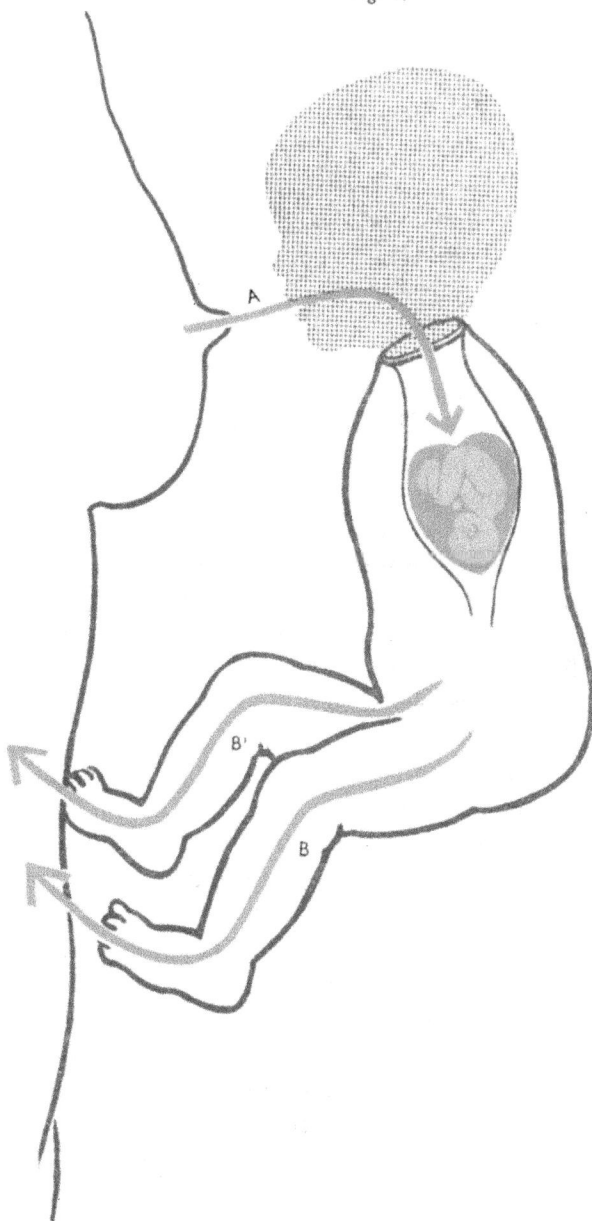

The Nature of the Self

THE FANTASY that the child's stomach is his mother's womb with him inside it, a fantasy illustrated in Figures Sixteen and Seventeen, inevitably leads to the fantasy of anal birth [113], in which the child feels that his fetal self is born out of his own rectum. The experience of anal birth does not, however, involve the sense of being dropped away from the body—at any rate, not at first. Rather is there the sense that the head-as-fetus which had been sucked down into the stomach, has come out at the other end as the child's own bottom [116], which is not unsuited to the task of providing a rough physical basis for that analogy. The buttocks are not unsuited to the role of the cheeks; the anus is simply the mouth displaced to the other end of the gastrointestinal tract, having its own crude crying (flatus); the legs, owing to their feeling-connection with the eyes [Figures Fifteen and Sixteen], are sometimes felt as eyes [116]. The artist has been hard put to it to try to convey this sense of the head at the bottom without making a drawing that was either offensive or ridiculous. It might be well, at this juncture, once again to proffer the reader's mind some defence against the inevitable suggestion that he is being asked to consider purposeless illusions of infancy—illusions which, so far from being dwelt upon, should be dispelled as soon as possible. The reader should remember that all these illusions are the by-product of a vital necessity, namely that of retaining the link between the feelings and that cosmic impress which is the very essence of the self. The cosmos has at root the sole purpose to set a nucleus inside a periphery and, after fructification, to secure a new emergence. That is the sequence of events detected by the umbilical blood, and it is the memory of it that imposes itself upon the feelings associated with the infant's physical processes. These processes, since they are concerned wholly with taking in and giving out, are ready-made to accept the cosmic impress, and this is especially true of that major bodily process, the combined acts of ingestion and of excretion. This general configurational accommodation is the driving power behind the making of all the illusions and fantasies illustrated here. These must not, therefore, be regarded as absurd fallacies, but as indispensable stages in the development of the human self.

Fig. 18

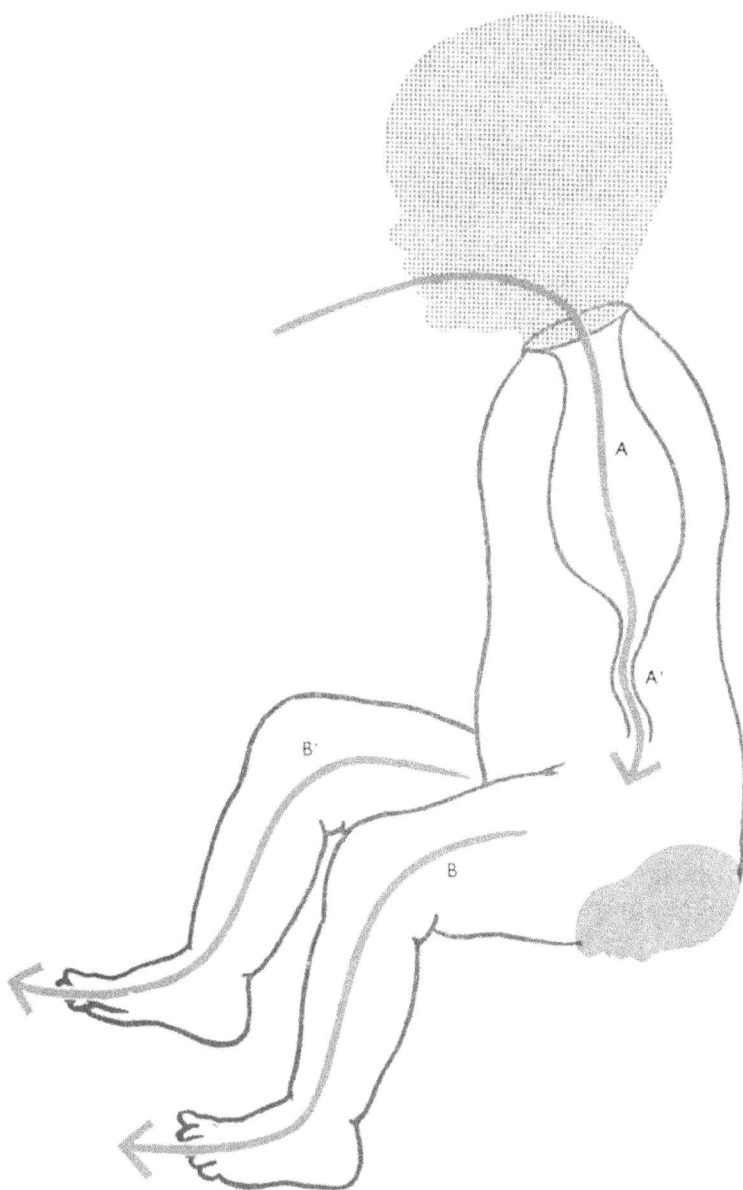

The Nature of the Self

THE HUMAN LEGS are the locus of a primary struggle in the human feelings. The legs begin their existence as little more than vascular appendages of the umbilical arteries [31], and the child tends to feel them in this form for a considerable time after birth. He feels them to be excretory ducts, just as the umbilical arteries were. The great struggle comes about when the child is called upon to use the legs for assuming the upright posture, a struggle which also involves the sense of the hardening bones necessary for supporting the child's weight. The child is now called upon to relinquish the sense of the legs as excretory tubes, and to accept the rectal and urethral ducts as the natural organs of excretion. Specifically, the left leg yields up its excretory feelings to the rectal passage, while the right leg yields them to the urethra. The infant resists this changeover because the umbilical arterial 'hangover' in the legs represents the last direct link with its mother, so that the abandonment of the sense of the legs as twisted umbilical arteries calls for a 'new birth' away from the mother. The struggle between the sense of the legs as excretory tubes and as instruments of walking is crucial in a sense that transcends the individual, because it comes near to the struggle between the downthrust to the earth through excretion and the upthrust to 'the sky' through the upright posture. The struggle is thus, in a sense, a struggle between bone and excrements—between the downgoing thrust of the feces and the upgoing thrust of the bones as they lift the organism from the earth. This struggle can be seen in a definite confusion (experienced by every infant) between bone and feces. This confusion centers in the left leg, and arises as follows: insofar as the left leg is felt as an excretory tube (and as the rectum) it feels to contain feces, and insofar as it is felt as truly a leg, it feels to contain bone. Thus bone and feces come into a strange feeling-confusion which forever haunts the human feelings [112]. In Figure Nineteen-A the artist has tried to suggest the confusion between bone and feces by making a 'fuzzy' spill-over between left leg and rectum, while in Nineteen-B he has sought to suggest the manner in which the upright posture of the child is haunted by the older feelings of the self with the 'twisted umbilical legs'.

Pictorial Recapitulation

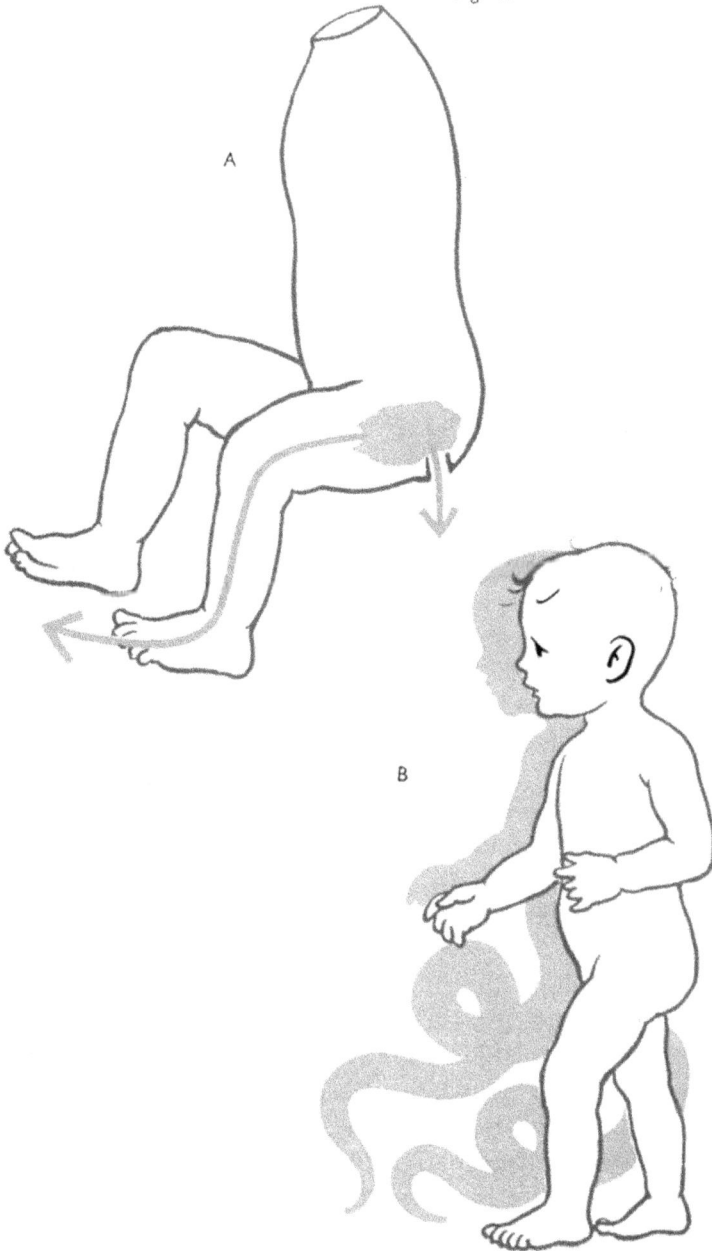

Fig. 19

A

B

The Nature of the Self

As THE LEGS PROGRESSIVELY shed the sense of being umbilical arterial tubes or indeed excretory tubes of any description, so the excrementory sense is taken up more and more by the rectal and urethral tubes [114]. And in the degree that this is achieved, the rectal and urethral tubes take on the residual sense of the umbilical arteries. The rectal and urethral tubes now feel to become umbilical vessels discharging blood—and discharging it into the earth [119]. The earth itself now assumes all the feelings once associated with the placenta and with the infantile sense of the mother. And just as in the womb the fetus felt that it was constantly sucked down into the placenta and destroyed [28], so now the child feels that his nuclear virtue (his fetal selfhood) is sucked down into the earth [122] and destroyed, but as constantly reborn. And just as the fetus seems to gain from the placenta some mysterious knowledge of the past [48], so now the infant feels to receive from the earth a mysterious link with certain organic knowledge stored somehow in the depths of the earth [123]. Whether there be an actual store of hereditary material in the earth, or whether this be only a placental superimposition upon the earth it is impossible to be sure. But my analyses strongly suggest that the earth contains some kind of memory-elements which are carried up into the child's body. The artist has sought to show this in Figure Twenty opposite. The child, standing upright upon the earth's surface, is shown as excreting down into the earth mysterious energies represented by the arrow *a* from the urethra and *b* from the rectum, while receiving back a response from the earth represented by the arrow *c*. The reader should clearly understand that it has not been possible so far to detect any actual energies leaving the human body for the depths of the earth and returning therefrom. The actual situation may be that there is a subtle circulation of energy between the earth and the organisms on its surface, and that the reaction of the human organism to this earth-circulation is in some way modulated by the excretory process. Or it may be that there is a circulation of energy between the center of the earth and its surface, and that this circulation acts as a carrier upon which affective elements may be superimposed.

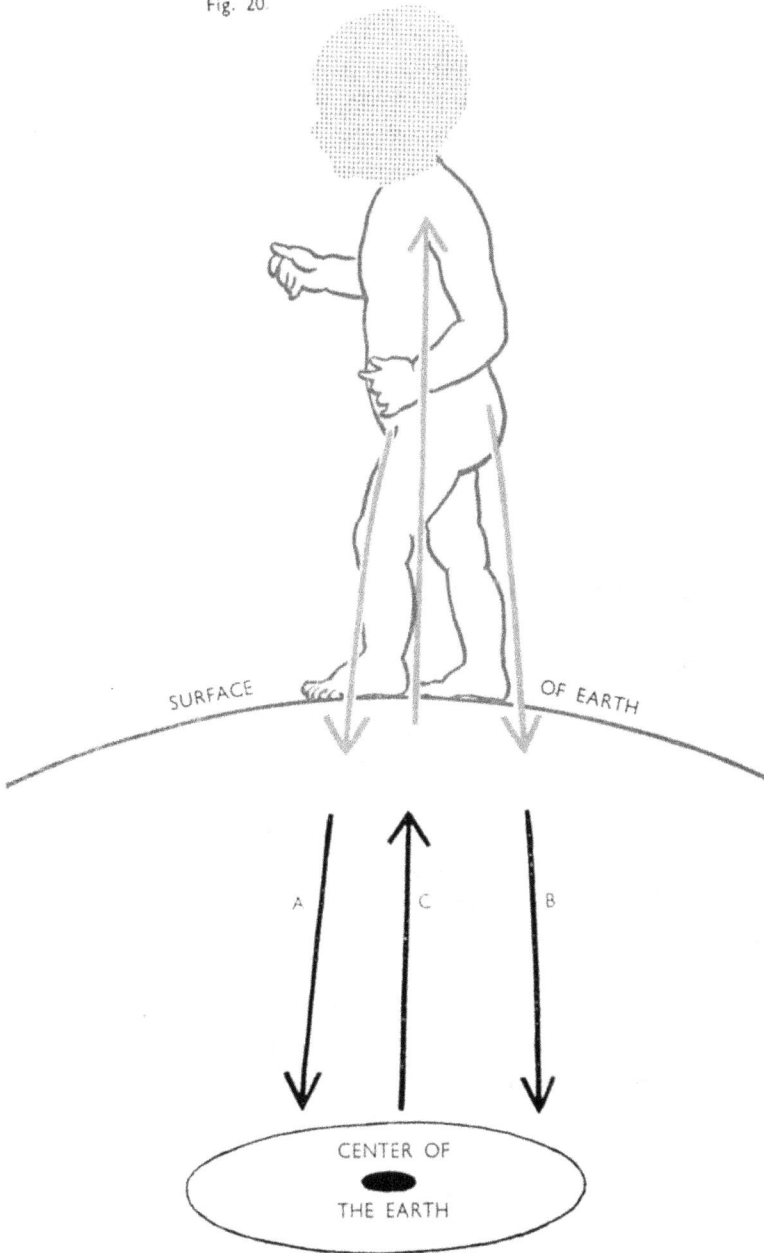

Fig. 20.

SURFACE   OF EARTH

A   C   B

CENTER OF

THE EARTH

225

The Nature of the Self

As ONCE THE FETUS felt the placenta as an aggressive entity [21], so now the infant feels the earth [122] to be an aggressor which thrusts upwards and threatens to penetrate its lower parts. The threat is first felt in relation to the anus and (in the case of the girl) the vagina also. There is a strong 'temptation' in the feelings to accept this upthrust from the earth into the anus [126], and this 'temptation' is no doubt related to an incipient confusion in the feelings between the two ends of the gastrointestinal tract [126]. There are many indications in dreams that the infant first feels that the earth is the mother, and that the upthrust is a sort of 'nipple' which can be 'suckled' by the anus. This 'temptation' must be resisted if mental and physical health are to ensue through later years. In addition to this, the little girl feels that the upthrust seeks to enter her vagina [126], and both the girl and the boy also undergo the strange sensation that the earth is male, just as the placenta was also felt to be [181], and is seeking to enter their bodies sexually. And since this primary male is identified with father [188], the earth is felt to be father—a monstrous and incestuous father who seeks to penetrate his children in this fashion. If both these improper forms of entry into the lower orifices are rejected by the child, then there follows a third possible wrong acceptance of it, and this is depicted by the artist in Figure Twentyone opposite. In this third experience the energy from the earth, having failed to find entry into the child's body (either in the above wrong forms or in the proper form to be illustrated overleaf), is felt to flood up over the body [127] and to cover it with a covering of material that is felt to be a mixture of the original fetal skin feeling [9] with blood, earth and feces [127]. This most peculiar fact, which is of undoubted objective truth for the infant feelings, seems to suggest that the thrust from the earth is a true energy which, denied entry into the lower orifices, spreads out and floods up over the trunk, just as a jet of water might meet an impenetrable body and flood or spray up over its outer surface. The whole subject matter of this book is complicated by the doubt as to whether we are dealing with a true energy or with pure affect, or some variable mixture of the two.

226

Pictorial Recapitulation

Fig. 21

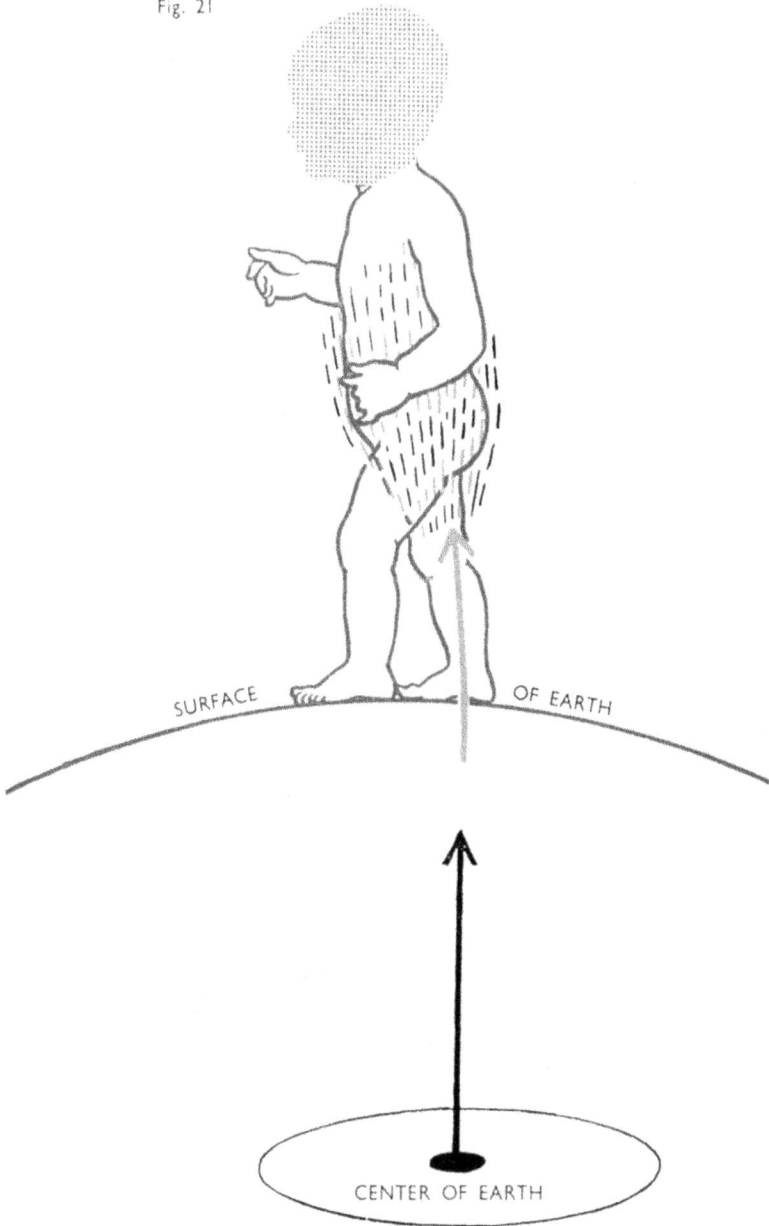

SURFACE   OF EARTH

CENTER OF EARTH

The Nature of the Self

THE BOY PROPERLY ACCOMMODATES the upthrust of the earth into his spine and his penis [129], the major upthrust being taken into the spine. This fact the artist has sought to illustrate by Figure Twentytwo-A opposite. The girl, after a brief illusory hope that she may also be able to make the same accommodation reconciles herself to the fact that her accommodation must be wholly through the spine [130] as illustrated in Figure Twenty-two-B opposite. This primary difference between the feelings of the boy and the girl appears to predate the awakening of sexual realization however precocious, and to set the style of the later feelings and reactions. As we have had cause to see in these pages, the umbilical pattern of one-versus-two [see Appendix L] is fundamental to the sense of the uterine pattern, and with the development illustrated on the page opposite it will be obvious that the boy feels his connection with the earth to be one down (from rectum) and two up (to spine and penis), whereas the girl continues to feel the original connection illustrated in Figure Twenty. It is a fact, therefore, that the boy's relation to the earth has about it elements of the placenta's relation to the fetus, while the girl's relation is just the reverse. This relationship felt between the lower parts and the earth is the determinant of the later feelings which will develop between the head and the sky. As the boy feels to make a single thrust down to the earth and to receive back what appears to him a dual thrust [129] so at the head he feels to make a single thrust up to the sky and to receive two back, the converse being true of the girl [see Figure Twentynine]. The fact that the earth's upthrust is divided between spine and genitals (though only fleetingly in the case of the girl) is the source of a number of confusions between spine and penis or between spine and clitoris. Women who suffer from various forms of backache are often found, upon analysis, to have transferred the sense of injury of the clitoris to the spine. The boy tends to confuse spine and penis so thoroughly that the penis is felt like a miniature self. The converse is also true, namely that the body is frequently felt as if it were a penis, the head being felt as the glans penis. Peculiar bodily movements can, in fact, not infrequently be traced to this confusion, as has been described by Jung.

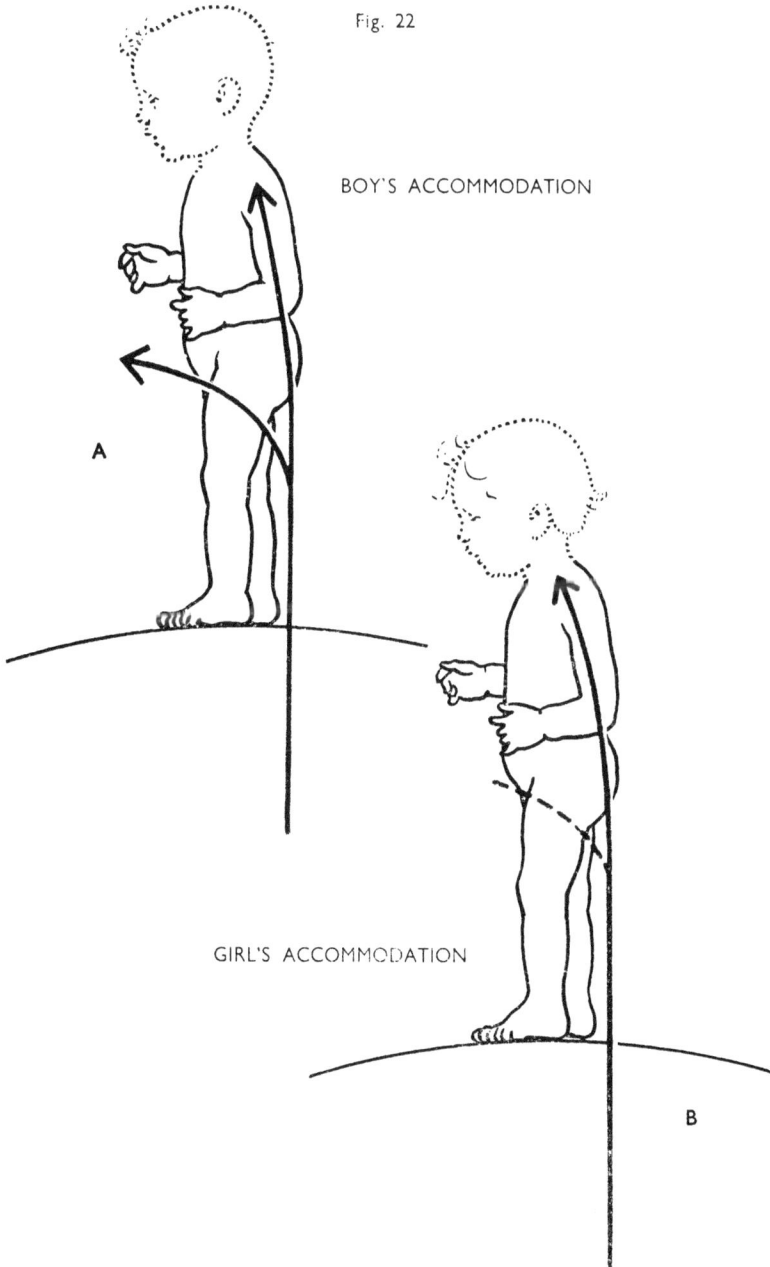

Fig. 22

BOY'S ACCOMMODATION

A

GIRL'S ACCOMMODATION

B

229

The Nature of the Self

THE CHILD FEELS that the upthrust from the earth, as illustrated in Figures Twenty, Twentyone and Twentytwo, is responsible for the existence of the skeleton in the body [129]. The precise *rationale* of this undoubted feeling is not understood, though certain suggestive elements are known. That there is a relation between the sense of the skeleton and the sense of the earth is understandable because bone equates in the feelings with fecal matter [112], and fecal matter with earth, but even this explanation is only partial, since we do not know the exact cause of the affinity between the earth and the feces in the feelings. It would appear that the infant feels that his major thrust into the earth (see Figure Twenty) is fecal or associated with feces. And since feces are closely related in the feelings with bone, the infant feels that it is bone that he is thrusting into the earth. This being so, it is not surprising to find that the upthrust from the earth is also felt to be related to, charged with or even composed of feces and bone. Moreover, since the emission of feces is related in the feelings with the birth of the self [113], this thrust down into the earth is felt to be a sort of 'descent' of the wrecked and ruined self into the earth, and the backthrust is felt to be the 'resurrection' of the self from the depths. The skeleton, therefore, is felt in part to be the lost fetal self who, after temporary lodgment in the stomach-as-womb, was born at the anus, thrust down into the earth and restored again [129]. In all such peculiar feelings the reader will see the efforts of the postnatal organism to keep alive the feelings of loss, destruction and recreation first evoked in the umbilical cord. In this way, by the multiple superimposition of feeling-images, the strange feeling of the skeleton is built up of a lost fetal and fecal self that has been down into the earth and is restored again in the body. If to this picture yet another layer is added, namely that of the earth as an upward-raping father [193], then we get the apparently absurd and even perverse idea that the skeleton is the self generated in us by the upthrust from the earth as father [194]. THE READER MUST ALWAYS KEEP IN MIND THAT THE GOVERNING FACTOR IN THE MAKING OF ALL THESE FANTASIES IS THE NECESSITY FOR PRESERVING THE UTERINE PATTERN AS THE CORE OF THE SELF.

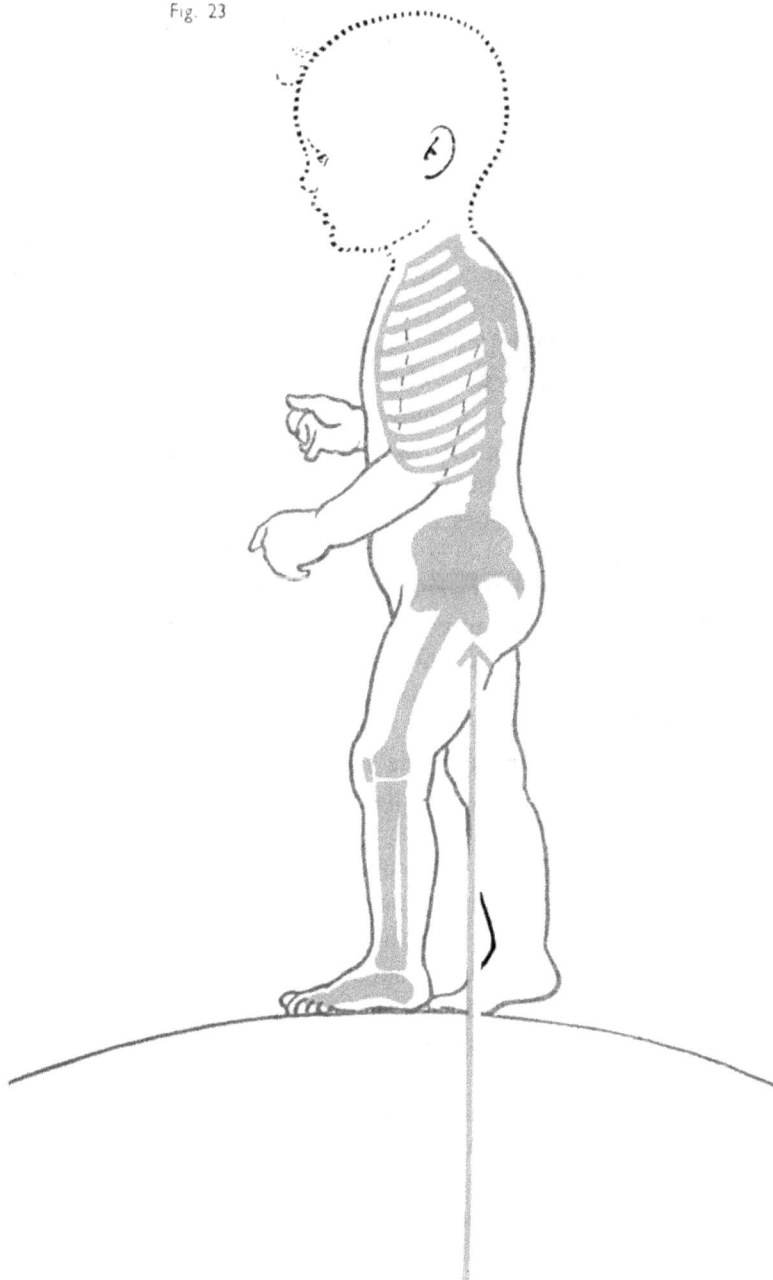

Fig. 23

The Nature of the Self

THE NEXT STAGE of the development of the feelings comes about when the skull is felt to be extruded upwards from between the shoulders. No doubt it seems more than extraordinary to suggest that the little child does not possess that anatomical orientation which commonsense would affirm, but the facts are testified to in both dreams and myths. The child feels that his head, which he identified with his fetal self [96], which was sucked down into the gut [103], born at the anus [113], thrust down into the earth and restored as skeleton, is now extruded up through the shoulders to its former place—not now as a solid head, but as a hollow skull [131]. Moreover, the skull feels to be a hollowed-out ball of feces. This strange situation is illustrated schematically in Figure Twentyfour-A opposite, where the trunk is represented as a tube extruding a solid ball at the lower end and a hollow one at the top. This is, of course, a vast over-simplification of the stages involved, as the narrative will have made reasonably plain, but in effect the basic feeling is that what the trunk does at the lower end, namely to extrude a solid ball of feces, is matched at the upper end by a sense that the skull is a ball of hollowed-out feces. The infant feels that his head is some-how lifted up out of its trunk by the downthrust of his arms and hands. This suggests, of course, that the feelings here described concerning the 'extrusion of the skull' are related to the infant lifting of the head as a result of the thrust of his arms in the act of crawling. Be this as it may, the fact is that the upthrust of the skull is felt to be a sort of outcome or product of the thrust of the two arms. The child feels this neuromuscular pattern in terms of the umbilical pattern of two-out-and-one-in—see Appendix L. The child also senses another aspect of the umbilical beat in the feeling-patterns illustrated opposite, namely the fourfold-seven-fold space-time configurations [37, 38, 39]. Briefly, the maternal nipple is felt as the *point*, and the passage of liquid through the gut evokes the sense of the *line* which, in its turn, develops into the sense of the *plane* of the buttocks, from which emerges again the sense of the feces as *point-solid*. There then develops the sense of the spine as *line*; the hollow skull as *plane*, and the thalamus as the new *point*.

Fig. 24

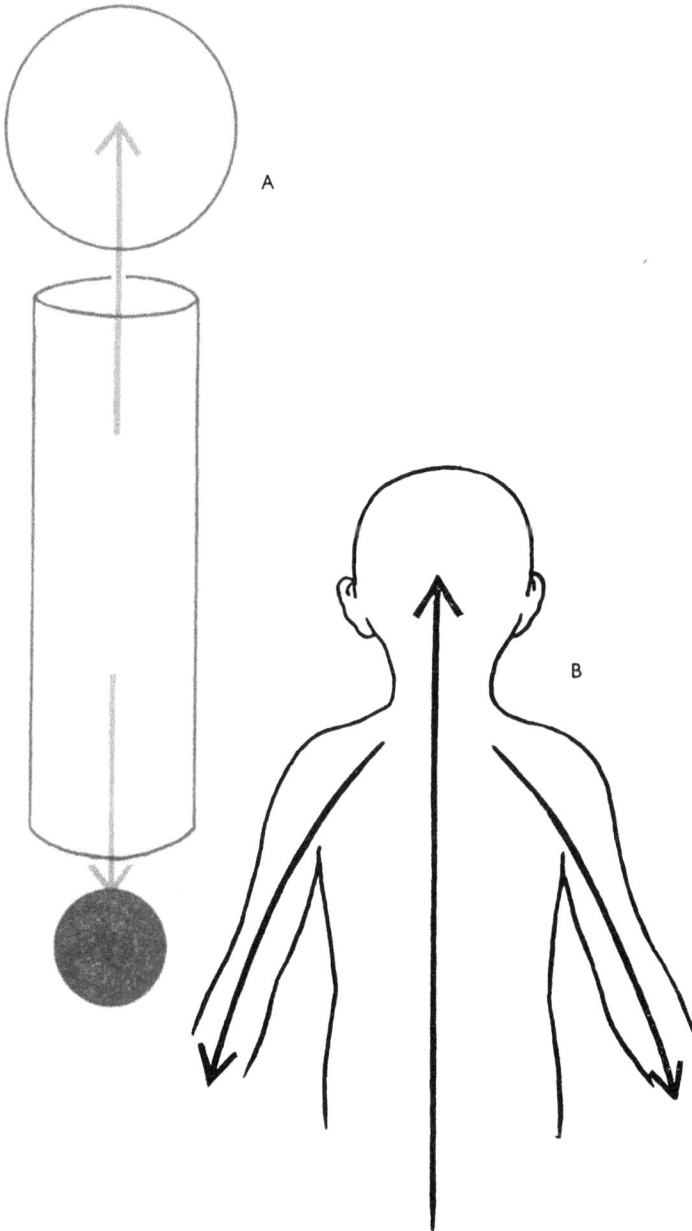

A

B

233

The Nature of the Self

SUDDENLY in the development of the feelings the skull ceases to be felt as the self, and instead the brain becomes identified with the whole uterine organism, the skull being then felt as mother's womb [141], but a hard and intractable one. This sudden reversal of feelings is typical of the experiences described in this book [141]. The outcome of this strange development is shown in Figure Twentyfive: the right side of the brain, *c* is felt as the fetal self; the left side, *b* is felt as the placenta; and the thalamocortical circulation *a, a'* is felt as the umbilical circulation joining the two. The outcome of this strange polarization of the brain is that the left side of the body is felt to be more nuclear, more fetal, while the right side is felt to be more peripheral, more placental [154]. Another fantastical feeling is also experienced in relation to the brain, and that is that the whole self is suddenly sucked up into the skull and incarcerated there [155], a fantasy which the artist has sought to illustrate by means of Figure Twenty-six opposite. The two fantastical situations illustrated opposite represent only the major feelings which beset the head. There is also a sense that the whole head is a sort of mannikin which walks upon the neck as upon a single leg. There is also another fantasy in which the head is felt as a creature 'walking upon its lower jaws', the ten deciduous teeth of the lower jaw being related in the feelings with the ten toes [161]. The imposition of the feelings of the lower parts upon the face is an old Freudian doctrine. But the Freudian idea seems to be that it is the anal and genital feelings *per se* which seek to displace themselves upon the face. In this idea one senses the dominance of the primary concept that mind is *libido*, a natural but mistaken view which I have exposed in Chapter Thirteen [178]. This book explains the displacement of the anal and genital feelings upon the head as no more than the by-product of the migration of the primary uterine pattern which, as it moves through the body of the infant, carries to each new station a compounded memory of its earlier *loci*. One should never forget, indeed, that the very feelings of the lower parts were themselves originally developed in association with a transfer of feeling from the head to the bottom—a displacement which has been dealt with in Chapter Eight.

Pictorial Recapitulation

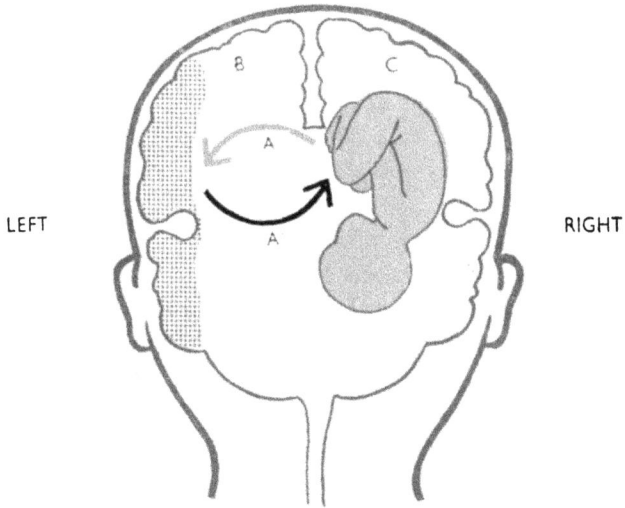

LEFT

RIGHT

Fig. 25

REAR VIEWS OF HEAD

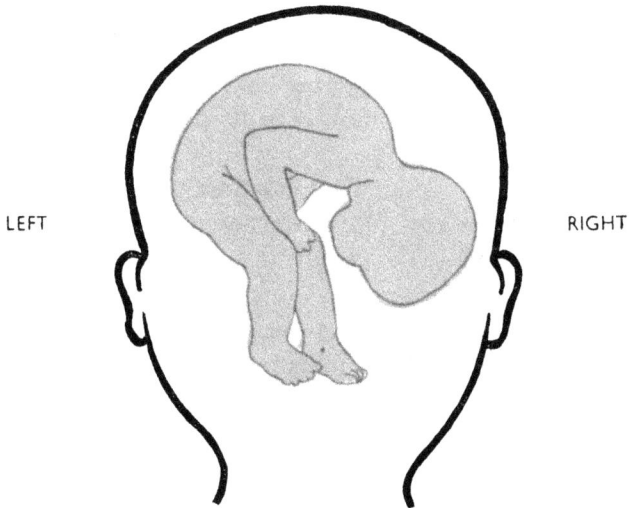

LEFT

RIGHT

Fig. 26

The Nature of the Self

DURING THE UNBORN state the thalamus (represented by a, a' in Figure Twentyseven) becomes identified with the fetal skin [14], and hence with the nuclear and time-elements of the cosmos. When at birth the cortex of the brain c, c, c', c' becomes activated and begins to play its role of spatial orientation [142] with placental undertones, it is thus all set to play the peripheral-placental role *vis-à-vis* the nuclear-fetal sense of the thalamus. And since this fundamental polarity is mediated by the two-way flow of neural energy between the thalamus and cortex, it is inevitable that this two-way flow assume umbilical undertones. Thus it is that the brain in the skull 'imitates' configurationally not only the Universal Design [71, 77] but also the fetal pattern which first evokes that design in our living flesh and blood, so that *two* main imprints of the Universal Design are felt in the brain—see Figures Twelve and Twentynine. But the brain and its neural activity appear to be involved in *two* major circulations, and these are illustrated roughly by Figures Twentyseven and Twentyeight opposite. The first neural circulation is that which takes place between the brain and the total environment of the human organism, and is depicted in Figure Twentyseven. Neural impulses flow up the spinal cord into the thalamus a, a' and spread out through the tracts b, b' to the cortex c, c, c', c', where they give rise to responding motor impulses d, d'. (N.B. For the sake of simplicity any decussation of the tracts is ignored in these sketches.) The second neural circulation of the brain is involved in the first, but assumes a 'life of its own' [147], and this is depicted roughly in Figure Twentyeight. This 'internal circulation' comes about because of the fact that the flow of neural energy between the thalamus and the cortex is not a one-way flow as shown in Figure Twentyseven b, b', but is a two-way flow [146] as shown in Figure Twentyeight, b, b, b', b'. The overlapping of these two major elements in a single neural circulation seems to suggest an answer to the problem as to the distinctive but interlocking aspects of mind, namely that aspect which is related primarily to the external world (Figure Twentyseven) and that which tends to have a purely subjective character (Figure Twentyeight). These two neural circulations offer a new view of both sleeping and dreaming.

Pictorial Recapitulation

Fig. 27

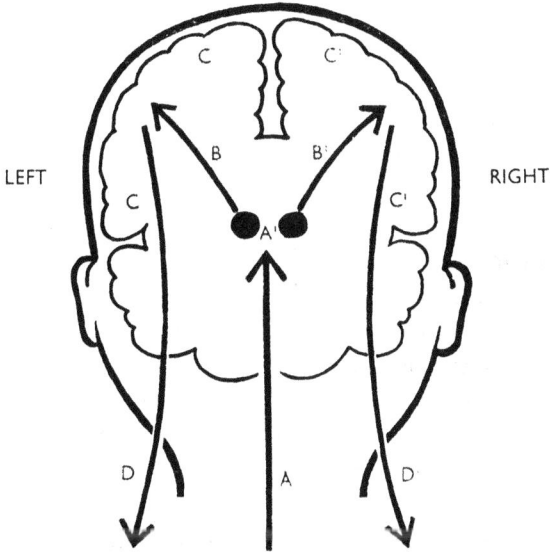

LEFT

RIGHT

REAR VIEWS OF HEAD

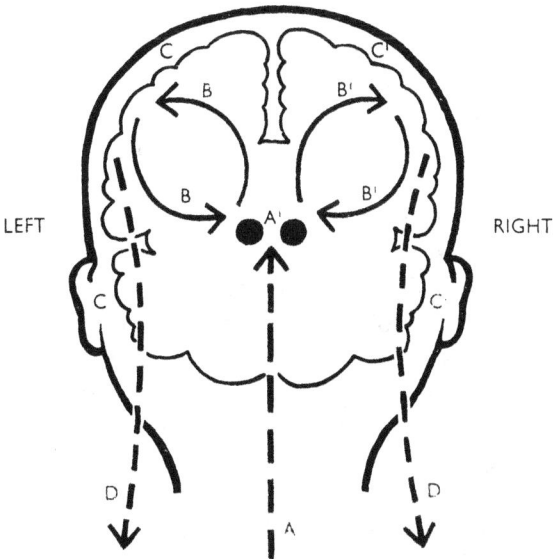

LEFT

RIGHT

Fig. 28

The Nature of the Self

As THE UTERINE ORGANISM offered a configurational sympathy
with the cosmic pattern [16], so also does the brain [164, 165].
Thus there arises a very definite sense in the brain that it is
related to 'something in the sky'. And yet something more than
this seems to become eventually evoked, for in some degree the
whole head feels either to become nuclear or peripheral to 'something in the sky' [164]. In the case of the normal human male the
head appears to take on a more peripheral feeling, the sky being
felt as nuclear. This results in the male head assuming certain
'placental' elements of feeling *vis-à-vis* the sky, with the result
that the circulation between the man's head and the sky is felt
in terms of a single upflow of energy balanced by two streams of
energy down into it. This situation is probably entirely subjective,
having no basis in any actual numerical pattern in the presumed
energy-flow between the head and 'the sky' [167]. The converse
is true of the relation between the female head and 'the sky'.
The woman's head normally feels to be nuclear in its relation
with 'the sky', and hence it assumes a more 'fetal' character, and
this is reflected in the fact that just as the fetus gave out two
(arterial) thrusts of blood and received back a single (venous)
thrust [20], so the female head feels to thrust up two streams of
energy to 'the sky' and to receive back a single thrust [168].
These different aspects of the head-sky circulation are depicted
opposite in Figure Twentynine. It will be observed that the artist
has not shown the links in their umbilical form, namely with the
two streams helically disposed around the one, but merely as
curved arrows. Yet it is an incontrovertible fact that we all feel
these circulations in their umbilical serpentine configuration,
though it is supposed that this feeling is purely subjective and has
no warrant in the flow of actual energy between head and 'the
sky', though on this point so far no certainty exists. This 'head-
sky' circulation is apparently felt by every child at a certain age,
but in most people appears to become atrophied. One might say
that the skull tends to shut off the head-sky link, while the sensory
activities of the brain, plus their uterine, gastrointestinal and
genital undertones, effectively inhibit this higher function in
the majority of people.

238

Fig. 29.

239

EPILOGUE

THIS BOOK has presented the human self as a specific product of that integrative principle which has left its signature upon external creation, and which in consequence of this ubiquity may be regarded as truly universal. The creation of mind has been depicted as taking place by means of two distinct impressions of this design: the first being made upon the unborn organism; the second upon the postnatal brain. Unlike the second, the first impress goes through many changes before it is registered in the brain. This book outlines those changes. It shows how the uterine impress, its organs disrupted by birth, secures postnatal accommodation in the body; how it migrates through the body and the earth, until at last it reaches the brain. In the brain it comes into relation not only with the central, neural integration of the body, but also with the direct impress from the sky.

I would be the last to claim that this book offers more than an outline of these events, but I do most emphatically claim that *as an outline* it is complete. By analogy with history, I might say that my book does not pretend to give details of marches and battles, nor with the associated politics and economics, but it does give a first outline of the *whole* campaign. It shows where the battles were fought, and why they were fought, and it shows also the sequence of their occurrence. Not only am I compelled to insist that my outline is complete in this sense, but I am also compelled to claim that it represents the *sine qua non* of all approach to the mind. In short, if what I write is even approximately correct, then there can be no fruitful approach to or discussion of the mind which ignores this outline. That my outline is, indeed, something more than 'approximately correct' is urged by the fact that it has already permitted me to achieve what had hitherto seemed impossible, namely the interpretation of the great myths and *märchen* and the demonstration that they all have a unitary source that also is the source of the dream.

Epilogue

No matter where we look in the fields of psychology, mysticism and religion, we fail to find the least sign that any of the orthodox and accredited authorities know the elementary facts of mind as herein stated. Indeed, this is too negative a statement, for I can show very plainly that a number of the explanations given in these fields are incorrect in the light of my discoveries. The lack of knowledge of the basic facts of mind places the exponents of psychology, religion and mysticism in the strange position of knowing a vast deal of detail that stands upon no true base. I am conversely in the difficult position of knowing the true base while yet inevitably knowing relatively little about the detail which remains to be adjusted to this base.

If asked to assess the position in which I am placed by my discoveries, I should liken it to that of the first men who used the experimental method to challenge the mass of dogma and opinion which formed the corpus of scholastic philosophy. These men used the authority of an *organon* to combat the goliath of ecclesiastical-political authority. I, too, have evolved an *organon* for the application of the experimental method to the depths of the feelings, and it is on the authority of that organon that I dare to present this most peculiar-seeming material.[1]

One reader of my manuscript has expressed disappointment that I have not dealt with the mental or spiritual aspects of the self. This is a common human reaction; the mind thirsts for meanings and results. It was this natural impatience which delivered our forebears into the tyranny of wild speculation about external nature, and it has performed the same disservice for mental science. Indeed, one of my biggest problems has been that almost nobody will take an interest in psychological principles, but that almost everyone is prone to rush after a little pragmatic psychotherapy or magic. Few people seem yet to see that pragmatism in mental matters is foredoomed to end in disillusionment, whereas devotion to principle will inevitably yield results some day that will make all magic and pragmatic psychology look as cheap as it intrinsically is.

[1] Appendices H and P offer some slight indications as to the nature of this organon, but the subject demands a volume to itself.

The Nature of the Self

In my approach to the mind, I have shunned speculation and have concentrated upon the facts revealed by my methods. This has involved an emphasis upon physical anatomy and physiology in a way that was quite unanticipated. When I began my researches I supposed that I was going to find the contents of thoughts and feelings *as such*. I certainly never dreamed that I should find myself dealing with umbilical and gastrointestinal tubes. By analogy one might say that I set out to study music, but ended up by delving into the inside of the piano—in the course of which, however, I have neither forgotten nor devalued the music *qua* music. A witty friend, observing my preoccupation with bodily tubes, has called my book a manual of cosmic plumbing. I appreciate the humor, but I think analogy with an orchestra would be more to the point. For I have shown how the bodily instruments, originally formed for entirely biological purposes, have become enlisted in the production of that mysterious and frequently dissonant symphony we call the human self.

Implicit in this discovery is an entirely new view of the relation of mind to brain, which brings in its train also a new light on the problem of the relation of spirit to matter. The demonstration that this relation is configurational is of the greatest possible importance. Moreover, new light is thrown also upon the hiatus which at present exists in the description of the evolution of man from the anthropoid. We can now see that the 'missing link' is the moment at which evolution of the animal body gave place to the use of that body as the instrument of configurational entities. There need no longer in principle be any mystery as to the relation between the animal kingdom and man. The emergence of animal form on this planet resulted in the production of a configurational instrument. Soul is the music, one might say, played upon the instrument provided by the anthropoid and his upright stance.

The contents of this book make for the doubt that man is now on the road of normal evolution. Instead of the highest human science being concerned to understand the configurational nature of man and to develop it according to its own self-evident principles, human science has been devoted almost exclusively to the preservation of the body and to machinery for extending its physical powers. But inevitably this misdirection contains the seeds of its own failure, and now the fear is that science will destroy and not develop man. Unlike those who see the alternative to destruction in terms of an atomic wonder-age, I am compelled by the facts of this book to wonder if *either* alternative fulfils the natural destiny of man. It seems to me that the human race must have got right off the lines so far as its civilized section is concerned. For if we study the myths and rites of primitive men, it seems patent that these myths were a first crude science 'of the configurational use of the body, and that the rites were a first crude technique for applying that knowledge. It is evident that at some fateful epoch in history this science of man became lost so far as the forerunners of modern civilized men were concerned. There are indeed relics of this ancient science and technology preserved in the spirit of archaism and superstition. Of such are the dogmas and the rites of Christianity and of the Masonic Temples, to mention but two instances. So far from scoffing at these things, I believe that they derive from true sources, but that they are now relics that have lost all contact with conscious understanding. The symbols have become things in their own right, and as such they oppose their own true source.

Indeed, the mere discarding of these religious and mystical relics by intellectual undercutting has got us nowhere. The tremendous elation of the rationalists as they undermined the historical bases of religion has ended in a frightened squeal of dismay. Modern psychology, which claimed to be so much more concrete than religion, has cast out the symbols of the uterine life and the rites related to them, and has put in their place a dizzy stratosphere of words and ideas. The Christian Communion, for instance, is manifestly an effort to pierce to the inner core of the self, whereas modern psychology remains utterly unaware of the existence of that core. In this context I would refer to my own psychology as 'a nuclear psychology'. In terms of this analogy it might be said that modern psychology deals with the peripheral phenomena of the mind (thoughts and feelings related to external events) just as chemistry and pre-nuclear physics deal with the peripheral phenomena of the atom—its electronic structures and their valencies. By contrast, my psychology penetrates to the core of the self, where there exist elements that are completely inaccessible to ordinary introspection or to analysis devoted to the peripheral phenomena of the mind. In a word, I might be said to have penetrated the nucleus of the mind as the nuclear physicist has penetrated the nucleus of the atom. Indeed, one might carry the analogy further and say that as the internal economy of the atomic nucleus does not respond to the ordinary laws of physics, so the internal structure of the 'ego' does not respond to the ordinary laws of external logic. Nothing we know with the conscious mind could, for instance, incline us to suspect that a child experiences his head as his own fetal self, or that he senses his head to go down through his trunk and back. This feeling-experience, though susceptible of being translated into conceptual statement, as I have demonstrated in this book, bears no relation to perception and conception as the conscious mind ordinarily knows them. It is thus that I call my psychology a 'nuclear psychology', and it is my hope that as nuclear physics has led to the transformation of matter into energy, so my new concepts may lead to techniques which will transform the feelings into new spiritual energies, and so achieve the transformation of man himself. It would, of course, not only be impossible for me to outline in advance what form these changes might take, it would indeed be quite wrong of me to try. But I am sure that the outline offered in this book can become the means of changes affecting the whole evolutionary status of the species *homo sapiens*.

APPENDICES

Appendix A

NOTES ON THE FACT THAT THE FETAL SKIN FEELING IS FREQUENTLY SYMBOLIZED BY SMALL, REGULAR PIECES

SYMBOLIC REPRESENTATION of the fetal skin feeling frequently takes the form of, or is associated with, small regular pieces. Sometimes this appears in the form of a cloak or mantle made of regular squares or patches, a circumstance which reminds us that Joseph's Coat of Many Colors is perhaps more correctly a Coat of Many Pieces. I have seen the skin feeling related to the regular squares on the skin of a crocodile or on the carapace of a tortoise. I have seen it represented as the scales of a fish or reptile; as regular tattoo-marks on a human skin; or even as a pattern of sunlight cast upon a human skin by the leaves of a tree. I have seen it symbolized by the button-covered coat of a cockney and by the chain mail of a medieval knight. I have seen it in the shape of a sequin-covered dress. Sometimes it is not directly related to the skin or its coverings, being represented by such impersonal things as a tile-mosaic, a formation of dominoes or of bricks.

So far I have not been able to account for this pattern, but so persistent and so consistent is the symbolism that I am sure it is a fact of the feelings. The question as to its mechanism still concerns me, for I am sure that the solution of this problem would cast a strong light upon the whole subject of the fetal skin feeling.

At first, lacking any alternative, I was inclined to suppose that it might be due to the nature of the fetal skin itself. I noted, for instance, that the disposition of hair upon the skin follows a rather strict pattern. It is said to be related to the original pattern of the reptilian scales, a fact which made me wonder if this could be the reason why the fetal skin feeling is so often symbolized by a reptilian skin. It is a remarkable fact that the hair on the skin

247

tends to take the form of a single large hair associated with two smaller ones. This seemed worth noting, since it is the same pattern as that which is strongly felt in association with the umbilical vessels. Also, the evolution of hair is closely associated with the evolution of the mammal, a fact which gives us a plausible link between the hair and the umbilical cord. Such considerations were, however, tempered by the fact that sometimes the hair-pattern is not two-and-one, but four-and-one. Certainly there is no apparent reason for this similarity of configuration, but owing to the close link between the fetal skin feeling, the hair and the umbilical blood these considerations are worth noting.[1]

I have wondered whether the small regular pieces might not represent the fact that the fetal skin feeling is created by the movements of tiny hairs regularly situated upon the fetal skin. Or by the regular beat of some electrical element in the umbilical blood. Or perhaps it might be due to the fact that a nerve-current is never continuous, but takes the form of discontinuous pulses, due to the fact that a nerve always rests after discharge.

Later still in my researches I have come to wonder whether these little regular pieces are prenatal in origin, or whether they are perhaps imposed upon the original skin feeling by the eyes. For, as I have shown, the eyes at birth are felt to be identical with the fetal skin.[2] The retina of the eye is composed of a mosaic of rods and cones which act as the detectors of light. I have been led to wonder if the 'little regular squares' associated with the fetal skin feeling might be the result of some early reaction of the brain to the impulses from the eyes? Is it possible that the child's first sense of the stimulation of his retina might be that of a mosaic pattern dictated by the neural structure of the retina? Naturally I am in no position to check this hypothesis.

However, that there *is* a relation between these regular pieces and light is certain. Symbolic representations of these 'regular pieces' often have the element of light strongly marked. The little squares or pieces of skin feeling are frequently linked with fish-scales that gleam; pearl buttons or sequins that glitter, etc.

[1] See Chapter Two.
[2] See Chapter One.

Appendix B

POST SCRIPTUM TO THE EXPOSITION OF A UNIVERSAL DESIGN

THE CONCEPT of a universal design outlined in this book is the outcome of two distinct inquiries. This fact should be understood, for otherwise grave misunderstanding of my methods and authority is bound to ensue. In the course of my life I have carried on forays, as it were, into *two* distinct fields of knowledge. This book represents the unification of the results of *both* forays. These results blend perfectly together into a single whole, but if anyone supposes that they were derived in the course of a single straight-line inquiry, he will get an entirely false picture. The simplest way to separate the two ingredients of this book is to present them in the chronological order of their discovery, and this I shall now attempt very briefly to do.

From about the age of twentyone I became fascinated by the concept that all creation is the product of a single order or pattern of relationships. This idea was not mine. I inherited it from another. I followed it up enthusiastically, studying the fields of science as best I could. At last I became so convinced of the reality of this concept that I abandoned business life and devoted my time and slender resources to a deeper and more professional quest. In the course of this quest I made journeys to various parts of the world and came into contact with many men of science. I found a considerable proportion of these men actually were sympathetic to my quest, and this sympathy they demonstrated by their readiness to receive me again and again, to carry on such correspondence as they had time for, and to introduce me to fellow scientists. I was encouraged by this to feel that my inquiry was not regarded *a priori* as pointless.

Well before I reached the age of forty I had gone as far as I could in this inquiry. I had found myself able to demonstrate that external creation can be summed up into seven distinct levels of integration, and that on each level the governing pattern was of the same order. What more could I do? If the concept did not attract the specialists, there was little I could do about it. Certainly I could not go into each separate field and become a specialist. In practice this would demand a number of lifetimes, and even so it would, in principle, be fruitless. For it was not more specialism that was required, but a different order of thought altogether.

I realized that I must find some way of applying my concept of a universal design, so as to create my own authority, and thereby to avoid the appearance of being merely an unofficial commentator upon science. I quickly saw that the next logical step was to demonstrate that the human mind is created by the influence of the same pattern as that which I had already traced in external nature. If I could use my theory of creation to guide me to discover the nature of mind, then my circle of proof would be complete. The problem was to find the appropriate *organon* for the investigation of mind. I came eventually to select dream analysis as my method, and I made it my specialism.

Thus at about the age of forty I opened up the second era of inquiry, this time into the nature of mind. As I have said before in these pages, I began my quest assuming that I might find patterns of thought and emotion which somehow would show me that the mind is the product of the same pattern as that already seen by me in the atom, the solar system, the living cell and so on. Instead I found the universal pattern impressed upon the feelings of organs created for quite mundane purposes. I was faced with the possibility of creating what I have called 'the configurational anatomy' of the body. This concrete anatomical element lent force to my discoveries, but my primary interest still lay in the fact that I had discovered the structure of the mind as the reflection of the same design as that perceived in external nature.

This implies that one can find in the depths of the human

feelings elements of pattern also to be found in external phenomena. It suggests that the fetus already has experienced the impact
upon its organic feelings of the forces which have shaped the
external world. I had spent half my life unearthing evidence for
a common pattern in all external forms, only to find that my fetal
self, in common with all fetal selves, had 'known it all' long before.
The very self that knows is the product of the pattern which has
formed the atoms, stars and cells or, if you will, according to
which they had been formed. Moreover, just as I had noted in the
external world a tendency to fourfold and sevenfold rhythms, so
now I saw that the fetus had experienced the source of this bias
in terms of its own umbilical beat. I saw this similarity between
internal and external pattern as the source of those elusive sympathies and intuitions which men have always felt for external
nature. Sometimes this was passive, but at other times it was
active, as when the umbilical beat, assumed into the thalamocortical circulation, influences the brain to perceive optical stimulations in terms of color, and aural stimulations in terms of music.

Science has been compelled rigorously to exclude the influence
of the inward pattern of the self upon the observations of the
mind. This exclusion, useful in its proper field, has unfortunately
overlapped into realms where it is highly improper. My task has
been to see both the inward and the outward manifestations of
the pattern while yet not confusing them.

This seems to be the place to notice the two opposing forms of
mental action here involved. The triumph of science has been
largely the outcome of a rigorous exclusion of all emotions from
the concept, culminating in those highly polished and brittle
conceptual instruments, the mathematical symbols, which can act
like exquisite chessmen in the great game of scientific logic.
This kind of thinking I have followed as best I could in the
formulation of my unifying concept of nature. But when I turned
to examine the nature of mind, I was compelled to invent techniques which would permit the mind to dissolve its concepts and
to yield the feeling components from which thought and the
scientific method have abstracted them. And yet in doing this, I
have had at the same time to watch the product of this dissolution

with the same logical faculty which, in the mind of the analysand, I was temporarily putting in abeyance.

In Figure Thirty I have tried to represent schematically the essence of this present discourse. The sketch seeks to represent the fact that both mind and matter derive from the same pattern, and that the mind imposes upon matter its own patterns, though these are not really foreign to matter, since both derive from the same primal source.

The sketch also helps to demarcate my own two lines of inquiry. My first period of inquiry led me into the field 'B', and in the course of that inquiry I became reasonably satisfied that a common pattern may be traced into the root of all forms. My second period of inquiry led me into field 'A', and here I found, by means of dream analysis, the same pattern again.

Figure Thirty shows not only the two distinct spheres of the universal impress (namely the spheres of matter and of mind) but also seeks to represent, by means of the arrow marked x, the relation which exists between the two fields. This relation is purely one of sympathy of pattern. There can be no other basis of contact between matter and mind save through their common unity of pattern. This fact, as I see it, governs all knowledge, and sets the pace for all thinking about the outside world. It has its correlate, incidentally, in the two systems of neuromuscular activity illustrated by Figures Twentyseven and Twentyeight, which show how 'pattern for action' and 'pattern for subjective thought' are both served by the single instrument of the thalamo-cortical circulation. And it is precisely here, I suspect, that one may find the source of two heretofore puzzling links between mind and matter, namely the phenomena of color and music. Why should it be that the impact of electromagnetic vibrations on the eye should give a sense of color related to a periodic element in the vibratory phenomena? And why should the impact of air vibrations on the eardrum result in a periodic sense of form which we call music? I think this is a case where the two impressions of the universal design, shown in Figure Thirty as field 'A' and field 'B', come into specific relationship. The organism, having acquired the periodic sense of flow through the umbilical

Fig. 30

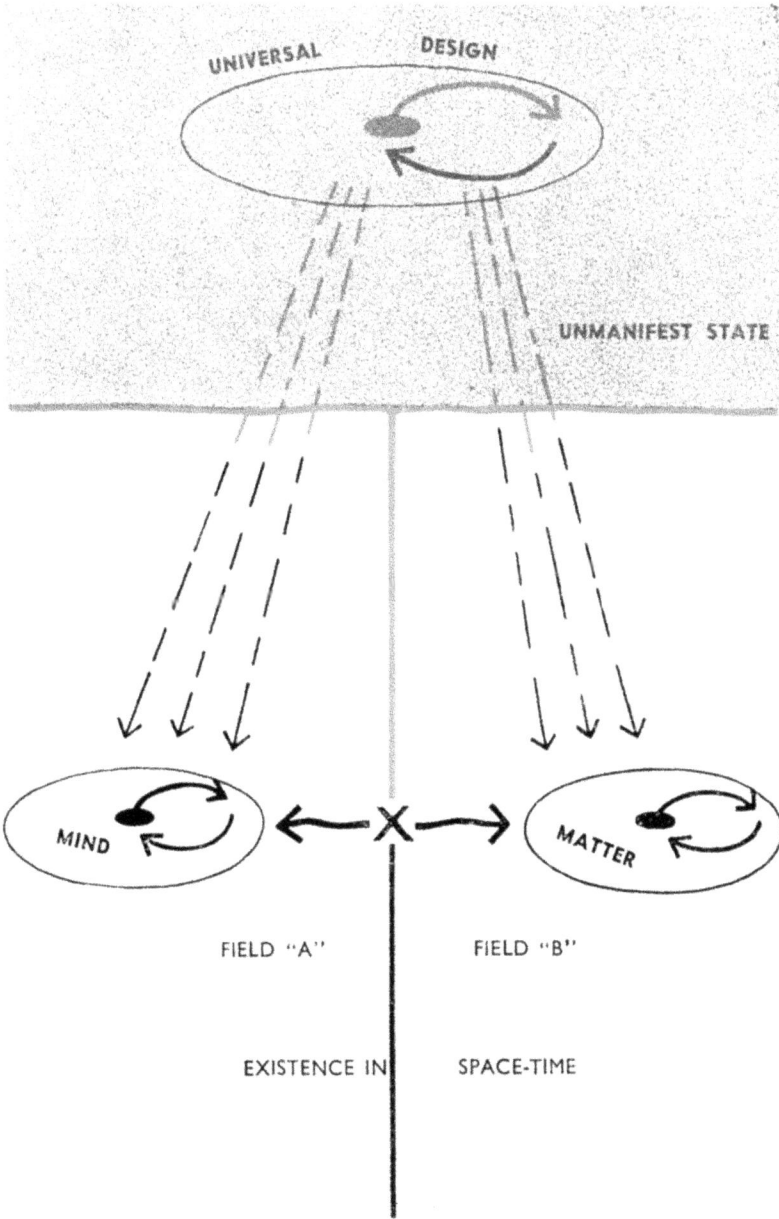

beat (see Figure One), experiences its remobilization in the meta-umbilical flow of neural energy in the brain. The senses of smell and taste show signs of a similar tendency to periodic organization.

Appendix C

HOW MANY PLACENTAS?

THERE IS, of course, only one placenta. But this uterine organ generates certain feeling-patterns which cannot be lost if the mind is to develop. Therefore this mysterious Twin with which we occupied the womb is never lost to the feelings. It appears again and again in a variety of forms. It is the lungs, the mother's breast, the mother's body, the excretory pot, the eating pot, the earth and so on. In the degree that the legs are felt to be the umbilical arteries, the sense of the placenta is evoked at the feet, and in the degree that the umbilical feelings are ultimately transferred to the arms from the legs, the placenta is felt to be either the hands or attached to the hands. It has been made the subject of numerous literary references of all kinds, some avowedly unconscious and others partly intellectual. Of this last kind, I suppose, is Jung's effort to intellectualize 'the Shadow' as the counterpart of the individual.

One well-known representation of this persistent presence of the Twin (the placenta) is offered by the Gospel of St John, where there is told the strange tale of Thomas called Didymus. Thomas declares that he will not believe in the resurrection of Jesus unless he can see in his hands the print of the nails, and put his finger into those prints, and also thrust his hand into the wounded side of Jesus. The wounded side, I suggest, is the representation of the navel, the wound of birth. The wounds in the hands, like the wounds in the feet, represent the feeling of the original 'wound in the side' transferred to the feet and the hands.[1] Wherever these

[1] See Figure Six and Chapter Eleven.

255

umbilical memories appear, there at once appear also the memories of the placenta. The figure of Thomas called Didymus fits into this context like a hand into a glove, for the name Thomas is the Greek version of the Hebrew *tâ'ôwm*, meaning 'a twin', while the name Didymus is the Greek *didumos*, also meaning 'a twin' or 'twins'.

The story of Thomas Didymus (Mister Twin-Twin) appeals to the deep feelings, which know that whenever the umbilical 'wounds' appear in the feeling of any bodily organ, there at once will also appear the simulacrum of the (placental) twin, longing to find again the Lord (fetus) who was lost at birth.

Appendix D

SOME NOTES ON THE SYMBOLIC FIGURE OF
THE SHINING ONE AS UNIVERSAL
REPRESENTATIVE OF THE FETAL SKIN
FEELING

THOUGH THERE may be some doubt as to the precise cause of the
feeling that the fetal skin is related to *light, fire* or *gleam*,[1] there can
be no doubt at all that a great number of the ancient gods, heroes
and saviors were represented in terms of brightness. Sometimes
this quality is clearly stated; sometimes it inheres in an etymological link; sometimes it is made evident by the adventures in
which the hero becomes involved. But whenever there appears in
myths and legends the figure of this shining or gleaming hero,
then almost always the uterine context is discernable, sometimes
plainly, sometimes dimly. Conversely, whenever mythological
material yields a markedly uterine context, then some trace of
this luminous personage is almost always found. It would be
quite impossible here to indicate all the variants of this Shining
One, and certainly impossible to give each his appropriate
uterine setting. But the job *can* be done with a large measure of
success, and has already been done in my unpublished analysis
of the myths. Here I propose to give only a few examples.

I begin by indicating Zeus, the great Sky god of the ancient
Greek world. Not only did he hurl the lightning bolt, but his very
name is alleged to mean 'the Bright One'. In the Hymn to the
Diktean Zeus he was hailed as something akin to 'Almighty
Gleam'. Zeus was also very closely related, like Esau, to a hairy
skin, for his famous *aegis* turns out upon examination to be an

[1] See Appendix A.

unshorn goatskin. In some mythical figures the sense of fire or light was combined with the skin itself, a circumstance to be seen in the mythology of Herakles, who slew the Nemean Lion and wore its skin. The ancient peoples apparently tended to regard the lion as in some way specially related to, or representative of fire, so that a lion's skin readily serves as a combination of the fire and the *aegis* of Zeus. Such a combination is hinted at obliquely in the myth of Samson, whose name is in the Hebrew *Shimshôwn*, deriving from the word *shemesh*, which means 'to be brilliant' and refers also to the sun. The relation of Samson to hair is intimate, for when Delilah clipped his hair, Samson's power was gone. Samson's relation to the lion is obliquely represented by his slaying of the beast at Timnath. The great Leo Frobenius has demonstrated the considerable consistency of the primitive myths of the Sun Hero. One element in the basic myth appears to be that the Sun Hero lost his hair in the belly of a great fish which swallowed him. It is possible to demonstrate that this great fish which swallows the Sun Hero is the symbol of the placenta, and also to show a like meaning in the case of Delilah. Indeed, the myth of Samson contains a hidden link with this aspect of the general myth of the Sun Hero, in that when the Philistines finally capture Samson they give praise to the god Dagon, a name which derives straight from the Hebrew *dag*, meaning 'a fish'.

In the case of Joseph, son of Jacob, the symbolism of the Shining One is conveyed by the mysterious Coat of Many Colors, which has no obvious relation to hair, and only an indirect relation to light or fire through the sense of color. And even the sense of color here is uncertain, since the original description of the Coat appears to be 'A Coat of Many Breadths' or 'A Coat of Many Pieces'.[1]

Sometimes the figure of the Shining One is represented by the eyes or the sense of sight. Thus Reuben, the firstborn of Jacob, whose fetal nature I have demonstrated in my unpublished work on mythology, has a name which refers to the eyes. His father's description of him in Genesis 49 amply supports the view that

[1] This is, in fact, the translation given in the Douai bible, and it may have a relation to the material indicated in Appendix A.

Reuben refers to the fetal skin feeling, so that we may see him in terms of the fetal feelings in the eyes.[1] Sometimes the Shining One has the eyes all over his skin, and it has been alleged that the name of the great Egyptian Osiris comes from a word meaning 'many-eyed'. Such a name reminds us of the Greek figure of Argos Panoptes, the man with a hundred eyes dispersed all over his skin, who was set to watch the heifer Io.

There are not wanting signs that would identify Abraham, Isaac and Jacob with the Shining One. Sometimes this identification is etymological. The name Abram is apparently a contraction from *'Ăbîyrâm*, which is composed of the word *'âb*, meaning 'father', and *rûwm*, 'to be high'. The 'high father' already vaguely suggests the sun, and this is supported by the fact that he comes from Ur, a name which derives from the word *'ûwr*, meaning 'flame'. Abram's sojourn in Haran is also telling in such a context, for the name Haran, though it appears to refer to the sense of height, is identical in outline with the Hebrew *Chârân*, which means 'parched', and which comes from *chârar*, meaning 'to glow'. The name Isaac, though it is reputed to mean 'the laughing one', from *tsâchaq*, 'laughter', could equally well be derived from an extremely close word *tsâchar*, which means 'to dazzle'. As for Jacob, though at first he is the enemy of the fetal Esau (and hence not in that role a candidate for the role of the Shining One), he comes at last to be Israel, a name which can be shown to have a suggestive link with the sun. It is at the ford Jabbok that Jacob becomes Israel, and it will be noted that his crossing of the ford coincides with *daybreak*, and that the myth states that the *sun* 'rose upon him' as he passed over. Moreover, it is conceivable that the name Israel does not mean, as is commonly supposed, 'a prince of God', but that it means something more like 'the shining one of God', being derivable from the words *yisra El*, the word *yisra* being from the root *yizrach*, meaning 'to shine forth'.

The ancient symbolism of the zodiac (which has fallen into so much undeserved disrepute as a result of the associations it has

---

[1] The name Reuben is in Hebrew *Re'ûwbên*, from the root *râ'âh*, 'to see'. The reference to Reuben in Genesis 49 represents him as the incestuous source of his father's strength and being.

acquired in modern times) contains a highly suggestive link between the lion, the sense of fire, the ego and the uterine pattern. In the zodiac, the sign of the Lion is related direct to the sun, and is related also to the human 'ego' through the fact that those born under its influence are reputed to be markedly egotistical. Its relation to the uterine pattern can be seen in the following circumstance: there are three so-called 'fire signs' in the zodiac, namely Leo, Aries and Sagittarius. Leo is represented by the Lion, Aries by the Ram, and Sagittarius by the Centaur-archer. This is highly suggestive because the ram has coiled horns, which could well symbolize the dual, twisted umbilical arterial thrust, while Sagittarius shoots a single arrow, which could equally well symbolize the single, straight placental thrust through the umbilical vein.[1] It seems to me highly likely that this ancient symbolism of the 'fire signs' of the zodiac is a method of representing the uterine organism in which the nuclear feeling (fire) is generated. The Lion in such a context would symbolize the fetal skin feeling, while the other two signs would symbolize the two opposing elements evoked in the uterine organism by the back-and-forth thrusts of blood in the umbilical cord.

[1] See Chapter Three for some comments on the horse and the centaur as symbols of the placenta. In my unpublished work on mythology, I have shown the horse in many a strong placental context.

Appendix E

HOW MANY BIRTHS DO WE SUFFER?

THE READER will have observed that I refer again and again to the experience of *emergence* in terms of *birth*. Thus the feces are felt to be the self 'born' out of the anus; the skull is felt to be the self 'born' out of the trunk through the neck. Is this just a loose manner of speaking? Indeed it is not. Every emergence is felt by us as if it were actually our own selves being born. Moreover, this is not merely a postnatal feeling-expression, for the same thing is felt retroactively in terms of the constant movement of the nuclear energy through the umbilical cord. The fetal nuclear self seems to be 'born' out of the navel, and out of the placenta back to the fetal body again.[1]

It was, in fact, this very cirumstance which was one of the major factors in facilitating my discoveries. When I started my analytical work I seemed to see in dreams nothing but birth symbolisms, plus a few hints of a dim prenatal memory. But as I persisted, I began to notice an odd thing about these memories of birth, namely that they were not invariably simple memories of parturition, but often seemed to consist of parturition-memories overlaid by other elements of extrusion or emergence. Thus, for instance, I found many birth dreams in which fecal and bowel symbolisms could be detected. There were births involving the supposed emergence of the head out of the trunk, and births related to the act of breathing. All these 'births' tended to coalesce, and they all seemed to have overtones of actual parturition.

This remained a mystery until at length I was driven to try the

[1] See Chapter Two.

261

hypothesis that birth is not felt by the human being merely in terms of parturition, but in terms of *emergence*. Every emergence is for the feelings a birth, of which actual parturition is simply the most violent and real. The concept of the Universal Design soon made it clear to me that there is only a very simple pattern of events at the root of the feelings, and that it is from this pattern of events that the unity of birth-feelings derives. This simple underlying pattern of birth may be stated thus: the Nucleus enters or penetrates the Sphere and fructifies it; is destroyed and renewed, and then emerges as the restored Nucleus. In human terms: The Father enters the Mother and is destroyed there and renewed, and is then Born as Child, and in turn becomes again the Father, ready for a new cycle.[1]

The feelings are dominated by this sense of birth, so that there are felt to be as many 'births' as there are emergences both by and from the body. Every neuromuscular thrust, say of the arms or legs, is very definitely felt not only as an excretion [112] but also as a birth. And wherever such a 'birth' is felt, the feelings of actual parturition are remobilized. It is for this reason that psychosomatic disturbances frequently have about them elements of a birth replay, as if the feelings are going through birth all over again, and making their effect felt upon the body. The birth shock includes such diverse phenomena as sense of falling, sense of cold, sense of the activation of the eyes, the ears, the nose and lungs. Another is a sense of violent head damage or compression. There phenomena are often manifested psychosomatically when the infant goes through the stages outlined in this book, as for instance in the experience of excretion and of the restoration of the sense of the head on the shoulders. Thus birth is a very wide term, and phenomena of the birth shock are produced in the body when any emergence is achieved. This is also true of those who, in the course of analysis, succeed in achieving or completing an emotional emergence delayed beyond its normal infancy time.

[1] See pages 40 and 186.

Appendix F

HINTS FOR THE ANALYTIC READING
OF
THE DEVIL AND THE THREE GOLDEN HAIRS

In case the reader may not be aware of the origins of the Grimm fairy tales, it should be said that none of these stories was invented by the Grimm brothers. They were collected by these wonderful men, who went into the villages and wrote down many of the stories from the lips of the story tellers. Mercifully for us, they did this at the moment when modern civilization was about to bring to an end this inheritance of folk mythology in Europe.

Résumé of the tale of the Devil and the Three Golden Hairs

A boy was known from birth to be fated to marry the King's daughter. This was known of him because he was born wearing a caul. The King, determined to prevent this marriage, got possession of the child and threw him into a river. The river carried the child to a mill, where he was rescued and adopted by the miller. Years later the King discovered the boy's existence at the mill, and again sought his life. But through the intervention of fate the boy arrived at the palace during the King's absence and was married to the princess. The King, returning home, was furious, and in a last effort to rid himself of the young man, sent him down to hell to fetch three golden hairs from the devil. On the way to hell the boy stopped at a town where stood a barren tree that once grew golden apples. He was asked to explain why the tree no longer bore fruit. At yet another town he found a dry well that once ran with wine. He was asked to explain why the well dried up. Then he came to a river across which he was ferried by an old man, who wanted to know why he was doomed to row back and forth. The boy reached hell and got the three golden hairs from the devil, and learned the answers to the three questions which had been posed to him in the course of his journey.

Interpretation of the Story

1. A boy born with a caul is fated to marry the King's daughter.

1. The caul represents the fetal skin feeling 'brought over' into the postnatal life. Since the fetal nuclear feeling is fated to find its placental counterpart, the meaning of the tale is obvious.

2. The child is thrown into a river and rescued by the miller.

2. The river represents the gastro-intestinal tract. The mill is a common symbol of the anus. The boy at the mill represents 'the face and fetus at the bottom'.

3. The boy cannot really keep his princess until he has been down to the devil.

3. The feelings must achieve the right relation with the depths of the earth before they can achieve their right relation in the head.

4. The boy is sent to get three golden hairs from the devil.

4. The number three suggests an umbilical meaning. The fact that the hairs are gold, and down in the earth, suggests that what is meant is that the umbilical pattern of the excretions (gold) must be rightly adjusted in their relation with the earth.

5. The meaning of the barren tree that once grew golden apples.	5. This is a representation of the umbilical cord in its excretory sense.
6. The meaning of the fountain that once ran wine.	6. The umbilical cord may be regarded as a fountain that once ran with wine (blood).
7. The ferryman rowing back and forth.	7. The ferryman represents the two-way flow of the blood in the umbilical cord.

It will be observed that not only are there three hairs to be gained, but also that there are three questions to be solved. So that not only can each individual question be shown to have an umbilical meaning, but the total number of the questions contains the same indication in numerical terms.

The above hints may raise as many questions as they solve, and this is inevitable when dealing in so small a compass with so elusive a subject. However, I have dealt with this fairy tale at much greater length in the context of my general work on the myths, and hope that it may soon be available for study. Lacking this wider extension of my analysis of the myths and *märchen* the reader may at times think that I have abandoned myself to wishful thinking whenever this seems to suit my case. As an example of this, he might think that it is the height of loose guesswork to assert, as I have done on page 264, that the caul represents the fetal skin feeling brought over into the postnatal life. But investigation of this subject would show that this old folk attitude to the caul is all part and parcel of a general superstitious reverence felt by our forefathers for everything belonging to the prenatal existence. Thus, for instance, Frazer tells us that savage and peasant peoples made a great deal of the umbilical cord and the placenta, as well as of the amnion. Either all or some of these had to be carefully, even ceremoniously preserved, and were believed to represent or to contain the spirit double of the child. This strange procedure is easily comprehensible in the light of the present book. It is not difficult to imagine that the more primitive peoples, whose minds are not shut off from their feelings, would have a strong intuition of the reality of the prenatal consciousness associated with the umbilical cord, the placenta and the fetal skin —for which last the amnion would make a suitable representative. What more natural than that these people, unable to separate the emotional elements from the fleshly relics of their origin, should preserve the pathetic bits of skin as their nearest approach to the lost reality. This little extension (and justification) of my interpretation of the caul (amnion) could be greatly increased, and the same applies to all the other assertions made in respect to the fairy tale of *The Devil and the Three Golden Hairs.*

Appendix G

THE PLACENTA FELT AS ANDROGYNOUS

EXPERIENCE HAS taught me that a few objects have an unchanging symbolic meaning both in ancient myth and modern dream. For instance, the Sun and the lion, seem always to symbolize the fetal skin-feeling. Similarly the ass and the dog seem always to appear in a context which suits their interpretation as anal symbols. I have learned to save time by trying out such familiar meanings before looking for an alternative, but I never permit myself any absolutely final assumption in such matters. In any case the number of objects having this consistent symbolic meaning is quite limited.[1]

With this in mind the reader will not accuse me of loose thinking when I say that in my experience a sexually indeterminate figure in a dream *invariably* symbolizes the placenta. Or, shall we more discreetly say that, in my experience, such an interpretation has always permitted the extraction from dreams of a perfectly consistent context. I have as yet found no exception to this rule. When I see in a dream the figure of a masculine woman or a downright Lesbian, or a feminine type of man or homosexual, I am at once alerted to try the placental meaning.

Indeed, I have used this knowledge in a way that is very confirmatory of my whole method. On several occasions when I have been confronted with a dream figure of manifestly placental nature, but in respect to which no sexual indications have been given, I have asked the patient or subject whether the individual was in real life a little sexually unorthodox. Again and again I

Anything even remotely approaching the idea of a dictionary of dream symbols is, of course, utterly foreign to my whole concept of the dream.

267

have been able to confirm the precision of my analytical methods in this way, namely by correctly guessing the character of an individual from his or her part in a patient's dream.

The reason for this particular placental symbolism is evidently the fact that the fetus feels the placenta to be by turns both nuclear and hollow, which is to say, by postnatal retrospection, both male and female. It is a readily demonstrable fact that any androgynous figure appearing in a dream will invariably fit the role of a placental symbol. When I say androgynous, I mean to indicate a category which covers the most extreme reaches of sexual uncertainty. Sometimes the symbol will be no more precise than that of a woman who always wears trousers, or of a man who has a rather high-pitched voice.

This symbolism is to be observed in the myths. It is particularly noticeable, for instance, that the famous twins which abound in mythology consist almost always of a very strong and masculine boy and a rather weak and effeminate boy. Mr A. B. Cook has stated that the theme of the strong and the weak twin is a recurrent feature of myths. The famous Dioskouroi were often represented as one bearded and the other beardless. There are not wanting signs that the beardless and weaker twin was effeminate, for indeed in some cases he was represented as a female. Thus the mystical school of Epiminides maintained that the Dioskouroi were male and female twins, and Mr Cook tells us that Apollo and Artemis were in all probability originally regarded as twins. In the myth of Esau and Jacob, Esau was not only the fetal symbol, but was also the more masculine figure, the cunning hunter especially linked to his father. Jacob, on the other hand was the symbol of the placenta. He stayed behind in the tents; was mother's favorite, and by implication beardless in contrast to his hairy brother.[1] The implication is that whereas Esau was powerfully male, Jacob was effeminate, a representation which is thoroughly consistent with their roles as symbols of the fetus and the placenta.

---

[1] And so had to have hair put on his hands and neck in order to pose as Esau.

Appendix H

NOTES ON THE NATURE OF A CONCEPT AND THE RELATION OF IT TO DREAMS AND THEIR ANALYSIS

OUR FIRST feelings of the external world are generalized. But as we begin to distinguish between different phenomena, so we gradually divide our feelings into finer and ever finer 'pieces'. These pieces have the character of memory. They tend to become integrated by education and language. Experiences are given labels, and the feelings associated with those experiences tend to form the nuclei to which new experiences adhere. The mental entity thus formed is, I believe, what we ordinarily call a concept.

We tend, however, to overlook the fact that the event in our mind which responds to these conceptual labels stems back to feelings now completely forgotten. Every concept in our minds, no matter how clear and sharp it has become in the course of the years, has an ancestry in the deep feelings. This ancestry we inevitably forget. We use words to express events without recalling the origins of those words. The process of thought uses the concept as a chess-player uses his chessmen. The composition of the concept is no more consciously present in the thinking mind than the molecular structure of the chessmen is in the mind of the chess-player as he concentrates upon the game.

But when we sleep, and the concepts cease to play in the mind, the constituent feelings become aware of their older existence. No longer is it the concept as a whole which the mind uses, but the feelings which constitute the raw material of the concepts. It is then that the mind becomes conscious of the original contents of the feelings. This consciousness we call a dream.

The Nature of the Self

When we awaken and remember a dream, we are really remembering the old context of the feelings, and not the conceptual wholes into which they have become integrated. But we cannot express the old context of the feelings, for the conscious mind knows nothing of it, its consciousness being based upon the existence of the very concepts into which the old feelings are bound. It is as impossible for a conceptual state of mind to know the content of a concept as for an eye to see its own constituent molecules.

But the conscious mind may realize that some of its concepts have been mysteriously used in an unfamiliar way during the night, and it may remember a strange context fleetingly caught. This context is, of course, what we call a dream. Though but vaguely connected with known externalities, it does not entirely make the kind of sense which the conscious mind expects.

Let me illustrate this by means of a rough analogy. A fisherman ties a line to a cork float, and on the line he puts ten baited hooks. He throws the line over the side of a boat and waits. One thing is certain: no matter which hook is bitten by a fish, the cork float will be agitated. The cork float represents a concept in the mind. Each baited hook represents one of the feelings of which the concept is composed. The point is that no matter *which* feeling becomes involved in a dream context during sleep, the concept (the cork float) will be agitated, and will appear in the dream context.

Let us take a very simple example of how this works. It must be simple only because there would otherwise be no room to represent it on a single page. A man dreams: 'I went into a house and met George Smith'. Now, the dreamer, when called upon to comment on this, says that he has never known a man called George Smith. But he recalls that he had a great friend named George who married a girl named Smith. In this way we derive three basic concepts from the dream: (1) George, (2) Miss Smith, and (3) a house. The artist has sought to make a pictorial representation [Figure Thirty-one, page 273] of the nature of a concept and the relation of its structure to both conscious thought and dreaming.

Appendix H

When each of these three concepts is probed, the following result is achieved:

GEORGE: (1) Boyhood friend, (2) Red face, (3) Full name was George Tanner, (4) Not a tanner, but a farmer, (5) Beer drinker, etc., etc.

MISS SMITH: (1) I courted her before George, (2) She wanted to wear the trousers—strong minded girl, (3) Good cook, (4) As good as a man on the farm, (5) Had big family, etc., etc.

HOUSE: (1) Stood in a wood, (2) Looked lonely, (3) It reminds me now I come to think of it of the house I spent my honeymoon in, (4) Maybe haunted, (5) Big windows, etc., etc.

I have made this imaginary subject give five associations with each of the concepts. These associations represent certain feelings and memories presumed to be bound up in the concept. I should make it clear, however, that these associations are very simple and superficial. I have made them so merely to illustrate the structure of a concept and its relation to both dreaming and to the analysis of dreams.

Let us now use these three concepts and their associations in connection with the analogy of the cork floats and the baited hooks. Each of the three concepts is represented in Figure Thirtyone by a cork float, and each of the five associations by a baited hook attached to one of these floats.

In terms of Figure Thirtyone, a dream might be likened to the passage of a fish across the lines, which bites at one hook on each line as it passes. The sequence of baited hooks thus bitten represents the hidden context of the dream. But the context which will appear in consciousness upon waking is the context provided by the bobbing of the cork floats on the surface—which is to say, by the activation of the concepts which contain the feelings relevant to the hidden context. The dream is not telling us about George, Miss Smith or the house, it is indicating feelings associated with each of these three which, when strung together, make a 'feeling-communication'.

The Nature of the Self

In the light of this book one context leaps quickly to the eye. If you take No. 3 in the first line (tanner), and add it to No. 2 in the second line (wore pants), and No. 3 in the third line (honeymoon house), you will see that the dream *could* have the following hidden context:

> A man who tans skins (a tanner obviously indicated by being contrasted with a farmer) married a girl who acted like a man (wore the pants) and lived in my honeymoon house.

In this can plainly be seen the possible statement that the dreamer is talking about a memory deep in his feelings of the fetal skin feeling (tanner = skins) living a life of love (honeymoon) in the womb with the 'androgynous' placenta.

The art of dream analysis is to find such hidden contexts. It should be borne in mind, however, that no single dream can offer proof of any kind. Proof comes only through the consistency to be observed in a growing accumulation of such contexts. All I seek to do in this brief appendix is to indicate how the nature of a concept, as described in Chapter Eleven, explains both the nature of a dream and the method of analysis. Analysis always consists of eliciting from a dreamer a series of associations as roughly illustrated, and then of tracing a plausible context by linking up the associations. The contents of this book have been built up over the years by analyses vastly more complex than anything I can illustrate here. Starting from a very small first perception, namely indications of birth, I gradually expanded my knowledge of the feelings step by step, by making hypotheses and watching for their possible confirmation in dream context. When confirmation was discovered in dream after dream, so the hypothesis would harden into fact, and would then become a starting point for a new hypothesis, which in turn was compelled to stand the test of my analyses. As a mathematical physicist formulates equations which may or may not have any application in 'nature', and submits them to the laboratory worker as guides for inquiry, so I have done the same thing. But I have had to be my own theoretician and my own practical worker.

My culminating certainty has come from the fact that after I

Appendix H

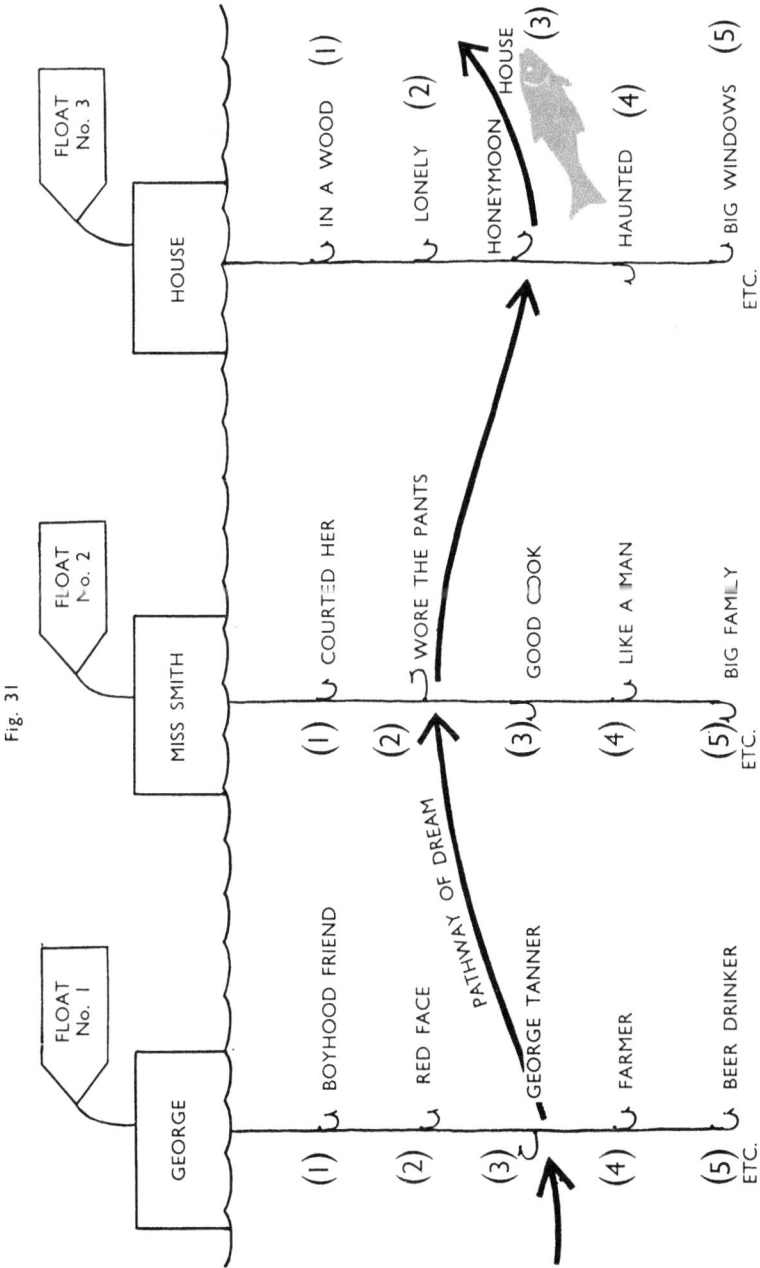

Fig. 31

FLOAT No. 3

HOUSE

(1) IN A WOOD
(2) LONELY
HONEYMOON HOUSE (3)
(4) HAUNTED
(5) BIG WINDOWS
ETC.

FLOAT No. 2

MISS SMITH

(1) COURTED HER
(2) WORE THE PANTS
(3) GOOD COOK
(4) LIKE A MAN
(5) BIG FAMILY
ETC.

FLOAT No. 1

GEORGE

(1) BOYHOOD FRIEND
(2) RED FACE
PATHWAY OF DREAM
(3) GEORGE TANNER
(4) FARMER
(5) BEER DRINKER
ETC.

273

have completed each new view of the nature of the feelings, I have been able to use it in its turn to interpret those ancient symbolisms we call myths. The persistent coincidence of the symbolisms has made it impossible to doubt both that my picture of the feelings is correct, and that it is universal both to modern man and to all men from the most primitive times.

Appendix I

BRIEF ANALYSIS OF THE MYTH OF ADAM AND EVE[1]

THIS WONDERFUL myth has been presented to successive genera-
tions of Western mankind as if it were a story of the origins of
mankind in an anthropological sense. In this form it has been
mistakenly accepted and equally mistakenly rejected. If one
examines it carefully, paying due heed to the peculiar nature
of the Hebrew language, it can be seen as a symbolic representation of the fact that each human self does indeed originate in the
interrelations of the fetus and the placenta through the umbilical
cord. Moreover, the myth gives powerful indications that the
human sense of gender derives from the same source.

The name Adam is from the Hebrew word *'âdam*, which appears
to relate to a flush of blood in the face. This idea makes a fair
start, for we know that one aspect of the fetal skin feeling is
derived from the blood in the skin. But the skin feeling is also
evoked by the hair and, although the Bible says nothing about
Adam's hair, yet it links him direct with Esau because Esau has
a second name, Edom, which is from the same root as the name
Adam. Esau, as we know, is born covered with a hairy coat,
and he eventually becomes closely associated with Seir, which
name is derived from the Hebrew root *sâ'ar*, meaning 'to shiver'.
But this word is identical in outline with the Hebrew word for
hair. Esau is thus very much the hairy one, but he is also red all
over, and the word for 'red' used by the Hebrew Bible in this

---

[1] All Hebrew words are rendered in transliterated form, using the style of
Smith's Bible Dictionary.

275

context is *'admônîy*, which derives from the same root as Adam. That Esau is a symbol of the fetal skin feeling is to be seen not only from the fact that he is born red and covered with hair (blood in the skin and hair on it), but that he has a twin named Jacob who is born holding onto Esau's heel. A twin in mythology is always suspect of being a placental symbol. And when we know that the fetus, owing to the link between the legs and the umbilical arteries, feels that the placenta is attached to the ends of his legs,[1] why then we can hardly doubt that the twin clinging to the end of his brother's leg is the symbol of the placenta. We can see, therefore, that the symbolic figure of Esau supplements the symbolic figure of Adam as representative of the fetus.[2]

As Esau has Jacob, so Adam has Eve. That Eve is the symbol of the placenta seems plain on the surface, but it is supported by the fact that her name is from the Hebrew *châyâh*, which signifies a life-giver. The word actually means 'to revive, to nourish, to quicken and to repair', all of which are certainly functions of the placenta. That Adam and Eve symbolize together the 'uterine organism' seems to be plain from the quaint tale that Eve was taken from Adam's rib. This tale is very much akin to the legend of certain primitive Australians (the Aranda), who say that the first people were stuck together or grown together. The eyes and ears of this primitive pair were closed, and they had only a small hole for a mouth. They were then cut apart by a lizard wielding a stone knife.

Wherever one finds fetal and placental symbols it is wise to look for the symbolism of the umbilical cord. And what could better represent that organ than the serpent and the tree of the knowledge of good and evil. The tree or staff with a serpent (or twin serpents) wound upon it is an age-old symbol of the umbilical cord. This snake-wound tree is simply a variant of that rod or staff associated with or entwined by snakes: the rod of Moses; the staff of Teiresias which slew the snakes; the *kerykeion* of Hermes. The

---

[1] See Figure Six.

[2] Those who doubt the propriety of using the symbolic figure of Esau to supplement the figure of Adam, might turn to Appendix P, where indications are offered to show that all myths are variant representations (in whole or part) of a single theme—namely the theme of this book.

fact that the Bible speaks of a single Edenic serpent does not diminish the adequacy of the umbilical symbolism, for in both dreams and myths the single serpent appears frequently in a context which is overwhelmingly umbilical-arterial. A prime mythological example of the single serpent is that which Apollo slew and buried at Delphoi (womb-town), marking its grave there with a stone called the *omphalos*, which is simply the Greek word for the navel.[1]

The Edenic tree with which the serpent was concerned was the tree of the knowledge of good and evil. To eat of the fruit of that tree was to become as a god, knowing good and evil.[2] The serpent told Eve that if she and her husband ate of the tree their eyes would be opened, and they would *know* good and evil. But as soon as they ate they found their eyes opened to something else —the fact that they were man and woman.[3] Here we see the plain indications that the sense of consciousness is related to the sense of gender. This Bible myth supports at every point the assertion made by me in Chapter Two, namely that these first intimations (of consciousness and gender) were engendered in connection with the sense of solidity versus hollowness. This assertion is plainly made in the myth of Adam and Eve, namely in the etymology of their sons' names. The name Cain derives from *qayin*, meaning 'a lance', while the name Abel is from *habêl*, meaning 'emptiness' or 'vanity'. Thus do the children, through the etymology of their names, act in an adjectival sense towards their parents, and in the birth of Cain and Abel to Adam and Eve we see symbolic representation of the fact that the outcome of Adam's thrust into his placental wife evokes the sense of a spear striking (Cain) into a receptive state of hollowness or emptiness (Abel).[4]

The order of the eating of the forbidden fruit is of interest. The serpent beguiled Eve, and she took and ate the fruit, where-

---

[1] At Knossos a similar 'navel stone' (omphalos) was actually believed to mark the spot where the navel string of Zeus fell. Mr A. B. Cook [Zeus: Vol. II, pp. 189-191] believed that the omphalos at Delphoi was of the same order.

[2] Genesis 3 : 5.

[3] Genesis 3 : 7.

[4] The ubiquitous 'umbilical three' appears in the fact that Adam and Eve had three sons. The third, Seth, has no obvious etymological significance.

upon she gave the fruit to Adam, so that he also ate. It is true that the serpentine umbilical arteries do 'feed' the placenta with blood, and that the placenta in turn may be said to 'feed' the fetus. This eating of the fruit provided by the co-operation of tree and serpent brings death into Eden. This is a perfectly satisfactory representation of the fact that our primary sense of death is generated in the umbilical flow (the thrust of Cain) from the fetal body into the hollowness (Abel) of Eve. It is the woman who destroys and who gives life. With this primal knowledge of life and death, right and wrong, solid and hollow, there comes also the sense of male and female. As soon as they had eaten of the fruit Adam and Eve knew that they were naked—they became aware of the distinction of gender.

The deep and fearful sense of the cosmic origins of this knowledge is represented in the myths in terms of God's jealousy and apprehension. God is represented as saying of the Edenic pair:

> 'Behold, the man is become as one of us, to know good and evil: and now, lest he put forth his hand, and take also of the tree of life, and eat, and live for ever: therefore the Lord God sent him forth from the garden of Eden.'[1]

God is represented also as wrath with Adam and Eve for knowing that they were male and female. Yet the earlier myth of creation in Genesis plainly asserts that this was the badge of their cosmic origins, for it was through being made male and female that they bore the image of God.

> 'So God created man in his own image, in the image of God created he him; male and female created he them.'[2]

It would be difficult for the myth to say more explicitly that God's essential nature is male and female. That is what the words say. The image of God is male and female, and this image he impressed upon man.[3] Why, then, should God be angry that man becomes aware of this? This is an anthropocentric slant, as

[1] Genesis 3 : 22, 23.
[2] Genesis 1 : 27.
[3] Here we have direct biblical-mythical support for the idea that the creative nature of the cosmos is nuclear (male) and peripheral (female), and that this is the image which Creation imprints upon the uterine organism.

is inevitable. By this means man is trying to express the fact that the impress of God upon his unborn organism is made in circumstances which must be purged from the emotions. The feelings of the womb are 'incestuous' feelings, and have a terrible power over the emotions unless some insulating barrier is erected against them in the mind. That this is no mere isolated piece of symbolism is evident from the fact that similar elements appear in the myth of the Greek seer Teiresias, who was punished by God for knowing too much about the divine nature.

The myth states that as a boy of seven, Teiresias was wandering on Kithairon, called 'the Mother mountain'. There at a place where three roads met,[1] he came upon a male and female snake in copulation. He struck at the snakes with his staff, killing the female, whereupon he himself was transformed into a female. Seven years later, after being a girl for that time, he again came upon a similar event, and once again he struck at the snakes. This time he slew the male, whereupon he became a boy again. Meantime, Zeus and Hera had been arguing about sex. Zeus claimed that women had more enjoyment in the marriage bed, while Hera asserted to the contrary. In order to settle the argument, they called Teiresias up to Olympos and said to him in effect: 'You, Teiresias, have been both man and woman; *you* tell us which enjoys most the sexual encounter'. Teiresias answered that the woman receives most joy, whereupon Hera in anger blinded him, but Zeus gave him inward sight as a compensation.

The blind Teiresias, possessed of inward vision, makes an excellent representative of the fetus. The fetus is 'blind' inasmuch as his eyes are not called upon to register.[2] The total overall function of the uterine organism does indeed confer upon him, as this book demonstrates, an inward vision that is entirely different from the divisive and extraverted perceptions of the special senses. The snake-killing staff is surely no other than a

[1] The meeting of three roads makes an excellent symbol of the umbilical cord in which three currents of blood 'cross' inasmuch as two arterial currents run counter to one venous current.

[2] Nor, indeed, any of his special senses though Sontag has shown that the fetus can hear through the maternal abdomen, and it has been said that the fetus may also see a dull, red glow through the same barrier.

variant of the Edenic tree of the knowledge of good and evil.[1] Moreover, it is plainly derived from a basic experience of gender, namely the copulating snakes and their male and female nature which became transferred magically to their slayer, Teiresias. The special interest of the Teiresian story is, moreover, the portrayal of the *alternating* feelings associated with the umbilical circulation. Teiresias is made female when he slays the female snake, and male when he kills the male snake. By this poetic imagery is represented the fact that the thrust of the umbilical arterial blood makes the fetus feel more nuclear (more male), while the thrust of the umbilical venous blood makes him feel more peripheral (more female). Teiresias is represented as experiencing this alternation just once in his life, but the event represents, I believe, what happens to the fetal feelings time and time again in tune with the beating blood.[2] The Edenic myth represents this alternation in terms of Cain and Abel, a single slaying of the 'empty one' by the 'striking one'.

I suggest that the anger of God against Adam is a mythological device akin to the anger of Hera against Teiresias. What is involved is the whole relation of man to God, by which I mean, of course, the relation of man's "I" to God. This "I" is imprinted upon the fetal organism in terms which become postnatally related not only to consciousness but also to sex.[3] Therefore man is faced with the truly terrifying proposition that God, consciousness and sex are all intimately related, for in our deep feelings we all know (as dreams every day reveal) that the origins of mind are in some way intimately linked with sexual feeling and with the cosmos.

Yet why should either the Greeks or the Hebrews feel concerned at this? They were afflicted neither by the puritanism of the Victorians nor by the self-conscious libidinousness of the Freudian

---

[1] Teiresias is not generally represented as bearing a snake-twined staff, but the implication of the staff and the two snakes is as clear as if he did.

[2] The myth says that Teiresias was seven years old when he first met the snakes, and that seven years elapsed before the second encounter. This, I believe, symbolizes the fact that in the cord the fetus gains its primary sense of periodicity, and *that* in terms of seven.

[3] See Chapter Thirteen.

era. It is not a question, as I see it, of any denigration of sex in the minds of those natural people. The roots of the fear lie deeper, and are more terrible. They lie in the fear of incest. So far as we can judge, the origins of the human race lie in the control of incest. To lie with the mother or the sister is the supreme human sin because this short-circuiting of energy is a blow at the very roots of our human mental status, which appears to depend upon a prevention, as it were, of the short-circuiting of the uterine energies. Freud long ago drew attention to the great importance attached by primitive peoples to the avoidance of incest, and indicated the relevance of their social institutions to this prime purpose. Freud ingeniously asserted that this primary social organization, and with it the 'totem feast', began in some primal forest when the expelled sons of a certain primitive father banded together, slew the old man and ate him, thereafter possessing their mothers and sisters. He adds:

> 'The totem feast, which is perhaps mankind's first celebration, would be the repetition and commemoration of this memorable, criminal act with which so many things began, social organization, moral restrictions and religion.'[1]

That isolated brutish acts of patricide, cannibalism and incest should be the foundation of human status, remembered forever in the breasts of all scattered humanity, is a fantastic suggestion. Freud, the great rationalist, here invokes a psychological miracle greater than any of the religious mystifications against which he rightly inveighed. The whole problem is illumined by my discovery that the fetus feels itself to be not only nuclear and hence male to the uterus and the placenta, but to be that *specific* male, its own father. More, the fetus feels to be not only father, but in this shape to enter mother [placenta] again and again, there suffering the loss of that 'father self' and becoming the son. And this new selfhood the fetus gains with each intake through the umbilical vein, so that the consummation of this drama is linked with the strange sense of eating the self. Freud saw the origins of the human state in a once-for-all drama enacted long ago by brutish

[1] Freud, Sigmund: 'Totem and Taboo'. London. George Routledge.

hominidae in some primal forest. Plainly the Freudian concept itself is only a myth. The reality is done afresh by every fetus in the 'primal forest' of the womb. For there everyone feels, in the umbilical circulation, to 'slay father' and to 'possess mother' and to 'eat the father' who is yet the self restored.[1]

[1] See pages 32, 186 seq.

Appendix J

THE DIFFERENCE BETWEEN THE SENSE OF SELF IN THE INFANT AND THE ADULT

IN CHAPTER SEVEN I stated that whereas the adult, when he *feels* the sense of "I", tends to identify it with his whole body and nature, the child tends on the contrary to feel that his body is a sort of ramifying structure through which his sense of self is wandering. The reader will already have become familiar with this strange idea from the contents of Chapter Two, which show that the fetus, so far from identifying his nuclear sense with a static skin feeling, identifies it rather with something that travels back and forth through the umbilical cord. That this nuclear sense seems to *originate* on the fetal skin (or in the thalamus stimulated by the nerve-ends of that skin) is certainly true. But though it may seem to *originate* there, and even to be specially *at home* there, it does not feel to *stay* there. The skin may be its proper home, but the nuclear feeling constantly leaves that home and as constantly returns. That, at any rate, is the testimony of the deep feelings.

So that from the very earliest times (at whatever time the umbilical feelings are first registered by the embryo or fetus) the self is not identified with the body, but is felt as something which moves about in that body or over it. This same sense is carried on after birth, as the self is felt to identify itself with the head, and in this association to move into the stomach, down into the earth and then up into the trunk and so to the head again. This feeling of dissociation between the self and the body is something which is abruptly changed when the new sense of the head is felt.

Just when this change takes place I do not know. It may take place in several stages. One is inclined to think that it may come about rather as the tide comes in upon a sea shore, coming in and then retreating and then coming in again. If this be so, and there are not wanting signs to suggest it, one might suppose that the first 'wave' of self-feeling which reaches the head is that which makes the child able to say "I".

At any rate, be this as it may, there is no doubt that the identification of the self with the body takes place with increasing rapidity after about the first year of postnatal life. There is no doubt also that the events described in this book can take place only so long as the final identity between body and self is deferred. Perhaps that is one of the reasons why the attainment of the 'head-sky' link does not develop—the full identification of self with body prevents any sense of the "I" being able to 'travel'.

I have found that that sense of inward space which we inhabit in dreams is always the space inside our own bodies, or that space related to the sense of the thrust down into the earth or up to the sky. And I have observed in the drawings of patients and subjects, and especially in those of children, definite signs that their sense of space is dominated by the limited personal space referred to above. This is true also of mythological and primitive forms, especially where these do not pretend to represent utilitarian things, but to represent idealized space such as is to be found in the dimensions and architecture of mystical or religious buildings.

For instance, the Temple of Apollo at Delphoi shows the most plausible signs of being a representation of the uterine feelings. The name Delphoi itself seems to mean something akin to 'place of wombs', and it was founded by Apollo who, though originally not a sun-god at all, became ultimately a manifest representation of the Shining One.[1] The fact that it was here that Apollo buried the serpent shortly after his birth, and that the grave is called the 'omphalos' (navel) all adds up to the same thing. Oddly enough, many of those whose task it is to know the facts of the Classical and Ancient Life seem to be emotionally incapable of accepting this obvious evidence at its loud-shouted face value. Thus I read

[1] See Appendix D.

recently the writing of a learned author who went out of his way to assert that the word 'omphalos' when used of the stone which marked the serpent's grave at Delphoi, did not mean navel at all, but 'center'. In fact, this seeming obtuseness is the product of that very change which the modern adult has suffered with greater completeness even than ancient man, namely the complete identification between body and self, brain and self. And this has entailed the loss of all memory of the earlier infancy and uterine state when indeed the navel (even the professor's own navel) was to his own self a gateway, and an objective piece of architecture in the ramifying building of his own body. Those nearer to the infancy feelings would naturally not feel it inappropriate to represent this old feeling in terms of an objective building made of stone.

Nothing is clearer than that the ordinary Christian church edifice is an effort to represent the human body in such a form that a worshipper may feel to occupy it in the way that he once occupied his own body. For, as I have already shown, the original intent of Christianity was manifestly to enable the individual to relive his uterine and infancy experiences and in this way to reinvoke old feelings in order, it might be supposed, to change them. This sense is entirely lost to Christianity, but the structure of the church building still proclaims it. The typical church building is designed after the nature of a cross, which in turn can hardly be divorced in the feelings from the form of the human body, as witness the nature of the crucifix.

Certainly the mystical story of Christ and especially the culminating events of the Gospels may be demonstrated to refer with perfect consistency to the movements of the self through the body. The sequence of the events, the nature of the events, and even the very names of the people and places involved, support such an interpretation to the hilt, as I have demonstrated in my unpublished work on the analysis of mythology.

Strange as it may seem, the events of the Gospels are essentially the same events as those represented in the myth of Jacob and Esau. Only the symbolism differs. Essentially, for instance, there is no difference between the stone which Jacob took for his pillow, and the rocky tomb in which Jesus was reputed to have been laid on Golgotha, which word means 'the place of a skull'. For indeed both the rock and the rocky tomb represent the skull, and it is from this skull that Jacob sees the 'head-sky' circulation of the angels on the Ladder, while from the same skull Jesus ascends to heaven.

Appendix K

SOME SUGGESTIONS AS TO WHY THE LEFT LEG SHOULD BE SPECIALLY RELATED TO THE RECTUM OR LOWER BOWEL

IN CHAPTER SEVEN I showed that there develops in the infant a strange but fateful connection between the feelings of the left leg and the rectum or lower bowel. This connection results in the feeling that the left leg is a tube which excretes feces, and also that the hardening bone in the left leg is a piece of fecal matter, thus creating a primary link between bone and feces which forever haunts the human organism.

The reason for the special relation between the left leg and the bowel has never been determined by me on the strength of any symbolic representations which I have been able so far to recognize. The fact of the identities I know. Their cause I do not know. But I have been impressed with certain anatomical facts which may give us at least a hint of the answer. As is well known to all, the passage of the fecal matter through the bowel performs a clockwise revolution. It passes down through the small intestines to the caecum at the lower right-hand corner of the abdomen, rises up the ascending colon, moves across the lateral colon and then down through the descending colon into the rectal passage and so out through the anal sphincter.

Now, in the final stages of travel, the descending colon runs in close parallel with the upper portion of the femoral artery, so that it is true that for a certain appreciable distance the feces in the lower bowel run side by side with the blood feeding the left leg. Since the left leg and the bowel both assume the umbilical excretory feelings (the former partly for physiological reasons and the latter for entirely configurational reasons), there is double reason why they might become confused together.

The situation is not parallel as between the ascending colon and the blood supply to the right leg. However, since we have reason, in the light of this book, to suspect a strong link between moral feelings and the movements of the gastrointestinal tract,[1] it is interesting to observe that the abdominal circulation does actually go *up* on the *right* side of the body and *down* on the *left*. This may help to explain why *up* and *right* are related, and why both are felt to be good, while *down* and *left* are also related, and why both are felt to be bad. Thus we are able to say that the good man is an upright man who always does right. The bad man is, on the contrary, a lowdown fellow who is extremely sinister (lefthanded). These terms are so widespread, and the anatomical geometry of morals so consistent, that the explanation offered here seems highly plausible—*especially when it is supported by the new material offered in the foregoing chapters.*

In conclusion I want to confess to a degree of uncertainty as to the exact nature of the feelings of the right leg. Whereas I have said that they are related to the urinary excretions, I have stated that the link does not appear to be strong. There is some possibility indeed that the right leg suddenly changes the character of its feelings and, instead of acting as one surrogate of the umbilical arteries, becomes instead the surrogate of the umbilical vein. In that case, the feelings associated with the two legs may develop into a complete picture of the umbilical pattern, the left leg feeling to be wound around the right leg, and carrying away excretions, while the right leg is carrying up the return flow.

Certainly there is a strong connection between the ultimate feelings of the right leg and those of the spine and the penis. The boy feels at a certain stage that his urinary sense is reversed by the sense of the erection of the penis. This may also be reflected in the feelings of the right leg, which may suddenly lose their urinary character and assume instead the sense of the phallic upthrust.

[1] See Chapter Seven.

Appendix L

NOTES ON THE NATURE OF THE UMBILICAL PATTERN

BY THE TERM 'umbilical pattern' is meant the memory-impress of a certain set of relations which always shows strong signs of being related to the flow of blood in the umbilical cord. This pattern is not so much the actual physical pattern of the cord as that of the flow of blood, or so it would appear. This 'umbilical pattern' is felt in numerical terms of three, and specifically in terms of *two* currents going in the opposite direction to *one* current. Very often the former are shown as twisting helically around the latter.

Is this pattern solely determined by the umbilical cord? Or has it some basis in a wider phenomenon? That is to say, does the uterine organism 'pick up' the nature of the back-and-forth flow of something vaster than itself, and impose the pattern of the umbilical cord upon it, or does that wider pattern itself have the same pattern as the cord?

This would seem to imply the further consideration: Does this wider pattern of flow, which I have tentatively called the 'cosmic pattern', influence the structure of the umbilical cord in the first place? There could hardly be any positive evidence of this, at any rate not in our present state of knowledge. But it is a fact that the structure of the umbilical cord is not entirely susceptible of explanation on ordinary grounds.

To consider first the numerical elements of the cord, namely the existence of two arteries and one vein. Why should this be so? Why not two arteries and two veins? Some creatures do, I believe, have this umbilical structure. The human embryo itself starts off with two arteries and two veins, but at an early stage one of the veins atrophies and the other swells. This is commonly alleged to be due to the development of the liver, but so radical a change does not seem to be called for on those grounds. I must add that the human being is not by any means the only mammal in which this change takes place.

As for the helical twist of the arteries around the vein, this has never been really satisfactorily accounted for, though there have been a number of theories. Why does the cord twist in this peculiar way, generally in a clockwise direction from the fetal body? I am not aware that any really conclusive answer has yet been offered. While admittedly the lack of a conclusive answer should not be taken as evidence that none is possible on the grounds of anatomical or physiological necessity, the fact remains that the strange development of the umbilical cord is unaccounted for, and that it does lend itself to explanations other than the physical.

It is conceivable that the uterine organism becomes operated upon at a very early stage by influences which are at present unknown, but which could register their effect in so plastic and so rudimentary an organ as the umbilical cord. The fetus *in utero*, resting in its watery bed, must be exceptionally sensitive to certain subtle influences imperceptible to the postnatal organism. The fetus is weightless and nondirectional in terms of the ordinary gross influences of the external world; therefore he might well in his very early stages make a series of turns which might be either the product of, or influenced by, some configurational element at work in space-time. The modification of the actual number of the vessels is, of course, of a different order.

This Appendix has simply the purpose to show that even the physical structure of the umbilical cord is derived in a manner not wholly understood at the present time. That this is important to the present book is obvious, since the cord becomes the instrument of mind by detecting a pattern in the cosmos, and there is obviously the possibility that this instrument might be in some degree itself the product of the very configurational forces whose operation it later detects and records.

Appendix M

THE PHENOMENA OF PUBERTY

THE READER may be surprised to find little mention in this book of the phenomena of puberty. In general the claim is that the configurational development of the body, including the sexual, is finished by the age of five to seven years of age. But puberty works such changes both in the body and the mind that it might be supposed that the story of this book cannot end at any time prior to puberty. I have no strong opinion on this matter. I know only that in the analysis of adolescents I have never seen anything that is not already implied and potential in the feelings of little children.

In temporary defence of this statement I would fall back upon the fact that the Freudians describe a period of latency lying between infancy and puberty, and as I understand it, they rather take the view that all that flowers at puberty is a second and more permanent surge of an energy which made a preliminary manifestation in infancy. My observations would suggest something of the kind, but in a negative rather than in a positive way.

The evidence suggests that the infant experiences the configurational energizing of the head (with sexual overtones added), and that this, so to speak, lays the essential foundations of feeling which puberty builds upon. Infancy is the overture, so to say, of a theme which is given full orchestration at puberty. But I do not think that anything *new* is added save, perhaps, the feelings associated with mammary development, though here I speak without much conviction.

How do I distinguish between what is felt at puberty and what is felt in infancy? What could there be in dream symbolism that would reveal any such distinction? The evidence lies in the context. I have always found the behavior and dreams of children to afford the whole picture given in the present book. I have no evidence to show that the dreams of pubic persons and adults contain any essential element missing from the dreams of children.

There are certain symptoms, however, which seem to indicate a valuable fact. The dawning of puberty certainly intensifies the accommodation of the earth's upthrust as described in Chapters Ten and Eleven. And this I have found evidenced in a very peculiar way. We all know that the pubic boy, and to a lesser extent the pubic girl, suffers from pimples and even boils on the face. The evidence of their dreams (and of adult dreams dealing with these experiences) strongly suggest that as a result of the earth's upthrust the trunk is emphasized in its directional confusion. For I have seen strong evidence to suggest that the boil is the outcome of a failure to know which is the excretory end. The result is that the body is reacting to the upthrust by trying psychosomatically to create little excretory organs on its upper parts. A boil is a mock anus.[1]

Though puberty, I repeat, makes great changes, I do not believe that I could adduce very much evidence in support of the idea that these bodily changes initiate any major new configurational sense. They certainly tend to excite, remobilize, amplify and make permanent the elements laid down by the end of infancy.

---

[1] I was fascinated to learn that when Karl Marx wrote 'Das Kapital' he was plagued by an enormous carbuncle on his neck. If my observations are to be accepted as having universal validity, it is therefore highly likely that the Father of Communism was trying to make his neck into an anus, and to excrete upwards. This possibility offers a potential new light upon the fact that the basis of Communistic philosophy lies precisely in the 'turning upside down' of Hegel's theory by Marx. Hegel asserted that 'all is mind', but Marx reversed that view by asserting that 'all is matter'. It is perhaps worth noting that Frederick Engels in his 'Ludwig Feuerbach' actually wrote: '. . . the dialectic of Hegel was (by Karl Marx) placed upon its head, or rather, turned off its head, on which it was standing before, and placed upon its feet again.' The struggle between the feeling of 'all is mind' or 'all is matter' is, in fact, in my experience, at root a struggle to determine which way up the human being is, as to whether he is excreting down the gut or up the spine—see Chapter Eleven, also Figure Nine. I should say, in the light of all this, that there is not wanting fair evidence for the suspicion that Karl Marx was very positively upside down in his feelings so that he did not in effect know his neck from his anus, and so felt that his brain was excrement. It is as fascinating as it is terrifying to think that basic Communist theory may be no more than the projection of this personal error upon the whole of humanity.

Appendix N

NOTES ON THE CATEGORIZATION OF FEELING

ALTHOUGH THE sense of self (the sense of being "I", or of having an 'ego') is unquestionably a feeling, it is of a different order from those feelings which the "I" experiences *outside* itself. That seems to go without saying. It is the "I" that feels, and all other feelings are possible only because of that "I". Without this, all feeling would be no more than a stream of sensations. In what lies the distinction between the two forms of feeling, namely that which constitutes the "I" and that which the "I" feels? I think the distinction lies solely in this: that the feelings which constitute the "I" are the total uterine feelings impacted into one unconscious whole. This encapsulation or impaction is brought about by birth. From birth onwards the postnatal feelings begin, as it were, to surround and to impinge on the central uterine core of feelings, and I suggest that the schema depicted in Figure Thirty-two does in fact represent a fair picture of the basic anatomy of mind in man.

Why should birth cause this impaction of feeling? The answer may be given tentatively in the following terms: Whenever an organ of the body evokes feelings and then loses the power to evoke them, and when those feelings are assumed by another organ of the body, then to the new organ those assumed feelings appear as 'unconscious' feelings. This principle is worth a little expatiation. Let us imagine ourselves back in the fetal state. I believe that in that state our experiences of the uterine life constitute a form of consciousness. That is, the fetus is as *aware* of his experiences as we are *aware* of our daily life. He is not aware in

293

the same terms, but the nature of his consciousness is the same as our own. Birth destroys the mechanism of that consciousness and initiates quite a different kind. But the old uterine consciousness does not disappear: it lives on in the feelings of the new organs in an entirely new form which we call psychological feeling as against conscious awareness or physical feeling.

The same principle applies to every change of awareness which occurs in the body. Thus I believe that the child lives *consciously* through each stage of the developments outlined in Chapters Six to Thirteen, but that each time the 'affect' changes its position, then the consciousness of the completed stage *becomes* feeling, without direct consciousness, while at the same time the new stage awakens a new experience of conscious awareness, to which all earlier stages appear as psychological feeling. The so-called Unconscious is therefore to be regarded only as a label for the totality of these sequential stages of submerged consciousness, each of which persisted for a time before being relegated by its successor to an inferior status.

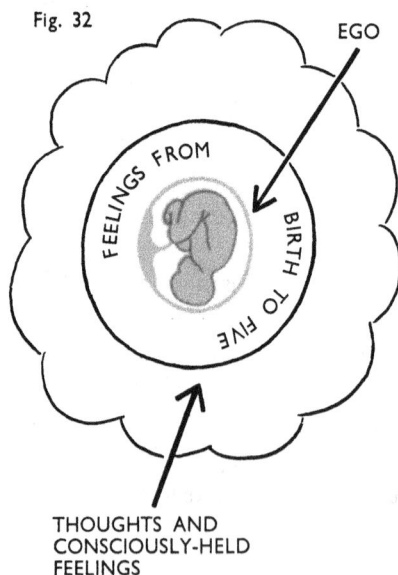

Fig. 32 — EGO — FEELINGS FROM BIRTH TO FIVE — THOUGHTS AND CONSCIOUSLY-HELD FEELINGS

Appendix O

THOUGHTS ON THEOLOGY AS THE QUEEN
OF THE SCIENCES

IN THE heyday of Christendom when, for better or for worse, it was still possible to speak of 'the Christian church', all thought was dominated, at least outwardly, by Christian theology. Every specialist, so far as his limited purview went, was regarded as concerned with some aspect of God's creation as represented in Genesis and as reported by Aristotle. Every specialist science and art from astrology to zoology was but an attendant before the throne of the Queen of the Sciences, whose name was Christian Theology.

This Queen of the Sciences, however, could not restrain her ardent handmaidens, and the reason for her failure is now obvious. For she was a synthetic product wrought by minds which had inherited the ancient symbolism of the feelings, but which had themselves no direct contact with those feelings. Christian theology was essentially the product of the syncretism of the many traditions which, in spite of their diverse social origins, all stemmed from the same root, namely the subjective awareness of the universal pattern that had created the mind in the womb. This syncretism was achieved under the impulsion of the fierce monotheism of the Hebrews and the need to find a super-tribal unity to fit a mediterranean world that was fast outgrowing the tribal traditions that had survived even in the polyglot cities.

There is every reason, in the light of this book, to see Christian theology as an effort to state the universal design in terms of a Hebrew messianism and Greek philosophy. This in itself is no refutation of the essential significance of Christian theology, for Hebrew religion and Greek philosophy alike were ultimately derived from the old but fading human ability to perceive the pattern of the cosmos in the feelings. The one thing more than any other that prevented this theology from being a true Queen of the Sciences was its fixed and dogmatic character, which was in turn inseparable from the nature of its creation. For when there is no method of exploring the mind's deep nature, and hence no science of the principles of that nature, then the choice is between dogma or nothing.

Theology, in order to be a true Queen of the Sciences, able to save science from its own specialisms, and to prevent it from becoming (as it now largely is) an end in itself, must be a living and demonstrable representation of the Creative nature at work *now* in the human soul, plus the overall demonstration that this same nature has left its signature upon all creation. This alone can enable theology to say to every man, and above all (in the terms of the present context) to the scientist: 'Go on with your specialisms. Do not think I wish to restrain you. I simply say to you that wherever you look you will find the reflection of that pattern and purpose which I declare to be the very heart of you yourself. There is no need for me to bind you with dogmas or to oppose you with sentiment. My task is to unfold the nature of *you*, as of all men, and to declare it abroad that this nature is also the nature of Creation and, by simple deduction therefore the nature of the Creator.'

This does not mean anything remotely approaching the Hegelian absurdity that all nature may be known by introspection, and that the specialist sciences are thus ultimately superfluous. Such a view is no whit better than the present pragmatic extreme that science is an end in itself and can dispense with theology. A true theology would defend the rights of specialist research and would not wish to create a universal theory to which the specialist must conform. We have seen in our own times that this kind of spurious unity was not a tyranny peculiar to Christendom, but can be true also for biologists compelled to work in a society dominated by the spurious theology of Dialectical Materialism.

Appendix O

It is truly an extraordinary experience to place Christian Theology and Dialectical Materialism side by side and to observe how both are an effort to present the Universal Design and method of creation. For what my researches have revealed is that each man's mind is created through the establishment of polar feelings *in utero*. This polar opposition is constantly *reversed* by the umbilical flow, so that the nuclear agent (the fetus) feels by turns nuclear and peripheral, or positive and negative, and feels the placenta as his alternating opposite.

Self-evidently this is the pattern of Dialectical Materialism, which posits a state of eternal opposition between what is called abstractly the Thesis and the Antithesis. This opposition is being constantly brought to Synthesis and to reversal, whereby a new Thesis and Antithesis are set up, and so *ad infinitum*. But this Marxian approximation is no modern discovery by Prophet Karl, for he achieved it by the superficial expedient of taking Hegel's Dialectic and turning it upside down.[1] And are we to suppose that Hegel created this pattern out of his own knowledge! Why, if he did, he was going to quite unusual trouble for so intelligent a man, since ancient thought and religion offered it to him on a plate. He had only to consider the Greek concept of the *eniautos daimon*, who came with the Spring, was slain in the Winter, as it were by his own dark self, the Enemy, and who rose again in the following Spring, to be hailed as Savior, and to start the cycle all over again. The Marxian dialectic is a primitive theology that has been through the Hegelian wringer and had all its human feelings removed.

Compare this with Christian theology, which declares that God the Father, through the Holy Ghost, penetrated an earthly Virgin and came forth as Son, who yet was Man and who was slain and buried and who rose again and was restored to the Father. This is the same story. It tells how the Nucleus is ever going out from itself to penetrate the Periphery and to be destroyed, and is ever being restored as Son and becoming again one with the Father. There is the same pattern of events as in the Greek concept of the *eniautos daimon*.

[1] See footnote to Appendix M.

The Nature of the Self

In the light of this book we see that the mind of man is rooted in this dialectical process. It begins in the polarity between the fetal body and the placenta. These are Everyman's Thesis and Antithesis. It is given dynamic existence through the reversals of the umbilical flow. This is Everyman's Synthesis leading to the start of a new cycle. And we know now, in the light of this book that in this cycle of events man feels the sense of the father and the mother; of the entry of the father into the mother and his loss and rebirth as son—a son who is yet also father.

Yet, miracle of miracles, this purely personal structure of the mind is not personal at all. For whence does it derive? When we compare the anatomy of the mind with the structure of the universe we see evidence to show that both derive from the same source. Therefore we are justified in saying 'This uterine pattern is not merely personal in any narrow sense: it is the signature of God'. And in saying this we are saying everything that Christianity and Communism say, but we are saying it in terms of positive and demonstrable science.

There is no doubt in my mind that the Creator may, without the least taint of blind anthropomorphism, properly be regarded as Father and Mother ever in opposition, but ever united by the rhythm of reversal. In this eternal rhythm the Father eternally enters the Mother, being destroyed there and reborn as Son, becoming thereby again the Father. This pattern is what you yourself felt as fetus. It *now* forms the nature of your mind. And that mind is able to look out through its eyes to nature, and to understand nature for the good reason that nature also is the product of that same pattern and process.

This quest into the human self (carried out on a collective basis and not by mere personal subjectivism) is the source of true theology. Christian theology failed because, although in many respects a faithful symbolic picture of reality, it was a syncretism created by men no longer able to look into their own natures. It was however a syncretism formed from the relics of such perceptions in an older time. I believe that this book indicates the first steps towards making theology a living science.

Appendix P

THE NATURE OF THE DREAM

THE DREAM is the link between the two distinct systems of logic which operate in the human psyche. The first is that system which we employ in our everyday, conscious and socially oriented thinking. By means of this logic we learn to separate and to distinguish between external objects and events. We formulate sharp concepts in the mind and, by their constant interaction, we create the patterns of thought. The second system of logic is that which works by association in the feelings. Its products are well illustrated in the pages of this book. It does not work by separating and distinguishing, but by creating identities and by imposing old relations upon new situations. We have seen in this book some of the strange results which proceed from this second system of logic. Thus, for instance, the lungs are identified with the placenta simply because the former take over from the latter the process of oxygenation. The child feels a single result from both these organs, and in the short period of changeover suffers agonies of fear and organic doubt, which welds the two organs close in the emotions. The result is not the awakening of a feeling of a new organ, but the creation of an artificial unity between two vastly different states of existence. The infant feels that the breath is the umbilical blood, and in this way imposes an old relation upon a new one.

The use of this 'feeling-logic' diminishes as the infant develops its postnatal system of logic under the guidance and impulsion of society. But the results of the older logic are not automatically caught up and transformed by the newer one. Both exist together in the same mind. The old feeling-logic works on under the surface of the newer one. Thus no matter how clearly the newer logic separates the lungs from the placenta (and, in fact, never sees any reason to give them any more than a similarity of function), the old logic holds its original concept of their identity unchanged. It would, I am sure, surprise a highly competent professor of anatomy to find that in his deep feelings he still completely identifies his lungs with his lost placenta, and that in this aspect of their common humanity differs not at all from the simplest citizen.

'The placenta still lies in mother's body and feeds me as fetus', say the deep feelings in one of their several layers, meaning 'My lungs are the placenta, my trunk is mother's body and my fetal self is in my own stomach'.[1] Of any such peculiar picture the conscious mind is singularly free. If it knows or cares at all about the lungs and the placenta it says something after this fashion: 'The placenta is an alimentary and excretory organ disposable at birth. It has been referred to as a sort of lung, and also as a liver, since it performs prenatally some of the functions of both'. The two sets of concepts are ordinarily quite irreconcilable. The dream alone offers them reconciliation. This assertion raises the next question: What is a dream that it can achieve this reconciliation?

I have shown already (see Appendix H) the way in which the structure of a concept operates both on the level of feeling and also on the level of conceptual thinking. Every concept is an integration of particulated pieces of feeling, and it is this fact which governs the strange 'coding' we find in a dream. Briefly, a dream uses concepts because of some constituent feeling. Conscious thinking uses the concept as a whole, and ignores the constituent parts. For reasons indicated in Appendix H, the dream becomes

---

[1] A dream will be found (refer to Appendix R) to be composed of two or more levels of memory imposed one over the other. In this way the original uterine imprint is repeated upon one or more sets of organs. The effect is by analogy slightly like that achieved by placing several photographs of the same person one over the other and looking through them. Unless one knows this, and devises means of separating these layers, dream analysis in any scientific sense is quite impossible.

involved in *both* systems of logic since, to revert to the analogy given in Appendix H, whenever a fish bites any hook on a line, the whole line is agitated and the float (the total concept) moves as certainly as if all the hooks had been taken. At night, when the ordinary conscious processes of the mind are in abeyance, the logic of the feelings, weaving in the subconceptual depths, can be experienced.[1] If the conscious mind, upon the individual's waking, is able to recall anything of this feeling-logic, it can only be in terms of the conceptual contents of that mind. But this conceptual result will not follow a true conceptual logic. That is why a great number of dreams are dismissed as ridiculous. 'I had my cat on my left shoulder' dreams a patient, 'and I suddenly realized it had no body—only a head'. How absolutely ridiculous! But when we know some of the feeling-particles contained in the concept of 'cat', and also of 'left shoulder', and also of a 'bodiless head', then the lineaments of a meaning at once appear. The fact is, the conceptual logic of a dream must get along as best it may, for the determining context lies not in the concepts but in their constituent feelings.

For purposes of illustration I propose to invent a simple dream of a kind which may be found any day in practice: 'AUNT HATTIE SAID THAT BEN ROGERS CALLED TO SAY THAT LITTLE TED JONES HAD FALLEN FROM A TREE AND HURT HIS HEAD.' Often in the case of such a dream one hears the dreamer dismiss it as quite absurd, for the reason that although he actually has an Aunt Hattie, and knows an old chap named Ben Rogers and a little boy named Ted Jones, none of them knows the others. How, then, could Ben Rogers tell Aunt Hattie anything about Ted Jones? It is quite obviously absurd. Or maybe the dreamer can offer a kind of reason for the dream. I will invent a typical piece of rationalization: 'Oh, I know why I dreamed this. It was Teddy Jones's birthday yesterday, and Aunt Hattie wrote to ask if we could spend Christmas with her. But I don't know why old Ben Rogers should have come into it—I haven't thought of him in twenty years'.

---

[1] On pages 236 and 237 I have given what seems a likely explanation of the physical bases of thinking and dreaming.

The Nature of the Self

When we take the trouble to probe into these concepts in the mind of the dreamer, we find that they contain prominent elements which offer quite a different possible explanation. I will invent a typical set of responses to the probing of the analyst. They are very superficial, of course, but they will serve to illustrate what I mean.

AUNT HATTIE

I think of her big eyes. She is my Father's sister. He says he used to call her 'saucers' as a child because her eyes were like saucers.

BEN ROGERS

He was an old navy man who used to take me fishing when I was a child. He was stone deaf—it was said that gunfire did it.

TEDDY JONES

Shall I ever forget the day that boy was born! It was during the war, and Joe, that's Teddy's father, had just taken off in an aircraft when the message came through, and I took a chance and radioed the news to him.

FELL OUT OF TREE AND HURT HEAD

I remember doing that.

Now, here we may see at once a plausible context which goes roughly as follows:

'I shall never forget that day of birth, because I fell and hurt my head and my eyes seemed huge and my ears deafened. . . .'

The reader may say, with some exasperation: 'How can you *prove* that?' The answer is, of course, that no single dream *proves* anything at all. One looks for a context in a dream, and notes it. It is the *persistence* of the same kinds of context in dream after dream after dream which ultimately yields the proof. But after a time, as experience grows, and one gains confidence as to the reality of the picture in the feelings, one realizes that such a dream as invented above is typical, and no matter how deeply analyzed would always yield the same content. To which the reader may again reply: 'You seem to find the same thing in every dream. Are you sure you don't just find what you are looking for?'

The answer here is both 'yes' and 'no'. One finds what one is looking for not in the sense of wishful interpretations, but because without some advance hypothesis it would be impossible to find anything at all. It is quite a mistake to suppose that a scientist observes phenomena without preconception, for unless he had a prior hypothesis to guide and direct his experimentation and observation he would never know what he was looking for. A man who does not know something about uranium would not know his fortune even if he stood in the middle of a desert completely formed of uranium-bearing rock!

But the much more important answer to the reader's last objection is that, contrary to popular opinion, dreams do *not* tell an endlessly variant series of tales. The outward conceptual form of the dream (what is called the manifest content) varies endlessly from dreamer to dreamer and from dream to dream. A few symbols seem to be consistent, but these are subject to vast variations of presentation. The outward form of the dream belies its hidden consistency. One of my most important realizations was that dreams are not endlessly variant in their significance. Dreams tell only one story, here a piece and there a piece, which *in toto* is the story of the evocation of the pattern of the feelings in the womb and their migration and transformation through the postnatal body. The story told in this book is the story the dream tells. I have pieced it together bit by bit over the years, like a mosaic. The more complete this mosaic becomes, the easier it is for its possessor to find in dreams an *immediate* meaning.

As I have said, there are endless variations of the dream's outward form, and one can demonstrate this very simply by making up a dream for oneself to express precisely the same meaning as that given above. Simply complete the following little formula:

1. I know a person with something unusual about sight or the eyes. His (her) name is X.
2. I know a person with something unusual about hearing or the ears. His (her) name is Y.
3. I know somebody whose birthday I have special cause to remember. His (her) name is Z.

Having done this, you may then rewrite the original dream about Aunt Hattie in your own terms, thus: 'I DREAMED THAT X CALLED (WROTE TO) Y TO SAY THAT Z HAD FALLEN OUT OF A TREE AND HURT HIS HEAD.'

What is more, you could switch the names of the three persons about without changing the meaning of this particular fragment, since the hidden context is concerned only with bringing together the memories of four elements of the birth experience:

1. The experience of the activation of the eyes at birth,
2. The experience of the activation of the ears,
3. The sense of falling, and
4. The sense of the compression of the head.

The dream merely expresses the fact that all these feelings lie close-compacted in the depths of the self. This simple fact can be expressed in an endless variety of dream narratives.

A great deal of what I have written about the dream applies with no less force to myths and fairy tales and to all manner of collective symbolisms. The great difference between a dream and a myth is that whereas the external conceptual form of a dream is likely to be personal and relatively trivial, the external form of the myth is likely to be conceived in terms of mighty personages and majestic events. The reason for this is fairly obvious: a man's own relations and experiences are important to him, but to hardly anyone else. Therefore what impresses him in a dream narrative would not mean anything to another person. Furthermore, the outward conceptual form of the myth must be of a kind that will attract collective attention and hold it over centuries. And it must have a rather close-to-the-surface relation between its conceptual and its subconceptual meanings.

Appendix P

Let us look at a simple mythological context. In this case it is not (naturally) an invented one, but it is a condensed piece of mythology:

> 'Apollo founded the city of Delphoi after he had, at the age of three days, slain the Python and buried it at a spot afterwards marked by the omphalos.'

Heaven knows what the archaeologists suppose this to mean, though they are quick enough to reject the meaning that lies close to the surface when that is suggested to them. Let us examine the fragment of mythology as if it were a dream.

APOLLO

He was not originally a sun god. But he was a great shooter of arrows. He acquired at some period a sort of sister-wife named Artemis, who also shot a great deal with the bow. Apollo was called 'the far-shooter', and he also acquired the epithet *phoibos*, which means 'the bright one'.

DELPHOI

This word means something like 'place of wombs'. It lies in a cutting in the rocks which acts like a veritable sun trap.

PYTHON

It was alleged to have chased Apollo's mother while she bore the young hunter in her womb. It was said in another myth to have been born from the slime left over from the great flood of Deukalion.

OMPHALOS

This is the Greek word for the navel. It is alleged by some to have been copied from Knossos, where a similar stone was erected, it was said, to mark the spot where the navel-string of Zeus fell to the ground. The omphalos of Delphoi has been found, and it is pierced by a piece of iron shaped like a knife.

From these bare associations we may obtain a very plausible and familiar context, thus:

> The fetal nuclear feeling is associated with the placenta, which it feels as a kind of sister-wife into whom it shoots umbilical arterial arrows, and from whom in turn it receives umbilical venous arrows. This fetal skin feeling is associated with a sense of light and is thus linked readily with the sun. Naturally, the proper 'home base' of this feeling is the 'womb place' where the sense of great shining was first generated. All that is left of it now is the navel, wherefrom fell the navel string which, like some persistent serpent, followed the pregnant womb everywhere and was only destroyed after birth.

The reader may say again, as he said of my analysis of the dream: 'O, you always find the same kind of things in the myths. According to you, the myths only tell the same story, or bits of it, over and over again' [303].

In reply I shall repeat what I said of the dream: 'One of my most important realizations is that myths do not have an almost endless variety of meaning, but under the ramifications of their outward stories they all tell the story of the evocation of the energy of the self in the womb, its migration and transformations through the born body.'

The reader could certainly 'make up a myth' just as easily as he made up a dream. That is, he could if he had at his fingertips enough legendary material to act as the raw materials of his myth-making. It is, in fact, possible to make up those little myths called fairy tales and nursery rhymes, and once the principle underlying all mythology is grasped, nothing could be easier. Certainly the reader can amuse himself, if he feel inclined, by browsing through the myths to see if he can find the content of the myth of Delphoi expressed in different external form. He may not find this an easy task, since sometimes a great deal of work and imaginative exploration is required to unearth the similarities under the differences. For instance, who at first sight could believe that in the famous old Bible tales of Genesis the same myth appears in variant forms over and over again, though not always with the same emphasis nor in the same degree of completeness. The myths of Adam and Eve, Lot and his wife, Abraham and Sarah, Noah and his Ark, Isaac and Rebekah, Jacob and Esau all tell in various ways the whole or parts of the same theme—the theme which this book has presented for the first time in the context of modern conceptual thought.

However, since these variations are too complex for analysis here,[1] let me offer the reader a simple instance of the way in which elements of the myth of Delphoi may be seen under a quite different guise. This alternative version is very well known:

> 'Noah made an ark in which he and his wife and three
> sons, Ham, Shem and Japheth, survived a great flood.
> When the flood was done, God put a rainbow in the sky
> as a sign of the covenant that he would not drown the
> world again.'

Many explanations of this story have been given. Archaeologists have noted that there are legends of great floods in many parts of the world. The Greeks had a great flood in their legendary history, and it is noted that Deukalion, the hero of that flood, also had three sons after whom the Greek nations were called. But let us analyze the myth as if it were a dream:

NOAH

The name is in Hebrew *Nôach*, and comes from *nûwach*, meaning 'to rest'. There is, however, a word *nûwr* (pronounced 'noor') which means 'to shine'.

HAM, SHEM AND JAPHETH

The name Ham is in Hebrew *Cham*, and is from *châmam*, which means 'to be hot' and 'to enflame'. The name Shem is in Hebrew *Shêm*, which seems to signify 'honor'. But one cannot overlook the fact that the

---

[1] Though they form a large and important section of my unpublished book on mythology.

Hebrew word *shemen* is linked to the idea of shining. The name Japheth is in Hebrew *Yepheth*, and is alleged to come from *pâthâh*, meaning 'to open'. But again one notes a word *yiph'âh*, which is from yâpha', meaning also 'to shine'.

COVENANT

This is in Hebrew *berîyth*, and means 'cutting'. It relates to the ancient Hebrew method of making an oath by cutting an animal in two and passing between the severed parts. We may note that in Greek mythology it was Iris, the rainbow, upon whose pouring of the stygian waters the gods swore their most solemn oaths. It will also be remembered that primitive peoples regarded the rainbow as a serpent because it supposedly sucked up water from the earth.

Here we see, hidden in this most familiar material, a possible context not at all unlike that much more obvious context in the Delphoi myth. The interpretation may be attempted thus:

The fetal nuclear sense of shining is related to that one who 'rests' in the ark or box of the womb. He is the enflamed one (Ham), the shining one (Shem and Japheth). This fetal one is related to the great rainbow serpent in the sky, which plays an umbilical role, and so is relevant to the rite which joins together the pieces of that severed animal, the uterine organism.

Appendix Q

STRANGE PERIODIC ELEMENTS EVIDENT IN THE STRUCTURE OF THE SKELETON

I CONFESS that it seems very strange to me that the deep feelings contain a strong sense of the architectonics of the skeleton. It is almost as if the formative forces of the body have used the skeleton as a means of their expression. Certainly the skull figures most powerfully in dream representations, as does the neck and its seven cervical bones, and also the ribs, the spine and the pelvis. In spite of my inability to discover the *rationale* of this feeling-awareness of the skeleton, I cannot deny that it is a fact so far as the feelings are concerned. Indeed, the skeleton contains several suggestive instances of numerical periodicity, and when it is viewed in its essential form shows strikingly 'musical' character. This is brought out very powerfully by the formalized picture of the human skeleton produced overleaf. This picture, I must add, was not drawn with any intent to support such views as mine, but is taken from a popular book on the human body produced in Germany some years ago. It presents the skeleton almost as if it were a violin or 'cello, a symbolism which in dreams some-times appears in a skeletal context.

Very often one finds in dreams the symbol of the piano, and this often lends itself to a context in which the keys of the piano evidently represent the vertebrae. I am not able to say that the whole of the vertebrae are thus symbolized, but I am *completely certain* that the seven cervical vertebrae are associated with the keys of a piano, and indeed with the seven notes of the musical scale.

Fig. 33

The Nature of the Self

I am quite unable to guess what physical link there might be between the seven cervical vertebrae and the cerebral mechanisms involved in the musical sense. Everything, indeed, goes to suggest that the link is affective and not neural, and that it derives from the sense of rhythm first evoked in the umbilical cord. Since this umbilical sense of rhythm is derived from some 'resonance' between the beat of the blood and the cosmos, the deep, cosmic elements poetically ascribed to music appear to have a very firm basis in fact. In order to try to check, if possible, the reality of the cervical link with the musical scale, I have applied musical frequencies to the seventh cervical bone, and have been interested to note that most subjects actually feel the notes of a scale to 'march up' the cervical stem, in spite of the fact that the vibrator has all the time remained applied to the lowest cervical vertebra.

Taken from *Man in Structure and Function*, by Fritz Kahn, M.D. Published by Knopf, New York.

Appendix R

A FUNDAMENTAL FEATURE OF THE DREAM AND ITS ANALYSIS

PAGES 87 seq. state a general principle governing the carry-over of uterine polarities from the prenatal to the postnatal state. Part Two outlines the strange feeling-devices which carry that principle into expression. The impression created by these evolutions of feeling may be illustrated by the analogy of a swarm of bees which constantly congregates and then dissolves and recongregates at another point, repeating this process a number of times. But such an analogy would not be complete unless these mysterious bees were endowed with the unusual faculty of being able to remember each swarming point, and to carry over to each point a memory of all the others. The affect is like this. It carries over from each station of integration (swarming) a memory which it will impose upon all the succeeding points. Thus it comes about that when these 'swarming bees' arrive at length in the brain, they bring with them the memories of all the previous locations at which they have 'swarmed'. The dream, being a record of this process in fragmentary form, reflects this repetitive process and its superimposed memories. Each dream contains elements of 'laminated' memory—see footnote to p. 300. A dream might be likened to a palimpsest in which the older writings remain partially visible, or to a pile of photographic slides of a single subject taken at different times and overlaid to form a confused composite. Failure to understand this element of dream structure inevitably leads to a failure to achieve a precise analysis of the dream. I must make it clear that my remarks here apply wholly to the hidden or latent content of the dream. The manifest content of the dream is *not* merely the surface lamination of a series. The 'laminated structure' to which I refer applies wholly to the latent content.

The result of failure to understand this aspect of the dream can be demonstrated very clearly from Freud's own published writings.[1] Freud has placed upon record one of his own dreams and its related associations and certain interpretations, and it happens that this dream lends itself spectacularly to the demonstration of the point I wish to make, a demonstration which inevitably gains force from the fact that it is made by challenging the analytic procedures of the father of modern dream research. The dream is translated by Mr Strachey thus:

'Company at table or table d'hôte . . . spinach was being eaten . . . Frau E.L. was sitting beside me; she was turning her whole attention to me and laid her hand on my knee in an intimate manner. I removed her hand unresponsively. She then said: "But you've always had such beautiful eyes." . . . I then had an indistinct picture of two eyes, as though it were a drawing or like the outline of a pair of spectacles. . . .'

This surprised Freud because Frau E.L. had hardly at any time been on friendly terms with him, and he had never consciously desired closer relations. The dream baffled Freud and he decided to investigate it deeper. Though I never claim to understand a dream until it has undergone full analysis, I often permit myself a glance at its surface material to see if the symbolism is plain enough to give a working clue. The reader who has followed this book with some attention will at once perceive that this dream offers extremely clear surface indications of its content. He will see that it suggests the theme of the displacement of the umbilical feelings upon the postnatal legs and eyes. A female figure which draws attention to the dreamer's leg and his eyes while at a meal is very suggestive of this basic theme. Freud cannot understand why spinach should figure in the meal, but

---

[1] *Über den Traum*, translated by James Strachey. W. W. Norton.

as a doctor of medicine he certainly knew very intimately that spinach is a prime source of organic iron and is therefore linked by close associations with the blood and its hemoglobin. We cannot ask Freud for amplified associations, but it is more than a fair guess that for Freud spinach meant blood, through the equation spinach = iron = blood. With this in mind, let the reader turn to page 217 where he will see Freud's dream actually illustrated, for thereon he will find two pictures of a baby 'eating spinach' (that is, feeling to be sucking blood), and in one case giving it out through his 'beautiful eyes' [Figure Fifteen], while in the second case [Figure Sixteen] he is giving it out through his legs [hand on the knee].

What makes Freud's dream of such specially compelling interest is the fact that it is a sort of minor symbolic representation of the tragedy of Oedipus. For Freud's dream almost certainly tells of the baby's feeling that it is giving out blood through the feet and the eyes, which is exactly the thing that the tragedy of Oedipus records. Oedipus had wounded feet as a baby, and in the end he put out his eyes. This classical myth is simply a projection of the feelings of Everyman. How ironical it must seem that Freud, who gave us modern dream analysis and who made Oedipus the symbol of his central complex of feelings, did not recognize Oedipus when he met him in one of his own dreams!

Freud is puzzled at the appearance of Frau E.L. in this particular dream context, and we may be forgiven for sharing his astonishment, since all we can learn of her from Freud is that she was the daughter of a man to whom Freud was once in debt. One could make a guess as to why this might make her a potential placental symbol for Freud, but it would be no more than a guess, and not a very impressive one at best.[1] It is much more likely that Frau E.L. was in some way suggestive (to Freud, at any rate) of a masculine woman—see Appendix G. But the rest of the dream powerfully suggests that Frau E.L. symbolizes the placenta.

---

[1] Here it is: I owe a great debt to my Father; anyone I owe a debt to is thus, in that degree, a father-symbol; Father's daughter is my sister, and a sister is frequently a symbol for the placenta, hence the daughter of a creditor-as-father-symbol is a symbol of the placenta.

The Nature of the Self

As in a crossword puzzle, it might be said that all the other pieces fit, and Frau E.L., though we do not know quite why she should, fits into the otherwise incomplete structure and completes it.

On the surface, then, the dream shows every sign of being a product of the following 'laminated' memories:—

1. The sense of sucking blood through the mouth and excreting it through the eyes,
2. The allied sense of sucking blood and excreting it through the legs,
3. The sense of this as essentially a sexual procedure.[1]
4. The sense of the placenta as a sexual partner from whom we took blood, and to whom we returned blood.

Freud's rather sparse and over-logical associative material yields nothing that detracts from the truth of the above remarks. Insofar as it yields anything at all, it is in the direction of confirmation and amplification. I will reproduce these associations in brief and add my comments.

'Company at table or table d'hôte' reminds Freud of taximeters that tick away and remind him of what he owes. He feels that he is getting the worst of a bargain. He recalls that he said this humorously to a friend who gave him a ride in a taxicab, and that he added some words from Goethe: *Ihr führt ins Leben uns hinein, Ihr lasst den Armen schuldig werden*. These seem unlikely words in such a context, for they are translated as: *You lead us into life. You make the poor creature guilty*. But is not the life in the womb a 'free ride' during which the constant tick-tick of the umbilical blood builds up in us the sense of the distinction between giving and getting? Is it not precisely this beat of blood which not only 'leads us into life' but which also at the same time makes 'the poor [fetal] creature guilty' of incest? Inevitably this constellation of feelings is related to the placenta, which after birth seems to attach itself to the eyes [Figure Fifteen] and to the legs [Figure Sixteen], so that the presence of the placental Frau E.L. is entirely comprehensible. But what is so interesting here is that Freud's dream now yields definite evidence of a memory that

1 Implied by the mildly sexual behavior of Frau E.L.

behind the uterine feelings loom the influences of the cosmic pattern, for the words quoted from Goethe are words taken from *Wilhelm Meister*, where the Harp Player addresses them to 'the Heavenly Powers'. The fetus itself might be termed a harp-player, learning the cosmic rhythms in the dark silence of his cave [50], and certainly it is not the mere 'ticking of the taximeter' of the umbilical blood that 'leads him into life' as a human SELF and 'makes the poor creature guilty', but the presence in the womb of the configurational forces which find resonance in the giving and getting of the blood.

'Table d'hôte' also reminds Freud of two things which are in keeping with the interpretation here offered. The first was an occasion when Mrs Freud gave her husband too little attention when they were dining together in the mountains, a fact which irritated him. The second was a caress which Mrs Freud gave him under the table when they were secretly courting. As to the first, the mountains are often used in dreams to signify the womb, presumably because our uterine sense is felt to antedate the first sense of falling, and the idea of eating in the mountains I have seen quite often as a symbol of the fetal life. It is there, indeed, that our 'wife' (the placenta) gives us her full attention and engenders the deepest feelings of love and incipient jealousy. Indeed, the onset of the cataclysm of birth is believed to be first indicated to the fetus by the failure of the placenta to fulfil its role, so that a wife's lack of attention may dimly echo these first horrible moments of uncertainty and arouse irritation even in a psychoanalyst! The second association is no less in keeping, for it presents this same lady (Mrs Freud) in the role of a secret lover, which indeed the placenta is felt to be. It will be noted that all these incidents, the original dream incident with Frau E.L. and the two actual ones with Mrs Freud, took place in association with eating. This is all of a piece, for the life in the womb is concerned with nothing but ingesting and egesting through the cord, in association with which all these umbilical feeling-phenomena arise.

Freud seems to have thought a good deal about Frau E.L.'s dream reference to his 'beautiful eyes', and in the end concluded that it could mean only this: 'People have always done everything for you for love: you have always had everything without paying for it'. Here we find another echo of the idea that giving and getting are at the root of his feelings. But later on in his book Freud links the 'beautiful eyes' with spinach in a new framework of ideas. He says that one of his children who had 'beautiful eyes' refused to eat spinach and was chided by his mother for it, which seemed to remind Freud once more of Goethe's strange words already quoted. We can see that the refusal to eat spinach by Beautiful Eyes is simply another representation of the affective link between sucking blood and giving it out through the eyes. The idea of 'getting everything for love' links with the sense of imbalance, and so with the sense of give and take first evoked in the cord in association with the sense of love. The reference to the scene at Freud's family table evokes the thought that Mrs Freud, when her children would refuse a dish (as Beautiful Eyes refused the spinach!), would urge them 'just to taste it', and this brings out the fact that the German words for taste and cost are the same, which once again brings up the relation between getting (tasting) and giving (costing).

It will be evident that anyone who ignores the 'laminated' structure of the dream is driven to try to find its meaning by indefinitely widening his inquiry-by-association on the level of adult-type thinking and feeling. Deprived of any idea that Frau E.L. might symbolize a lost bodily organ (the placenta) and its configurational legacies to his feelings, Freud was condemned to try to find some explanation of her, her action and her words, in ordinary feeling-events which, though they might not be conscious, were directly comprehensible. It is plainly inevitable that such inquiry must in the end lead the mind into sexual considerations, for as I have shown [178], the umbilical feelings have been entirely assumed by the sexual ones and swallowed up in them. For that reason, no doubt, Freud excuses himself from deeper (!) analysis of this dream, saying that it would compel him to reveal things of a personal nature which had better remain secret.